Deutsch in 30 Tagen

by Christoph Obergfell

Langenscheidt

Deutsch in 3o Tagen

Fachlektorat: Magdalena Obergfell
Gestaltungskonzept: Farnschläder & Mahlstedt, Hamburg
Zeichnungen: Claas Janssen, Frankfurt/Main
Corporate Design Umschlag: KW43 BRANDDESIGN, Düsseldorf
Umschlaggestaltung: Guter Punkt, München

Kostenloser Download Ihres Bonusmaterials

Gehen Sie folgendermaßen vor:

1. Gehen Sie auf die Seite www.langenscheidt.com/bonusmaterial
2. Geben Sie dort den Code **DE586** ein.
3. Klicken Sie auf den Button „aktivieren“.
4. Klicken Sie auf Ihr gewünschtes Zusatzmaterial (MP3-Audiodateien):
   - Audio-Wortschatztrainer
   - Dialoge

3. Auflage 2025

www.langenscheidt.com

Satz: Franzis print & media GmbH, München
Druck & Bindung: Publikum d.o.o

ISBN 978-3-12-563586-9

User Advice

Welcome to your new language course "German in 30 days". We're glad you want to learn German with us.
Once you've completed this course, you will be able to talk in German about common topics in easy, everyday and routine situations. This corresponds to level A2 of the Common European Framework of Reference for Languages.

How is this course built?

- The course consists of **30 consecutive daily portions** ordered in four sections containing six to eight days respectively.
- The modules are accompanied by an enjoyable **serial story**. Pierre, an engineering student from France, comes to Berlin for an internship. Iwona, a business woman from Poland, got sent to a new position in Germany by her firm. In Berlin they meet and become friends in a German class led by the friendly Martina. Martina and her boyfriend Jens, Pierre's colleague as it happens, make friends with the two as they encounter many everyday experiences together. We will accompany them in their language class, their everyday life, on a journey to Munich and in their business life. It's going to be interesting!
- First, a short quiz helps you find out what type of learner you are.
- This course starts with the chapter **Tips for learning German** in which we reveal helpful tips to make listening, reading, talking and writing in a foreign language easy for you. However, if you'd rather start right away, just skip the first day and start with day 2.
- As you know: practice makes perfect! Therefore we would like to encourage you to repeat what you've learned on a regular basis. For this reason you'll find a **unit for repetition** and a **short test** after 5–7 chapters. Here you'll be able to test how far you've mastered the material and where there's still need for practice. After day 30 you can find the **final test**, with exercises from the whole book.
- In order to assist you with your self-learning, we provide you with an extensive **appendix** at the end of the book. There you'll find a systematic short grammar to consult, a verb table for irregular German verbs, solutions to all the exercises and tests, scripts for all listening texts and an alphabetical vocabulary with all words from this course plus a phonetic transcription.

How is a lesson built?

At the beginning of each lesson we present the **learning goals**, so you know what awaits you.

Day 4 Family and Relationships

In this lesson you will learn
- to talk about your family
- how to ask others about their family
- to name some professions

1/9 1/10 **Und deine Familie?**

Martina stellt in ihrem Deutschkurs das heutige Thema vor.

Martina Heute sprechen wir über unsere Familien. Jeder fragt seinen Na zur Familie. Zum Beispiel: Wie heißt dein Vater? Oder: Hast du G O. K.? Dann los!

Iwona und Pierre sitzen heute am gleichen Tisch ...

Iwona Pierre, hast du Geschwister?
Pierre Ja, ich habe zwei Schwestern. Ihre Namen sind Julie und Camille
Iwona Und wie alt sind sie?
Pierre Camille ist 21. Aber Julie ist noch jung. Sie ist erst 14. Hast du auc eine Schwester?
Iwona Nein, ich habe keine Schwester. Ich habe einen Bruder. Er heißt R und er hat schon einen Sohn.
Pierre Dann bist du ja Tante! Wie alt ist Roberts Sohn?
Iwona Er ist ein Jahr alt. Er ist sehr süß und so klein. Was ist dein Vater
Pierre Mein Vater ist Architekt. Er arbeitet sehr viel. Meine Mutter arbe in einem Kindergarten. Was machen deine Eltern?
Iwona Mein Vater ist Rechtsanwalt. Meine Mutter arbeitet nicht mehr. Sie besucht jetzt sehr oft ihren Enkel. Roberts Frau mag das. Sie mehr Zeit für sich. Dann sind beide glücklich.
Martina So ... seid ihr fertig? Ihr macht das alle wirklich gut! Ich bin sehr

Read the **dialogue** while listening to the recording on the CD. Try to catch the general meaning of the dialogue as a first step without lingering on each new word.

You'll find the most important new words of the lesson in the **vocabulary** afterwards, neatly alphabetically ordered or summarised in small thematic tables. You can listen to the new vocabulary from each chapter in the Audio Vocabulary Trainer which you can download from **www.langenscheidt.com/bonusmaterial** (see page 2 for more information). You'll find the track numbers on page 285.

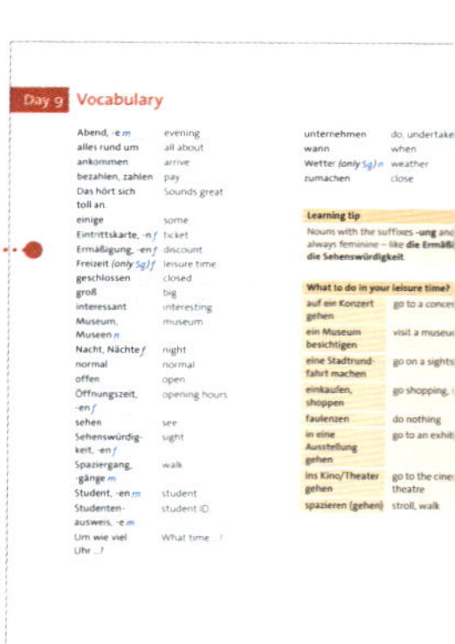
Day 9 Vocabulary

Abend, -e *m*	evening
alles rund um	all about
ankommen	arrive
bezahlen, zahlen	pay
Das hört sich toll an.	Sounds great
einige	some
Eintrittskarte, -n *f*	ticket
Ermäßigung, -en *f*	discount
Freizeit *(only Sg) f*	leisure time
geschlossen	closed
groß	big
interessant	interesting
Museum, Museen *n*	museum
Nacht, Nächte *f*	night
normal	normal
offen	open
Öffnungszeit, -en *f*	opening hours
sehen	see
Sehenswürdigkeit, -en *f*	sight
Spaziergang, -gänge *m*	walk
Student, -en *m*	student
Studentenausweis, -e *m*	student ID
Um wie viel Uhr ...?	What time ...?
unternehmen	do, undertake
wann	when
Wetter *(only Sg) n*	weather
zumachen	close

Learning tip
Nouns with the suffixes **-ung** an always feminine – like **die Ermäß die Sehenswürdigkeit**.

What to do in your leisure time?	
auf ein Konzert gehen	go to a conce
ein Museum besichtigen	visit a museu
eine Stadtrundfahrt machen	go on a sights
einkaufen, shoppen	go shopping,
faulenzen	do nothing
in eine Ausstellung gehen	go to an exhi
ins Kino/Theater gehen	go to the cine theatre
spazieren (gehen)	stroll, walk

Under the heading **Exercises** you practise what you've just learned in various ways. The symbols (see on p. 6) show you the emphasis of each exercise: listening, speaking, reading or writing.

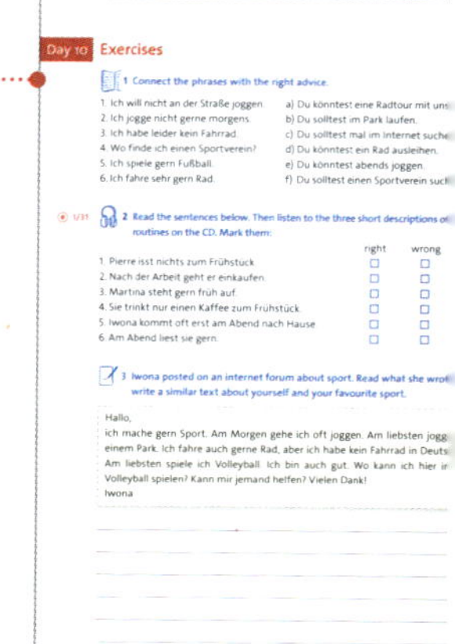
Day 10 Exercises

1 Connect the phrases with the right advice.

1. Ich will nicht an der Straße joggen.
2. Ich jogge nicht gerne morgens.
3. Ich habe leider kein Fahrrad.
4. Wo finde ich einen Sportverein?
5. Ich spiele gern Fußball.
6. Ich fahre sehr gern Rad.

a) Du könntest eine Radtour mit un
b) Du solltest im Park laufen.
c) Du solltest mal im Internet such
d) Du könntest ein Rad ausleihen.
e) Du könntest abends joggen.
f) Du solltest einen Sportverein suc

1/31 **2 Read the sentences below. Then listen to the three short descriptions o routines on the CD. Mark them:**

	right	wrong
1. Pierre isst nichts zum Frühstück.	☐	☐
2. Nach der Arbeit geht er einkaufen.	☐	☐
3. Martina steht gern früh auf.	☐	☐
4. Sie trinkt nur einen Kaffee zum Frühstück.	☐	☐
5. Iwona kommt oft erst am Abend nach Hause.	☐	☐
6. Am Abend liest sie gern.	☐	☐

3 Iwona posted on an internet forum about sport. Read what she wro write a similar text about yourself and your favourite sport.

Hallo,
ich mache gern Sport. Am Morgen gehe ich oft joggen. Am liebsten jogg einem Park. Ich fahre auch gerne Rad, aber ich habe kein Fahrrad in Deuts Am liebsten spiele ich Volleyball. Ich bin auch gut. Wo kann ich hier i Volleyball spielen? Kann mir jemand helfen? Vielen Dank!
Iwona

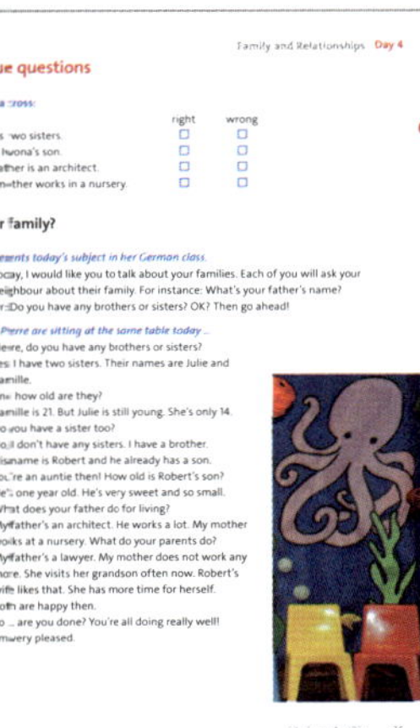

Family and Relationships Day 4

...ue questions

...a cross:

	right	wrong
...as two sisters.	☐	☐
...s Iwona's son.	☐	☐
...father is an architect.	☐	☐
...mother works in a nursery.	☐	☐

...r family?

...resents today's subject in her German class.
Today, I would like you to talk about your families. Each of you will ask your neighbour about their family. For instance: What's your father's name? Or: Do you have any brothers or sisters? OK? Then go ahead!

...d Pierre are sitting at the same table today ...
Pierre, do you have any brothers or sisters?
Yes I have two sisters. Their names are Julie and Camille.
And how old are they?
Camille is 21. But Julie is still young. She's only 14.
Do you have a sister too?
No, I don't have any sisters. I have a brother.
His name is Robert and he already has a son.
You're an auntie then! How old is Robert's son?
He's one year old. He's very sweet and so small.
What does your father do for living?
My father's an architect. He works a lot. My mother works at a nursery. What do your parents do?
My father's a lawyer. My mother does not work any more. She visits her grandson often now. Robert's wife likes that. She has more time for herself.
Both are happy then.
So ... are you done? You're all doing really well!
I'm very pleased.

fünfunddreißig 35

If you answer the following **dialogue questions**, you'll see, that you've already understood a lot.

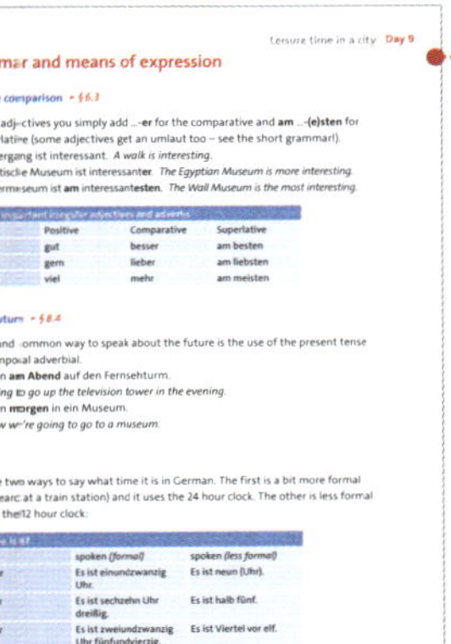

Leisure time in a city Day 9

...mar and means of expression

...e comparison → §6.3

...adjectives you simply add ...-er for the comparative and am ...-(e)sten for ...rlative (some adjectives get an umlaut too – see the short grammar!).
...iergang ist interessant. *A walk is interesting.*
...tische Museum ist interessanter. *The Egyptian Museum is more interesting.*
...ermuseum ist **am interessantesten**. *The Wall Museum is the most interesting.*

...important irregular adjectives and adverbs

Positive	Comparative	Superlative
gut	besser	am besten
gern	lieber	am liebsten
viel	mehr	am meisten

...uture → §8.4

...and common way to speak about the future is the use of the present tense ...mporal adverbial.
...n **am Abend** auf den Fernsehturm.
...ing to go up the television tower in the evening.
...en **morgen** in ein Museum.
...w we're going to go to a museum.

...e two ways to say what time it is in German. The first is a bit more formal ...ear at a train station) and it uses the 24 hour clock. The other is less formal ...the 12 hour clock.

	spoken (formal)	spoken (less formal)
	Es ist einundzwanzig Uhr.	Es ist neun (Uhr).
	Es ist sechzehn Uhr dreißig.	Es ist halb fünf.
	Es ist zweiundzwanzig Uhr fünfundvierzig.	Es ist Viertel vor elf.
	Es ist zwei Uhr fünfzehn.	Es ist Viertel nach zwei.

einundsiebzig 71

Under the heading **Grammar and means of expression** new grammar is explained in a plain manner. There are also references to the **short grammar** in **the appendix**, where the topics are presented in a more comprehensive way.

Sport and hobbies Day 10

...rtipp Germans and football

Football is one of the most popular sports in Germany – even before the World Cup in Germany in 2006. A lot of Germans spend Saturday afternoon in a football stadium or – after 6 pm – in front of the television watching the **Sportschau** with the results of the **Bundesliga** *German Football League*. The matches of the national football team draw an even greater TV audience or – since 2006 during the World or European Cup – there is **Public Viewing** (yes, that's German!), where the matches are shown on big screens open to the public.

Thanks to the great successes of the women's national football team, women's football has become very popular and is one of the fastest growing sports in Germany.

...nt to play sports actively check out the local **Sportvereine** *sports clubs* where ...participate in your favourite sport for small fees.

...t can you already do?

...dvice		→ Ü1
...bout your daily routine		→ Ü2
...t your interests, hobbies and favourite sports		→ Ü3

...g a foreign language is like sport. You have to stay on the ball. And if you do, ...t better and better and it's as much fun – but with a lot less sweating! ...'t forget that learning a language is a team sport. Sooner or later you're out ...mpeting" – why not already assemble a team for training?

neunundsiebzig 79

The last page of each lesson – under the heading **Culture tip** – offers interesting hints and information about Germany and its people.

The last part of each lesson is entitled **What can you already do** and allows you to evaluate your learning success.

What symbols are used?

1/2 This text or exercise is on the CD. The first number is the CD's number, the second the track's number. We've recorded the dialogues from day 2 to 13 in two different rates. Once in "normal" everyday life speech and once a bit slower.

exercise with emphasis on speaking

exercise with emphasis on listening

exercise with emphasis on reading

exercise with emphasis on writing

► *§1 reference to short grammar | exercise | lesson*

Achtung:
important grammar note

The author and the editorial staff at Langenscheidt wish you a lot of fun and success learning German.

Content

Deutsch

User Advice 3

Pronunciation, stress and spelling 13

Alphabet and abbreviations 15

Which learner type are you? 16

Basics – Let's start with German!

Day 1 **Tips for learning German** 18

Day 2 **Greetings** 22
Communication: introduce yourself | say hello and goodbye | numbers 1 to 12
Grammar: personal pronouns | singular verb conjugation | basic word order | gender and the definite and indefinite articles
Culture tip: Saying hello and goodbye

Day 3 **Introductions and small talk** 28
Communication: start a conversation | ask how others are and answer | talk about your place of origin and length of stay | exchange basic information about work
Grammar: questions (Wh/Yes/No) | plural verb conjugation
Culture tip: Wie geht's? (Small talk)

Day 4 **Family and relationships** 34
Communication: talk about your family | ask others about their family | name some professions
Grammar: haben and *sein* | negation | the nominative and accusative case
Culture tip: Du or better *Sie*? (The correct address in German)

Day 5 **You know more than you think** 40
Communication: say that you don't understand | ask for help | deal with false friends
Grammar: the modal verbs ***können*** and ***müssen*** | word order: modal verbs and sentence frame | use of definite and indefinite article | more about nominative and accusative
Culture tip: German and English

Day 6 **Repeat and practise** 46

Intermediate test 1 52

Everyday life – German for every day

Day 7 **Shopping** 56
Communication: buy food | ask about prices | quantities and packaging
Grammar: imperative | the dative case | *Nullartikel*
Culture tip: Shopping in Germany

Day 8 **In a restaurant** 62
Communication: order in a restaurant | ask for the bill | speak about food
Grammar: polite forms | personal pronouns | three- and four-digit numbers
Culture tip: Eat and drink

Day 9 **Leisure time in a city** 68
Communication: talk about leisure time | express wishes and preferences | buy tickets for a museum
Grammar: adjective comparison | simple future | time
Culture tip: A weekend in Berlin

Day 10 **Sport and hobbies** 74
Communication: give advice | talk about your daily routine | present interests, hobbies and favourite sports
Grammar: ***trennbare Verben*** | the modal verbs ***wollen*** and ***sollen*** | advice
Culture tip: Germans and football

Day 11 **Forming new friendships** 80
Communication: introduce and get introduced | welcome guests | congratulate
Grammar: local prepositions with the dative | temporal and local statements
Culture tip: Happy birthday!

Day 12 **Home and chores** 86
Communication: say what you like and don't like to do | apologize | home, furniture and chores
Grammar: local prepositions with the accusative | *haben* and *sein* in the simple past

Day 13 **Information and entertainment** 92
Communication: talk about TV programs | search and present short information | mass media
Grammar: modal verbs in present and past tense
Culture tip: Media

Day 14 **Repeat and practise** 98

Intermediate test 2 104

Travel – German to go

Day 15 **Plan a journey** 108
Communication: make suggestions | talk about plans | gather information about a hotel | book a room online | ordinal numbers | dates and months
Grammar: coordinating conjunctions | temporal prepositions | ordinal numbers
Culture tip: The Oktoberfest in Munich

Day 16 **Means of transport** 114
Communication: read a timetable | look for a train connection on the internet | trains and other means of transport
Grammar: subordinate clauses with *dass* and *weil*
Culture tip: Travelling in Germany

Day 17 **Where is ...? Ask the way** 120
Communication: approach strangers | ask for help | ask the way | give and understand directions
Grammar: subordinate clauses with interrogative pronouns | prepositions with the dative
Culture tip: Munich's sights

Day 18 **In the hotel** 126
Communication: check-in to a hotel | fill in forms with personal data | hotel services
Grammar: reflexive verbs | nationalities
Culture tip: Bread

Day 19 **At the Oktoberfest** 132
Communication: talk about the weather | understand weather forecasts | write a simple text message
Grammar: impersonal *es*
Culture tip: Snack specialties

Day 20 **In case of an emergency** 138
Communication: talk about illness and health | give a short accident report | body parts
Grammar: the past tense *Perfekt*
Culture tip: German health care system

Day 21 **Report on the journey** 144
Communication: give a short verbal account of a journey | express likes or dislikes | express grade and frequency
Grammar: more about the *Perfekt* | temporal subordinate clauses with *wenn* and *als*
Culture tip: Tourism in Germany

Day 22 **Repeat and practise** 150

Intermediate test 3 156

Job – German for your job

Day 23 **On the phone** 160
Communication: say hello and goodbye on the phone | leave messages | ask about people
Grammar: indefinite pronouns
Culture tip: Phoning home

Day 24 E-mails 166
Communication: write formal e-mails | understand a formal e-mail | common salutations and valedictions
Grammar: conditional clauses
Culture tip: German (formal) e-mail style

Day 25 Making appointments 172
Communication: make appointments | agree to and decline appointments | date, time, days
Grammar: relative clauses | interrogative articles
Culture tip: German punctuality

Day 26 Making contacts 178
Communication: talk about clothes | prepare for a job interview | about networks and networking
Grammar: the indefinite pronoun *man* | other articles
Culture tip: My German job interview

Day 27 Meetings 184
Communication: welcome the members of a meeting | present a topic | moderate a meeting | presentations and presentation media
Grammar: adjectives
Culture tip: Body language

Day 28 Draw the balance 190
Communication: praise and criticise others | receive praise or criticism | have a conversation with colleagues and seniors
Grammar: more about adjectives | *deshalb* and *darum*
Culture tip: Intercultural misunderstandings

Day 29 Job-related plans 196
Communication: express and talk about wishes | express plans and intentions for the future
Grammar: the auxiliary verb *werden* | Futur I | wishes
Culture tip: Further education

Day 30 Repeat and practise 202

Final test 208

Appendix

Grammatical terminology 216

Short grammar 218

Irregular verbs 237

Solutions and listening texts 239

Alphabetical word list 262

Track list 285

Picture credits 286

Pronunciation, stress and spelling

Vowels			
[a]	a	similar to **a** in British English *cat*	gef**a**llen
[aː]	a, aa, ah	like **a** in *father*	B**ah**n, ein p**aa**r
[ɛ]	e	like **e** in *bed*	am b**e**sten, **e**ssen
[eː]	e, ee, eh	formed similarly to a long [iː] but the mouth a bit more open	l**e**sen, s**eh**en, T**ee**
[ə]	-e	non-stressed **-e** endings, like **a** in *about*	bitt**e**, dank**e**
[ɪ]	i	like **i** in *list*	du b**i**st, r**i**cht**i**g
[iː]	i, ie, ieh	like **ee** in *see*	Kant**i**ne, er s**ieh**t
[ɔ]	o	similar to **o** in *not*	**o**ffen, P**o**st
[oː]	o, oo, oh	formed similar to the [ɔ] but the lips more rounded and closed	**O**bst, w**oh**nen
[ʊ]	u	like **u** in *put*	**u**m, L**u**st
[uː]	u, uh, ou	like **ou** in *you*	**Uh**r, Radt**ou**r, J**u**ni

Diphthongs and umlauts			
[aɪ]	ai, ei (ay, ey)	like **y** in *my*	M**ai**, h**ei**ßen (Bayer, Meyer)
[au]	au	like **ou** in *mouth*	**Au**to, eink**au**fen
[ɔʏ]	äu, eu	like **oy** in *boy*	R**äu**me, n**eu**, t**eu**er
[ɛ]	ä	like **e** in *bed*	Erk**ä**ltung, H**ä**nde
[ɛː]	ä, äh	like **ai** in *fair*	erz**äh**len, Gespr**ä**ch
[œ]	ö	something between [ɔ] and [ɛ]	pl**ö**tzlich, **ö**ffnen
[øː]	ö, öh	something between [oː] and [eː]	nerv**ö**s, S**öh**ne
[ʏ]	ü	similar to [yː] but the mouth is a bit more open and it's short	M**ü**tter, m**ü**ssen
[yː]	ü, üh	formed like [iː] but the lips are formed for [uː]	Gem**ü**se, fr**üh**er

Consonants			
[ç]	ch	no English equivalent, can occur as an allophone of [h] in front of vowels (like *huge* or *hue*)	**ich**, wel**ch**e
[ɪç]	-ig	only as a word ending	wen**ig**
[x]	ch	after German **a**, **o**, **u**, **au** – no English equivalent, like the Scottish **ch** in *loch*	Na**ch**t, au**ch**
[f]	f, ff, ph, v	like the English **f**	**f**ünf, **V**ater
[j]	j	like **y** in *New York*	**j**a, **J**acke
[k]	k, ck, c, -g	like **ck** in *jacket*	Ja**ck**e, we**g**
[ŋ]	ng	like **ng** in *wrong*	lä**ng**er

Consonants			
[p]	p, pp, -b	like the English p	Pause, gib
[r]	r, rr	no English equivalent, like the Scottish r in *curd*	rot
[ɐ]	-er	similar to the English u in *but*	Lehrer
[z]	s	like z in *zero*	lesen
[s]	s, ss, ß	like s in *say*	Wasser, Straße
[ʃ]	sch	like sh in *show*	schwarz
[ʃp], [ʃt]	st-, sp-	combination of [ʃ] and [p] or [t] when sp and st are combined at the beginning of a word	Sport, studieren
[t]	t, dt, -d	like the English t	gut, Stadt, wird
[tʃ]	tsch	like ch in *chat*	deutsch
[v]	w	like v in *voice*	wirklich
[ts]	z, tz	like ts in *let's*	Zimmer, putzen

Some pronunciation rules

[ː] means that the previous vowel is a long vowel.
A lot of consonants (b, d, g, h, k, l, m, n, p, t) are generally spoken the same (or very similarly) to their English counterparts.
Vowels in front of double consonants are always short: **Treppe**, **passieren**
Double vowels, ie and vowel + h are always long: ***Tee***, **pass*ie*ren**, **s*eh*en**
b, d, g at the end of a word are spoken like p, t, k: **we*g***, **gi*b***, **wir*d***
h after a vowel is not spoken – it only prolongs the vowels: **s*eh*en**, **g*eh*en**
The German [r] is formed in the throat and spoken like when you are clearing your throat or gurgling.

Stress

Usually the first syllable is stressed in a word. However, the stress in German is relatively free and similar looking words can be stressed differently. The primary stress is signalled with [ˈ], the secondary with [ˌ].

Spelling

In German the beginning of a sentence and all nouns are written with a capital letter. Additionally all pronouns for formal address (**Sie**, **Ihr** ...) are written with a capital letter.

Alphabet and abbreviations

Alphabet									
A	[ɑ:]	F	[ɛf]	L	[ɛl]	Q	[ku:]	Ü	[y:]
Ä	[ɛ:]	G	[ge:]	M	[ɛm]	R	[ɛr]	V	[fau]
B	[be:]	H	[hɑ:]	N	[ɛn]	S	[ɛs]	W	[ve:]
C	[tse:]	I	[i:]	O	[o:]	ß	[ɛs'tsɛt]	X	[ɪks]
D	[de:]	J	[jɔt]	Ö	[ø:]	T	[te:]	Y	['ʏpsilɔn]
E	[e:]	K	[kɑ:]	P	[pe:]	U	[u:]	Z	[tsɛt]

Abbreviations

Pl Plural
Sg Singular
m masculine
f feminine
n neuter
Nom. Nominative
Acc. Accusative
Dat. Dative

Which learner type are you?

Not all people learn the same way. Using the statements below, try to establish which type of learner you are and adjust your learning habits accordingly. Remember that you don't always have to follow your own way of doing things. You could assume the methods of another type of learner, even if it may seem less agreeable at first.

Auditive learner

- ☐ You follow lectures easily and memorize the contents.
- ☐ You like listening to audio books and having things explained.
- ☐ You're able to quickly get along with listening to spoken foreign languages.
- ☐ You have few problems understanding different English accents.

Visual and reading learner

- ☐ You like to read and take the contents in with your eyes.
- ☐ You know which page a word is listed on in a vocabulary book as well as which words precede and follow it.
- ☐ You memorize new words with visual mnemonics.
- ☐ You read grammar rules several times.

Writing learner

- ☐ You mark keywords and write them down.
- ☐ You like written exercises.
- ☐ You quickly want to be able to write e-mails in the new language.
- ☐ You like word lists and mind maps.

Action and speaking learner

- ☐ You want to actively use the new language.
- ☐ You want to meet native speakers.
- ☐ You like to talk and don't worry too much about correct grammar at the start.
- ☐ You like to give new words and sentences a try in role plays.

Read the following chapter to learn more about which method of learning is the most effective for each type of learner to reach his individual goals.

Tips for learning German Day 1
Greetings Day 2
Introductions and small talk Day 3
Family and Relationships Day 4
You know more than you think Day 5
Repeat and practise Day 6

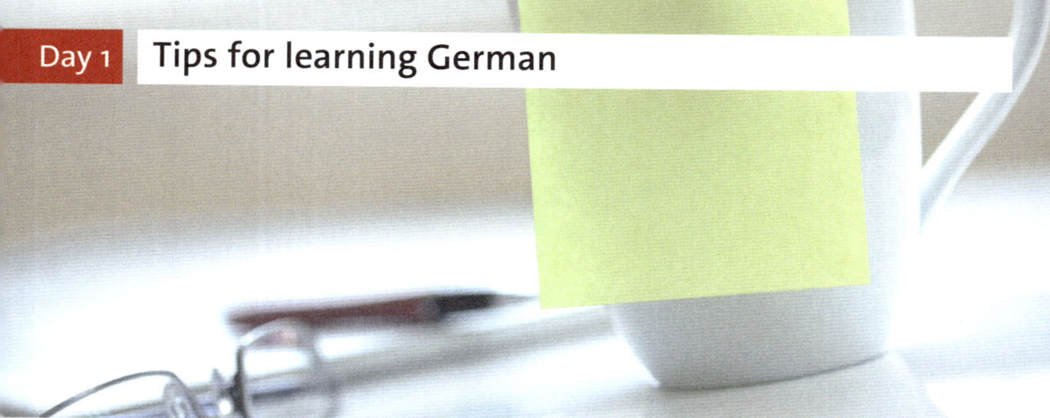

Day 1 Tips for learning German

Vocabulary learning tips

Have you ever been in a house or flat with almost every object labelled in a foreign language using little stickers or post-it notes? They were trying, probably with success, to memorize things of everyday use in another language. It's an apt technique. You are constantly reminded of the new word when you look at or take the object and say the related word in your head or speak it out loud. It won't take long for you to remember that the toilet tank is *der Toilettenspülkasten*, the rolling pin *das Nudelholz* and the wrench *der Schraubenschlüssel*.

If this method is a bit too cumbersome for you, you can try learning with vocabulary notebooks, index cards, mind maps or books with thematical vocabulary or you make use of digital media like computers, tablets and smartphones.

To learn your vocabulary we recommend e.g. a file card box with four or five compartments. Words you haven't learned yet stay in the first compartment. Keep going over your cards. Words you're still unsure of go to the next compartment. The better you know a word the further to the back it goes. Once it reaches the last compartment, it means you have learned the word.

Reading tips

Reading is an important task while learning a new language. Especially at the beginning reading tasks should be carefully planned and reading should be practiced regularly. There are three methods that can be used in turn.

Imagine three cars: a fast sports car, a (big/medium-sized) family car and a small city car. At the start of your learning career you can only afford the small car: You read single words slowly and repeatedly speak them out loud. You should look up the pronunciation in the vocabulary list in the appendix or in a dictionary if you are not sure. Don't fear the phonetic transcription; you'll know those few special characters soon enough. Wherever you have internet connection, the Langenscheidt dictionary online is easily accessible. For every foreign-language entry you can find a sound version spoken by a native speaker, so you can absolutely rely on the pronunciation.

Don't wait too long before changing to the family car and start reading whole sentences, slowly at first, then a bit faster. It's good to try to bear in mind the rhythm of speech typical to the country. As soon as you feel comfortable on the foreign roads, read bigger paragraphs at a time and so dare to get into the sports car at last. Keep in mind though: there is no reason to drive as fast as the locals. Enjoy the scenery of the language with medium reading speed and take the time to pause for a moment at certain terms – you might risk missing the beauty of single words – but also read fast sometimes to get a fair step ahead.

Speaking tips

Speaking is closely connected to reading. It's the hardest part while learning a foreign language since usually there aren't any native speakers around who could sensitively correct your mistakes. But maybe there's another learner around who would be happy to have someone to communicate with. Meet at home or at a café and try some small talk in your "new" language. Be courageous! Or read the dialogues from the textbook to each other and maybe even learn them by heart.

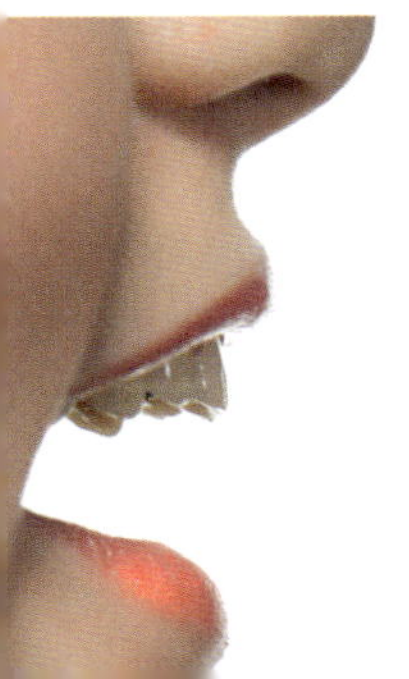

If there's no one to learn the dialogue with in assigned roles, do it on your own. Take over one part and try to think of what could be said additionally in each situation and have a conversation with imaginary partners. If you find this method slightly embarrassing, try it where nobody can see you, for example in the morning in front of your bathroom mirror.

Why not try it with lyrics or movies? Buy a German version of your favourite film – or maybe a German film you have heard of and would like to see – and watch it, particularly with German subtitles on.If you pause from time to time to write down single phrases or small sections and learn them, you can use them later as a starting point for short role plays. Put yourself in each particular situation and "chat" with the actors. You can practice this kind of communication even with yourself while jogging or having a shower.

Listening tips

Considerably easier than speaking is listening. The new media available these days offer a wide variety of possibilities which you didn't dare to dream of a few years ago.

You only need a few clicks to tune in to a foreign radio station or to listen to a podcast. Even if you don't understand much at first because they speak too fast for you, just accept it. Keep listening and get accustomed to the sound of the language you're learning – that's all that matters at the beginning. There's a good chance of getting into a holiday mood – and there's no harm in that, is there?

Listening and comprehending is like jogging. If you're a beginner running a marathon, you're likely to be soon standing breathless on the roadside. Take your time and be patient: Constant input will train the brain. That means: the more you expose yourself to spoken language, the more you keep listening, be it concentrated or just casually, the faster your listening comprehension will progress. You'll get the feeling for words and intonation. If you like listening to audio books or watching DVDs, pause from time to time and listen carefully to single sections a few times in a row. You

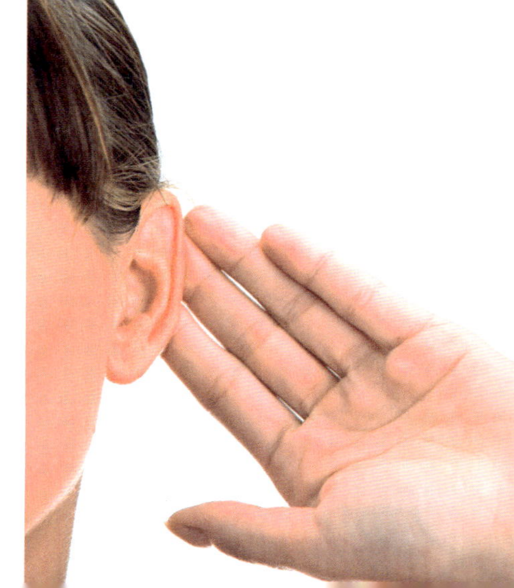

will see: at the third repetition you'll already understand a lot more. And if you make use of the text too – if you have it – you'll take a large step forward in comprehension.

Writing tips

Writing is an easy but very effective exercise. Even the mere copying of words or dialogues improves your understanding of a language considerably and helps you to easily memorize those words or sections.

You can start with writing down the exercises or dialogues from this book. As your next step, you can change them or even write new ones. Writing down short scenes in different situations is a brilliant exercise – not only for prospective writers. But you should try to find someone to read your writing and point out possible mistakes.

Of course this should not prevent an electronic exchange of ideas. Try to find chat partners, for example in social networks and write each other short messages. You can write about simple everyday matters. You'll see that it's not as easy as it sounds. Even writing just a shopping list for your spouse or child in the new language will require a lot of leafing through dictionaries. Make it a rule to write short messages for your family and friends in German or change the text recognition on your mobile phone to German and surprise your friends with "foreign" text messages. Who knows, maybe one of them will also write back "foreign".

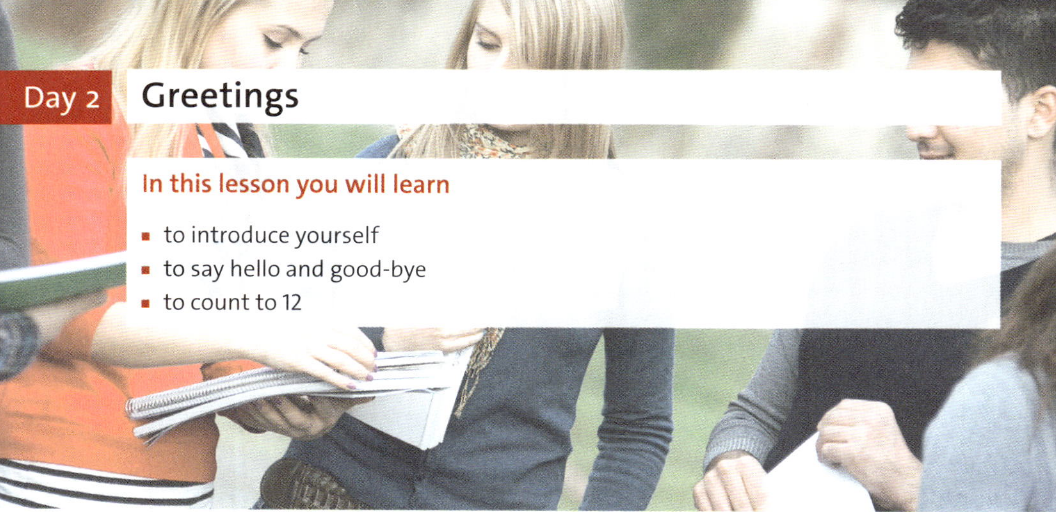

Day 2

Greetings

In this lesson you will learn

- to introduce yourself
- to say hello and good-bye
- to count to 12

Erste Stunde im Deutschkurs

1/2
1/3

Die meisten Lerner sind schon da. Iwona kommt zur Tür herein.

Iwona Guten Tag. Ist hier der Deutschkurs?

Martina Ja, genau. Dort vorne ist noch ein Platz frei ...

Iwona Danke.

Martina Hallo, herzlich willkommen. Wir sagen „du“ und benutzen den Vornamen. Ist das O. K.?

Die Lerner nicken zustimmend.

Ja? Super! Wir stellen uns jetzt vor – das ist nicht schwer. Ihr sagt einfach euren Vornamen, wie alt ihr seid und aus welchem Land ihr kommt. Ich beginne: Mein Name ist Martina. Ich bin neunundzwanzig Jahre alt. Ich komme aus Deutschland. Machst du bitte weiter?

Brian Ich? O. K. Hi! Ich bin Brian und ich bin neunzehn Jahre alt. Ich bin aus Australien.

Susan Hallo, mein Name ist Susan. Ich bin dreiundzwanzig Jahre alt und aus England.

Pierre Salut! Ich heiße Pierre. Ich bin vierundzwanzig. Ich komme aus Frankreich.

Iwona Hallo. Mein Name ist Iwona. Ich bin dreißig Jahre alt und ich komme aus Polen.

Yoko Ich heiße Yoko. Ich bin einundzwanzig Jahre alt. Ich komme aus Japan.

Die restlichen Lerner stellen sich der Reihe nach vor ...

Martina Vielen Dank, das war echt gut!

Dialogue questions

Cross out the wrong answer.

1. The teacher's name is *Iwona* | *Martina*.
2. Iwona learns *German* | *English*.
3. Martina is *19* | *29* years old.
4. *Brian* | *Susan* is from England.
5. Pierre is from *Australia* | *France*.

The first lesson in German class

Most students are already there. Iwona steps in.

Iwona Good day. Is this the German class?
Martina Yes, exactly. There's an empty seat at the front ...
Iwona Thank you.
Martina Hello, welcome. Let's say "du" and use our first names. Is that OK with you?

The students nod in agreement.

Yes? Great! We will introduce ourselves now – it's not difficult. You just say your first name, how old you are and which country you come from. I shall start: my name's Martina. I'm twenty-nine years old. I come from Germany. Will you continue?

Brian Me? OK. Hi! I'm Brian and I'm nineteen years old. I'm from Australia.
Susan Hello, my name is Susan. I'm twenty-three years old and from England.
Pierre Salut! I'm Pierre. I'm twenty-four. I come from France.
Iwona Hello. My name is Iwona. I'm thirty years old and I come from Poland.
Yoko I am Yoko. I'm twenty-one years old. I come from Japan.

The remaining students introduce themselves in turn ...

Martina Thank you, that was really good!

Vocabulary

alt	old
Auf Wiedersehen!	Good-bye!
bitte	please
danke	thanks, thank you
Deutschkurs, -e *m*	German class
Deutschland	Germany
Dialog, -e *m*	dialogue
die USA (*only Pl*)	USA
England	England
Frankreich	France
frei	free, empty
Hallo!	Hello!
Herzlich willkommen!	Welcome!
Hi!	Hi!, Hey!
ich bin	I am
ich heiße	my name is
ich komme aus	I come from
ja	yes
Jahr, -e *n*	year
Japan	Japan
Kontinent, -e *m*	continent
Land, Länder *n*	country
Lektion, -en *f*	lesson
Lerner, – *m*	student
Name, -n *m*	name
nein	no
Platz, Plätze *m*	here: seat
Polen	Poland
sagen	say
Schottland	Scotland
Stunde, -n *f*	hour, here: lesson
Tschüs!	Bye!
Vorname, -n *m*	first name
weitermachen	continue

Learning tip

You can listen to the new vocabulary from each chapter in the Audio Vocabulary Trainer which you can download from **www.langenscheidt.com/bonusmaterial**.

Learning tip

To memorize the gender of a noun, we think it's best to learn the definite article (**der/die/das**) together with the noun – and not **m**, **f** or **n** (see grammar on next page). You'll also see words or endings behind a noun: that's the plural (e.g. plural of **Dialog, -e** is **Dialoge** and of **Lerner, –** it's **Lerner** without an ending). Memorize it at once with each noun!

Greetings	
Guten Morgen.	Good morning.
Guten Tag.	Good day.
Guten Abend.	Good evening.
Gute Nacht.	Good night.

Continents	
Afrika	Africa
Amerika	America
Asien	Asia
Australien	Australia
Europa	Europe

Numbers from 1 to 12	
eins	1
zwei	2
drei	3
vier	4
fünf	5
sechs	6
sieben	7
acht	8
neun	9
zehn	10
elf	11
zwölf	12

Grammar and means of expression

Personal pronouns ► *§ 3.1*

ich	I	wir	we
du	you	ihr	you
er/sie/es	he/she/it	sie	they

Verb conjugation in the singular ► *§ 8.1*

Ich **komme** aus Frankreich. *I come from France.*
Machst du bitte weiter? *Will you continue?*
The following table shows you the endings for the singular of most verbs.

I	**ich** komme	**ich** mache	**ich** heiße
you	**du** kommst	**du** machst	**du** heißt
he/she/it	**er/sie/es** kommt	**er/sie/es** macht	**er/sie/es** heißt

Word order I ► *§ 10*

The "normal" word order in a declarative sentence (main clause) is similar to the English: subject – verb – object.
Mein Name ist Martina. *My name is Martina.*
However, the German word order is not so fixed. The subject doesn't always have to be in the first position. But: The conjugated verb is always in the second!

Gender ► *§ 1.1*

German nouns have three genders: masculine (*m*), feminine (*f*) and neuter (*n*).
But it's very often difficult to determine the gender of a noun. There are some rules – look out for them in the vocabulary sections!
Like English, German has a definite and an indefinite article. The definite article always shows the gender!

The German definite and indefinite article				
	m	f	n	Pl
the (definite)	der	die	das	die
a/an (indefinite)	ein	eine	ein	–*

* The indefinite article **ein** has no plural since it means not only *a* but also *one*.

Day 2 Exercises

1 These declarative sentences are a mess. Put them back in the right order.

1. ist / Pierre / Mein Name / .

....

2. aus Australien / Ich / komme / .

....

3. Yoko / 21 Jahre alt / ist / .

....

4. kommt / aus England / ist / Susan / und / 23 / .

....

5. komme / bin / aus / 30 / Ich / alt / Jahre / und / Polen / .

....

1/4 **2 Listen to the numbers on the CD, repeat them and cross them off the list. One number remains. Which is it?**

12 3 2 17 20 14 16 7 9 5 8

3 Read the sentences and fill in the missing personal pronouns or verb endings.

1. .... machst einen Deutschkurs.
2. Die Lehrerin heiß...... Martina. .... kommt aus Deutschland.
3. .... bin aus England.
4. Pierre komm...... aus Frankreich. .... ist 24 Jahre alt.
5. Ich komm...... aus Japan.

1/5 **4 Where are your fellow students from? Listen to the CD and complete the sentences.**

Australien den USA Schottland England

1. Paul kommt aus ....
2. Mary ist aus ....
3. Lucy kommt aus ....
4. George ist aus ....

Kulturtipp Saying hello and good-bye

Guten Tag! is the standard way to say hello in Germany and **Auf Wiedersehen!** is the most common way to say good-bye. The less official forms are **Hallo!** and **Tschüs!** respectively.

However, you will encounter many other forms of saying hello and good-bye during your stay in Germany. This depends where you are in Germany and whom you are talking to.

In Northern Germany you will hear **Moin!** all day long when people say hello (this is also used to say good-bye) or **Tach!**. In Southern Germany **Grüß Gott!** is usually used to say hello and the French word **Adieu!** or the adapted form **Ade!** to say good-bye. Among friends you can often hear **Servus!** in Western and Southern Germany as a way to say hello as well as good-bye.

Young people use **Hi!** or **Hey!** to say hello. The Italian **Ciao!** (or the German **Tschau!**) is used to say good-bye.

So you see, there are no boundaries for language!

What can you already do?

	☺	😐	☹	
▪ say your name	☐	☐	☐	► *Ü1*
▪ say where you come from	☐	☐	☐	► *Ü1*
▪ say how old you are	☐	☐	☐	► *Ü3*
▪ understand where someone is from	☐	☐	☐	► *Ü4*
▪ count to 12	☐	☐	☐	► *Ü2*

Welcome to the end of your first lesson! You've learned a lot already, haven't you? Don't worry, you don't have to know all by heart yet. The next lessons will allow you to deepen, extend and repeat your knowledge. Keep on and you'll see: practice makes perfect!

Day 3 Introductions and small talk

In this lesson you will learn

- to start a conversation, ask others how they are and answer such questions
- to ask and answer further questions about place of origin
- to talk about your length of stay
- to exchange basic information about work

1/6 1/7

Vor dem Sprachkurs

Vor der Sprachschule treffen sich Pierre und Iwona vor ihrer zweiten Unterrichtsstunde.

Pierre Hallo Iwona, wie geht es dir?

Iwona Gut, danke. Du bist Pierre aus Frankreich, ja?

Pierre Ja, ich komme aus Rennes. Das liegt in der Bretagne. Entschuldigung, woher kommst du?

Iwona Ich bin aus Polen, aus Rzeszów. Das ist in der Nähe von Krakau. Bist du schon lange in Deutschland?

Pierre Nein, erst seit einem Monat. Und du? Arbeitest du hier?

Iwona Ja, ich habe einen neuen Job hier in Berlin. Ich bin aber erst seit zwei Wochen hier.

Pierre Und was machst du?

Iwona Ich arbeite in einer Consultingfirma. Und du?

Pierre Ich studiere Maschinenbau. Ich bin fast fertig und mache jetzt ein Praktikum in einer deutschen Firma.

Martina und Jens kommen dazu.

Martina Hallo Iwona, hallo Pierre. Darf ich euch meinen Freund Jens vorstellen?

Iwona Freut mich ...

Pierre Was? Jens, Martina ist deine Freundin?

Martina Woher kennt ihr euch denn?

Jens Hi, ihr beiden. Pierre und ich arbeiten in der gleichen Firma.

Martina Das ist ja toll! Oh, die anderen kommen schon. Der Unterricht beginnt gleich. Gehen wir hinein?

Jens Gut, dann viel Spaß. Bis später!

Dialogue questions

Mark with a cross:

	right	wrong
1. Iwona is from Cracow.	☐	☐
2. Pierre has been in Germany for a month.	☐	☐
3. Iwona studies in Berlin.	☐	☐
4. Martina is Jens' girlfriend.	☐	☐
5. Martina and Pierre work at the same company.	☐	☐

Before the language class

Pierre and Iwona meet in front of the language school before their second class.

Pierre Hello Iwona, how are you?
Iwona Well, thank you. You are Pierre from France, right?
Pierre Yes, I come from Rennes. It's in Brittany. Sorry, where are you from?
Iwona I am from Poland, from Rzeszów. It's not far from Cracow. Have you been in Germany long?
Pierre No, only a month. And you? Do you work here?
Iwona Yes, I have a new job here in Berlin. But I have only been here for two weeks.
Pierre And what do you do?
Iwona I work at a consulting company. And you?
Pierre I study mechanical engineering. I'm almost finished and now I am doing a placement at a German company.

Martina and Jens join them.

Martina Hello Iwona, hello Pierre. May I introduce you to my boyfriend Jens?
Iwona Pleasure ...
Pierre What? Jens, Martina is your girlfriend?
Martina So where do you know each other from?
Jens Hi, you two. Pierre and I work for the same company.
Martina This is cool! Oh, the others are already coming. The class is about to start. Shall we go inside?
Jens Ok, have fun. See you later!

Vocabulary

arbeiten	work
beginnen	start
Bis später!	See you later!
Consultingfirma, -firmen *f*	consulting company
Darf ich Jens vorstellen?	May I introduce Jens?
Das ist toll!	This is cool!
dürfen	may
Entschuldigung! *f*	sorry
fertig	done
Firma, Firmen *f*	company
gehen	go
in der Nähe von	not far from
Job, -s *m*	job
kommen aus	come from
lang(e)	long
leben	live
Maschinenbau (*only Sg*) *m*	mechanical engineering
Monat, -e *m*	month
Praktikum, Praktika *n*	placement
sich kennen	know each other
sich treffen	meet
studieren	study
Tag, -e *m*	day
toll	cool
Unterricht (*only Sg*) *m*	class
Viel Spaß!	Have fun!
was	what
wie	how
Wie geht's?/ Wie geht es dir/ Ihnen?	How are you?
wo	where
Woche, -n *f*	week
woher	from where
wohnen	live (e.g. in a flat)
Wohnung, -en *f*	flat

Numbers from 13 to 100	
13	dreizehn
14	vierzehn
15	fünfzehn
16	sechzehn
17	siebzehn
18	achtzehn
19	neunzehn
20	zwanzig
21	einundzwanzig
22	zweiundzwanzig
23	dreiundzwanzig
24	vierundzwanzig
30	dreißig
40	vierzig
50	fünfzig
60	sechzig
70	siebzig
80	achtzig
90	neunzig
100	(ein-)hundert

Information about the length of the stay	
Ich bin hier seit einem Tag/ einer Woche/ einem Monat/ einem Jahr.	I've been here for a day/ a week/a month/a year.
Ich bin hier seit zwei/drei/... Tagen/Wochen/ Monaten/Jahren.	I've been here for two/ three/... days/weeks/ months/years.

Grammar and means of expression

Wh Questions ► *§ 3.3, § 10*

These questions always start with an **interrogative pronoun** (they all start with **W**).
Wie geht es dir? *How are you?*
Woher kommst du? *Where do you come from?*
Was machst du? *What do you do?*
Like in a normal positive sentence (• *Day 2*), the verb takes the second position in the sentence.

Yes/No Questions

This type does not involve an interrogative pronoun. Unlike Wh Questions, these questions can just be answered with a **Yes** or **No**. Like in English, the **verb takes the first position** in the sentence.
Bist du schon lange in Deutschland? *Have you been in Germany long?*
Arbeitest du hier? *Do you work here?*

Verb conjugation in the plural ► *§ 8.1*

In the previous lesson, you learned how the verbs conjugate in the singular.
Now take a look at some **verbs in the plural**:
Wir arbeit**en** in der gleichen Firma. *We work at the same company.*
Woher kenn**t** ihr euch denn? *So where do you know each other from?*
Die anderen komm**en** schon. *The others are already coming.*

This is how regular verbs conjugate in the plural			
we	**wir** arbeit**en**	**wir** kenn**en**	**wir** komm**en**
you	**ihr** arbeit**et**	**ihr** kenn**t**	**ihr** komm**t**
they	**sie** arbeit**en**	**sie** kenn**en**	**sie** komm**en**
you*	**Sie*** arbeit**en**	**Sie*** kenn**en**	**Sie*** komm**en**

* To address someone formally you use **Sie** (with a capital) for both singular and plural.

Exercises

1 These questions are totally mixed up. Put the words in the correct order and answer the questions.

1. a) du / woher / kommst / ? ....
   b) Answer: ....
2. a) geht / wie / dir / es / ? ....
   b) Answer: ....
3. a) ist / das / wo / ? ....
   b) Answer: ....
4. a) machst / was / du / ? ....
   b) Answer: ....
5. a) aus Deutschland / kommst / du / ? ....
   b) Answer: ....
6. a) schon / lange / in Deutschland / du / bist / ? ....
   ....
   b) Answer: ....
7. a) hier / du / arbeitest / ? ....
   b) Answer: ....

2 Choose the right forms of the verbs *arbeiten* and *kommen* from the box in the grammar section and fill in the gaps.

1. Woher ____________ ihr?
2. Wir ____________ in Berlin.
3. Wir ____________ aus England.
4. Pierre und Jens ____________ in der gleichen Firma.
5. Wo ____________ ihr?
6. Jens und Martina ____________ aus Deutschland.

1/8

3 You're talking to Jens now. Listen to his answers and then ask him the appropriate question after the beep. Choose your questions in the right order from the box. Listen to the correct question and answer again after each of your questions.

Wo ist das? Hallo Jens, wie geht's? Und was machst du? Woher kommst du?

Kulturtipp Wie geht's?

To start small talk with friends you can use the question:
Wie geht's?/Wie geht es dir?
How are you?
If you want to address someone formally use: **Wie geht es Ihnen?**
How are you?
Sometimes others use this phrase only to start a conversation. If you have the feeling that they don't really want to know how you are, then answer with one of the following:

(Mir geht es) prima/toll/super/sehr gut. *(I'm doing) great/OK/well/fine.*
Gut, danke. *Well, thank you.*
Es geht. *Not bad.*
So lala. *So so.*
Nicht so gut. *Not so good.*
Schlecht. *Bad.*

If you think the other person cares and you're feeling bad and you want to talk about it, then answer truthfully and tell your story. But – vice versa – be prepared to hear the full story if you ask someone how she/he is!
And of course you can counter with your own question by putting **Und (wie geht's) dir?** *And (how are) you?* after your answer.

What can you already do?

	☺ ☹ ☹	
▪ conduct a short conversation	■ ■ ■	► *Ü1*
▪ ask how others are and answer if you're asked	■ ■ ■	► *Ü3*
▪ ask and answer questions about place of origin	■ ■ ■	► *Ü1*
▪ ask others about the length of their stay	■ ■ ■	► *Ü1*
▪ answer questions about the length of your stay	■ ■ ■	► *Ü1*
▪ talk about work	■ ■ ■	► *Ü1, Ü2, Ü3*

Day 4

Family and Relationships

In this lesson you will learn

- to talk about your family
- how to ask others about their family
- to name some professions

Und deine Familie?

Martina stellt in ihrem Deutschkurs das heutige Thema vor.

Martina Heute sprechen wir über unsere Familien. Jeder fragt seinen Nachbarn zur Familie. Zum Beispiel: Wie heißt dein Vater? Oder: Hast du Geschwister? O. K.? Dann los!

Iwona und Pierre sitzen heute am gleichen Tisch ...

Iwona Pierre, hast du Geschwister?

Pierre Ja, ich habe zwei Schwestern. Ihre Namen sind Julie und Camille.

Iwona Und wie alt sind sie?

Pierre Camille ist 21. Aber Julie ist noch jung. Sie ist erst 14. Hast du auch eine Schwester?

Iwona Nein, ich habe keine Schwester. Ich habe einen Bruder. Er heißt Robert und er hat schon einen Sohn.

Pierre Dann bist du ja Tante! Wie alt ist Roberts Sohn?

Iwona Er ist ein Jahr alt. Er ist sehr süß und so klein. Was ist dein Vater von Beruf?

Pierre Mein Vater ist Architekt. Er arbeitet sehr viel. Meine Mutter arbeitet in einem Kindergarten. Was machen deine Eltern?

Iwona Mein Vater ist Rechtsanwalt. Meine Mutter arbeitet nicht mehr. Sie besucht jetzt sehr oft ihren Enkel. Roberts Frau mag das. Sie hat mehr Zeit für sich. Dann sind beide glücklich.

Martina So ... seid ihr fertig? Ihr macht das alle wirklich gut! Ich bin sehr zufrieden.

Dialogue questions

Mark with a cross:

	right	wrong
1. Pierre has two sisters.	☐	☐
2. Robert is Iwona's son.	☐	☐
3. Pierre's father is an architect.	☐	☐
4. Iwona's mother works in a nursery.	☐	☐

And your family?

Martina presents today's subject in her German class.

Martina Today, I would like you to talk about your families. Each of you will ask your neighbour about their family. For instance: What's your father's name? Or: Do you have any brothers or sisters? OK? Then go ahead!

Iwona and Pierre are sitting at the same table today ...

Iwona Pierre, do you have any brothers or sisters?

Pierre Yes, I have two sisters. Their names are Julie and Camille.

Iwona And how old are they?

Pierre Camille is 21. But Julie is still young. She's only 14. Do you have a sister too?

Iwona No, I don't have any sisters. I have a brother. His name is Robert and he already has a son.

Pierre You're an auntie then! How old is Robert's son?

Iwona He's one year old. He's very sweet and so small. What does your father do for living?

Pierre My father's an architect. He works a lot. My mother works at a nursery. What do your parents do?

Iwona My father's a lawyer. My mother does not work any more. She visits her grandson often now. Robert's wife likes that. She has more time for herself. Both are happy then.

Martina So ... are you done? You're all doing really well! I'm very pleased.

Day 4 Vocabulary

beide	both
Beruf, -e *m*	profession
besuchen	visit
erst	only
Familie, -n *f*	family
fragen	ask
glücklich	happy
jung	young
Kindergarten, -gärten *m*	nursery
klein	small
mehr	more
Nachbar, -n *m*	neighbour
nicht mehr	not anymore
Seid ihr fertig?	Are you done?
sprechen	speak, talk
süß	sweet
verheiratet	married
Verwandte, -n *m+f*	relative
wirklich	really
Zeit, -en *f* *(mostly only Sg)*	time

Family	
Eltern	parents
Mutter, Mütter *f*	mother
Vater, Väter *m*	father
Kind, -er *n*	child
Tochter, Töchter *f*	daughter
Sohn, Söhne *m*	son
Geschwister *Pl*	brothers and sisters
Bruder, Brüder *m*	brother
Schwester, -n *f*	sister
Großeltern *Pl*	grandparents
Großmutter *f*	grandmother
Großvater *m*	grandfather
Tante, -n *f*	aunt
Onkel, – *m*	uncle

Possessive pronouns (used like an article)	
mein	my
dein	your
sein/ihr/sein	his/her/its
unser	our
euer	your
ihr/Ihr formal, *Sg+Pl*	their/your

Professions	
Architekt, -en *m*	architect
Kindergärtner, – *m*	nursery teacher
Lehrer, – *m*	teacher
Rechtsanwalt, -anwälte *m*	male lawyer
Rechtsanwältin, -nen *f*	female lawyer
Kellner, – *m*	waiter
Professor, -en *m*	professor
Ich bin Lehrer.	I'm a teacher.

German professions don't take the indefinite article as in English!
Each profession also has a female form!
Normally you just add **-in** to the male form: e.g. **Kellner** *m* and **Kellnerin** *f*.

Grammar and means of expression

haben and *sein* ► *§ 8.5*

haben have		**sein** be	
ich habe	wir haben	ich bin	wir sind
du hast	ihr habt	du bist	ihr seid
er/sie/es hat	sie haben	er/sie/es ist	sie sind

Negation ► *§ 4*

As you've already seen in the previous dialogues you can use **nicht** (*not*) to negate words or sentences:
Das ist **nicht** schwer. *That's not difficult.*

Kein only negates nouns and stands right in front of them, just like the indefinite article (see table below):
Ich habe **keine** Schwester. *I don't have a sister.*

Cases: Nominativ and Akkusativ I ► *§ 1.3*

The German equivalent of the direct object is the accusative. It's used for things or people you have, see or in general do something with.
Ich habe **einen Bruder**. *I have a brother.*
The good news is: The noun usually does not change – only the little word in front of it. Here you can see the accusative forms of the indefinite article, **kein** or a possessive pronoun that are all very similar.

	m	f	n	Pl
Nom.	ein	eine	ein	–
	kein	keine	kein	keine
	mein, dein ...	meine ...	mein ...	meine ...
Acc.	ein**en**	eine	ein	–
	kein**en**	keine	kein	keine
	mein**en** ...	meine ...	mein ...	meine ...

Achtung:
Remember that there's no indefinite article for plurals!

Day 4 Exercises

1 ***Haben* or *sein*? Fill in the gaps with the correct forms of *haben* or *sein*.**

1. Mein Vater .... Architekt.
2. .... ihr aus Polen?
3. Ich .... 24 Jahre alt.
4. Jens und Martina .... noch keine Kinder.
5. .... du eine Schwester?

1/11

2 Listen to the questions on the CD and write the answers down.

1. Mein Name ist ....
2. Ich komme ....
3. Ich ....
4. ....
5. ....

3 Connect the questions with the right answers.

1. Wo arbeitest du?
2. Arbeitet deine Mutter viel?
3. Was macht dein Bruder?
4. Wer arbeitet in einem Kindergarten?
5. Bist du Rechtsanwältin?
6. Was machen deine Eltern?

a) Meine Schwester arbeitet in einem Kindergarten.
b) Er ist Kellner.
c) Sie arbeiten nicht mehr.
d) Ja, sie arbeitet sehr viel.
e) Ich arbeite in einer Firma.
f) Ja, ich bin Rechtsanwältin.

**4 Fill in the missing words in their appropriate form (gender, accusative). The numbers in brackets show what to use:
0 = *kein*, 1 = *ein*, all other numbers = this number as a German word.**

1. Ich habe .... Schwestern. (2)
2. Du hast .... Bruder. (0)
3. Wir haben .... Kinder. (0)
4. Sie hat .... Freund. (1)
5. Er hat .... Freundin. (1)
6. Ihr habt .... Brüder. (3)

Kulturtipp *Du* or better *Sie*?

Use **Du** and the first name with people you're familiar with and who you like. For all others, you're on the safe side with **Sie** and the last name.

If you're not sure, look around to see what others say and follow their lead. It's never a mistake to use **Sie** but it might be embarrassing to say **Du** (if someone hasn't proposed it yet).

Students often use **Du** and the first name with each other, regardless of age. But don't use **Du** with your professors and teachers (unless they propose it).

You can often read that a tie (and a suit) is accompanied by **Sie** (even if the wearer is a 12-year younger bank clerk). If you are new in a company, use **Sie**, especially with your managers. They'll tell you if they prefer it otherwise.

However, in some companies the hybrid form of **Sie** plus first name exists. It suggests more familiarity than **Sie** and the last name but not as much as the use of **Du** would. On the contrary, **Du** and the last name can be heard (especially with children) but is normally not used!

What can you already do?

	☺	😐	☹	
▪ introduce your family	☐	☐	☐	► *Ü3, Ü4*
▪ ask questions about family	☐	☐	☐	► *Ü1, Ü2, Ü3*
▪ answer questions about family	☐	☐	☐	► *Ü1, Ü2, Ü3*
▪ ask and answer questions about professions	☐	☐	☐	► *Ü2, Ü3*

Day 5

You know more than you think

In this lesson you will learn

- to say that you don't understand
- to ask for help
- to deal with false friends

1/12
1/13

Deutsch ist einfach! Oder?

Im Deutschkurs

Martina Brian, kannst du bitte den Beamer holen? Er steht dort hinten.

Brian Entschuldigung, das verstehe ich nicht. Kannst du das bitte wiederholen?

Martina Der Beamer. Für Filme und Präsentationen am Laptop.

Brian Oh, meinst du einen „video projector"?

Martina Ja, genau! Das Wort Beamer kennst du nicht? Es ist doch englisch ...

Brian Nicht wirklich, ich kenne nur „beam".

Iwona Das ist aber seltsam. Passiert so etwas oft?

Martina Ich weiß es nicht. Ich muss das nachschlagen. Aber es gibt sehr viele echte englische Wörter im Deutschen. So wie der Laptop hier zum Beispiel.

Pierre Heißt es übrigens der Laptop oder das? Ein Kollege sagt immer „das Laptop".

Martina Ja, das kommt vor. Bei Laptop ist beides möglich.

Brian Es gibt auch deutsche Wörter im Englischen: „Sauerkraut" zum Beispiel.

Martina Stimmt. Und ziemlich viele Wörter haben gemeinsame Wurzeln. Diese Wörter sind heute oft sehr ähnlich: „garden" und „der Garten" oder „fish" und „der Fisch".

Iwona Aber „Chips" sind hier etwas ganz anderes als „chips" in London.

Martina Ja, leider gibt es auch einige falsche Freunde! Wer kennt denn noch andere falsche Freunde aus seiner Muttersprache?

Dialogue questions

Cross out the wrong answer.

1. A Beamer is a *laptop* | *video projector.*
2. There are *some* | *no* English words in the German language.
3. Garden and fish have *similar* | *other* words in German.
4. Chips in London are *the same as* | *something completely different* than "Chips" in Berlin.

German is easy! Isn't it?

In the German class

Martina Brian, can you get the "Beamer", please? It's over there at the back.
Brian Sorry, I didn't understand that. Can you repeat, please?
Martina The "Beamer". For videos or presentations on a laptop.
Brian Oh, you mean the video projector?
Martina Yes, exactly. You don't know the word "Beamer"? But it's English ...
Brian No, not really, I only know "beam".
Iwona That's strange. Does this happen a lot?
Martina I don't know. I have to look it up. But there are a lot of real English words in German. Like "der Laptop" here for instance.
Pierre Is it "der Laptop" or "das" by the way? One colleague always says "das Laptop".
Martina Yes, it is used. With Laptop both are possible.
Brian There are German words in English too: "Sauerkraut" for instance.
Martina Right. And quite a few words have common roots. These words are very similar today: "garden" and "der Garten" or "fish" und "der Fisch".
Iwona But "Chips" here are something completely different than "chips" in London.
Martina Yes, unfortunately there are also some false friends. Who knows any other false friends in his native language?

Day 5 Vocabulary

ähnlich	similar, alike
Beamer, – *m*	video projector
dieser, diese, dieses	this/that
diese *Pl*	these
dort	there
echt	real
etwas ganz anderes	something completely different
Film, -e *m*	film, movie
Fisch, -e *m*	fish
Garten, Gärten *m*	garden
gemeinsam	common
Haus, Häuser *n*	house
hinten	(at the) back
holen	get, fetch
können	can
langsam	slow
Laptop, -s *m/n*	laptop
möglich	possible
müssen	have to, must
nachschlagen	look up
oft	often, a lot
passieren	happen
planen	plan, arrange, design
Präsentation, -en *f*	presentation
Restaurant, -s *n*	restaurant
sehr viel	a lot of
sehr	very
stehen	stand (here: be)
Stimmt.	Right.
verstehen	understand
wiederholen	repeat
wissen	know
Wort, Wörter *n*	word
Wurzel, -n *f*	root

Some false friends	
Chip, -s *m* *(mostly only Pl)*	crisps
Mord, -e *m*	murder
Mörder, – *m*	murderer
Pommes (frites) *(Pl)*	chips, fries
fast	almost
schnell	fast
Geschenk, -e *n*	gift
Gift, -e *n*	poison
Chef, -s *m*	boss, manager
Koch, Köche *m*	chef
bekommen	get
werden	become

Learning tip I

Most internationalisms or English words used in German have **-s** as a plural ending. E.g.: Chip**s**, Chef**s**, Laptop**s**, Single**s**, Restaurant**s**.

Learning tip II

German nouns with **-ion** as suffix are always feminine! E.g.: die Präsentat**ion**.

Grammar and means of expression

The modal verbs *können* and *müssen* ► *§ 8.6*

können		müssen	
ich kann	wir können	ich muss	wir müssen
du kannst	ihr könnt	du musst	ihr müsst
er/sie/es kann	sie (Sie) können	er/sie/es muss	sie (Sie) müssen

Modal verbs and sentence frame ► *§ 10*

Remember: In declarative sentences and Wh Questions, the conjugated verb (here the modal verb) is in the second place (the first in Yes/No Questions):
Ich **muss** das ***nachschauen***. *I have to look it up.*
Kannst du das bitte **wiederholen**? *Can you repeat, please?*
The second (uninflected) verb goes – as you see – to the last place and together they build this frame-like structure: the **Satzklammer** *sentence frame.*

Definite vs. indefinite article ► *§ 2.1*

The use of the appropriate article should in most cases be the same as in English.
Use the definite article with nouns when you refer to a singular distinct and known thing (or things).
Kannst du bitte **den** Beamer holen? *Can you get the video projector please?*
If you refer to a noun in general or something yet unknown, use the indefinite article.
Meinst du **einen** „video projector"? *You mean a video projector?*

Cases: Nominativ and Akkusativ II ► *§ 2.1*

Let's develop the table of accusative forms from the previous lesson. Here you can see the accusative forms of the definite article.

	m	f	n	Pl
Nom.	der	die	das	die
Acc.	den	die	das	die

Day 5

Exercises

1 False friends. Connect the German words with the correct translation.

1. die Chips	a) fast	4. fast	d) gift
2. das Geschenk	b) almost	5. das Gift	e) crisps
3. die Pommes	c) chips	6. schnell	f) poison

1/14

2 Read the phrases below. Now listen to the CD, repeat each sentence and strike it off the list. One phrase remains. Which one?

Heißt es der Laptop oder das Laptop? Dieses Wort kenne ich nicht.
Entschuldigung, ich verstehe das nicht. Leider gibt es einige falsche Freunde.
Das ist etwas ganz anderes. Kannst du das wiederholen?
Garten und *garden* sind sehr ähnlich.

3 Put the mixed up sentences in the right order. Remember the position of the modal verb and the infinitive. Translate them afterwards.

1. a) den Satz / wiederholen / muss / er / . ...
   b) Translation: ....
2. a) kannst / den Beamer / holen / bitte / du / ? ....
   b) Translation: ....
3. a) viel / arbeiten / musst / du / ? ....
   b) Translation: ....
4. a) diese Wörter / Iwona / muss / nachschauen / . ...
   b) Translation: ....
5. a) oft / unseren Sohn / besuchen / können / wir / . ...
   b) Translation: ....
6. a) ich / das / nicht / verstehe / . ...
   b) Translation: ....
7. a) wiederholen / Sie *(formal!)* / das / können / bitte / ? ....
   b) Translation: ....

Kulturtipp
German and English

You might have thought that English and German are not very similar. But as they both have Germanic origins, it's easy to spot similarities (either in writing or pronunciation): **das Haus** *house*, **der Mann** *man*, **gut** *good*, **singen** *sing*, **das Wasser** *water*.

But be careful! There are also some false friends as you've learned in this lesson. And it wouldn't be good to confuse *a gift* and **das Gift**!

You'll notice that the Germans use a lot of English words today – especially around computers and the internet. Those are either real English words: **Software aus dem Internet auf den Computer downloaden** *to download software from the internet on the computer* is actually a German sentence! Or (as in the dialogue) pseudo-anglicisms: **das Handy** *mobile/cell phone*, **der Beamer** *video projector* for presentations and **Bodybags** *shoulder/cross-body bag* for carrying your stuff.

What can you already do?

	☺ ☹ ☹	
▪ say that you don't understand	▪ ▪ ▪	► Ü2, Ü3
▪ ask for help	▪ ▪ ▪	► Ü2, Ü3
▪ detect some common false friends	▪ ▪ ▪	► Ü1

Congratulations, you've now mastered the first part of this book! Wasn't as difficult, was it? Now you can delve into the next lesson with a lot of opportunities to practise what you've learned ... Have fun!

Day 6

Repeat and practise

Here you repeat

- asking and answering questions about yourself and others
- talking about your family
- talking about professions
- conducting short conversations

1 Write the sentences again. This time use personal pronouns given in brackets instead of the names and don't forget to adapt the verbs.

1. Iwona arbeitet in einer Consultingfirma. (du) ....
2. Pierre studiert noch. (er) ....
3. Jeff ist aus den USA. (wir) ....
4. Monika ist Rechtsanwältin. (sie *Sg*) ....

2 The possessive pronouns are missing. Fill the gaps with the right pronoun in the nominative case.

1. Wir haben zwei Kinder. .... Kinder sind 7 und 8 Jahre alt.
2. Ich habe einen Bruder. .... Bruder heißt Michael.
3. Iwona und Pierre lernen Deutsch. .... Lehrerin heißt Martina.
4. Sie kommt aus Deutschland. .... Freund kommt aus England.
5. Ihr habt eine Schwester. .... Schwester ist verheiratet.
6. Haben Sie ein Kind? Wie alt ist .... Kind? *(Caution: formal Sie!)*

3 Two people are having a little chat but the phrases got mixed up. Can you put them back in their original order?

1. Ja, Rzeszów liegt in der Nähe von Krakau. Bist du aus Deutschland? ☐
2. Ich kenne Berlin. Ich arbeite dort. Arbeitest du auch? ☐
3. Hallo! Mein Name ist Iwona. Wie heißt du? ☐
4. Nein, ich studiere noch. ☐
5. Ich komme aus Rzeszów. ☐
6. Ich heiße Claudia. Woher kommst du? ☐
7. Ist das in Polen? ☐
8. Ja, ich bin aus Potsdam. Das ist in der Nähe von Berlin. ☐

4 Write the correct numbers in German in the puzzle. The coloured boxes will reveal another number when you've finished.

a) = 4
b) = 2
c) = 11
d) = 3
e) = 10
f) = 7
g) = 8
h) = 9

5 Listen to the CD. Then read the sentences below and listen to the CD again. Mark the correct information with a cross. 1/15

1. Martin ist a) ☐ Deutschlehrer. b) ☐ Architekt.
2. Martin ist seit a) ☐ einem Jahr b) ☐ fünf Jahren in Berlin.
3. Lynn kommt aus a) ☐ Deutschland. b) ☐ England.
4. Lynn ist Martins a) ☐ Schwester. b) ☐ Freundin.

6 Read the short word lists. Then choose the words from the box that go with each list and write them down. One does not fit!

Deutschland Guten Abend Geschäftsmann
Eltern Onkel Auf Wiedersehen Monat

1. Tante, Vater, Sohn, ...
2. Kellner, Lehrer, Architekt, ...
3. Stunde, Woche, Tag, ...
4. Frankreich, England, Polen, ...
5. Guten Tag, Hallo, Hi, ...
6. Großeltern, Kinder, Geschwister, ...

7 *Sie* or *du*? Which one would you normally use when talking to the people in the table below? Mark:

	Sie	du
1. dein Chef	☐	☐
2. deine Familie	☐	☐
3. ein Freund aus dem Deutschkurs	☐	☐
4. ein neuer Kollege	☐	☐
5. eine Kellnerin	☐	☐
6. dein Professor	☐	☐

8 *Kein* or *nicht*? Write the sentences in the negative.

1. Das ist schwer. ....
2. Martina hat eine Schwester. ....
3. Ich verstehe das. ....
4. Das ist ein englisches Wort. ....
5. Du weißt es. ....
6. Ich habe einen Laptop. ....

9 Read the short text. Then read the phrases below and decide whether they are right or wrong.

Martina ist Deutschlehrerin in Berlin. Sie lebt dort mit ihrem Freund Jens. Martinas Eltern wohnen nicht in Berlin. Sie wohnen in München. Martina hat eine Schwester, aber keinen Bruder. Ihre Schwester heißt Kathrin. Kathrin wohnt in Potsdam. Potsdam liegt in der Nähe von Berlin. Sie studiert und arbeitet als Kellnerin. Martina besucht sehr oft ihre Schwester in Potsdam. Jens hat keine Geschwister. Jens kommt aus Jena. Aber er lebt seit sechs Jahren in Berlin. Er arbeitet dort in einer großen Firma. Er ist Informatiker.

	right	wrong
1. Martinas Eltern wohnen in Hamburg.	☐	☐
2. Jens' Schwester heißt Kathrin.	☐	☐
3. Kathrin wohnt in der Nähe von Berlin.	☐	☐
4. Kathrin besucht sehr oft ihre Schwester.	☐	☐
5. Jens hat keine Schwester.	☐	☐
6. Jens arbeitet in Jena.	☐	☐

10 What do you say? Choose your replies from the box.

Hallo! Es geht. Bis später! Viel Spaß! Freut mich!

1. Wie geht es dir? – ....
2. Das ist mein Freund Jens. – ....
3. Der Unterricht beginnt. – ....
4. Tschüs! – ....
5. Hi! – ....

11 Build sentences. Use the information in their right forms.

ich / haben / 2 / Bruder *Ich habe zwei Brüder.*
1. sie *Pl* / sehen / 2 / Mann ....
2. wir / haben / – / Schwester ....
3. du / haben / 1 / Sohn ....
4. sie *Sg* / haben / 4 / Geschwister ....

12 Connect the short descriptions with the correct profession.

1. Er macht den Deutschkurs.
2. Er plant Häuser.
3. Sie arbeitet in einem Restaurant.
4. Sie arbeitet mit Kindern.
5. Er arbeitet an der Universität.

a) der Professor
b) die Kindergärtnerin
c) der Architekt
d) die Kellnerin
e) der Deutschlehrer

13 Pierre introduces himself and his family. Read the text and then introduce yourself following Pierre's example.

Hallo, mein Name ist Pierre. Ich komme aus Rennes. Das liegt in der Bretagne. Ich bin 24 Jahre alt. Ich studiere Maschinenbau. Ich mache ein Praktikum in einer deutschen Firma in Berlin. Ich habe zwei Schwestern. Sie heißen Camille und Julie. Camille ist 21 und Julie ist 14. Mein Vater ist Rechtsanwalt von Beruf. Meine Mutter arbeitet in einem Kindergarten.

....

....

....

....

....

14 The following sentences and questions are in a mess. Please sort them out. But be careful: all the verbs are in the infinitive and you have to put them in the right form!

1. sehen / können / den Mann / du / ? ……
2. ich / Deutsch / müssen / lernen / . ……
3. arbeiten / wo / du / ? ……
4. du / in einer Consultingfirma / arbeiten / ? ……
5. sehr viel / wir / müssen / lernen / . ……
6. sie (*Pl.*) / können / verstehen / diese Wörter / nicht / . ……

……

15 Read the short e-mail. Then write back answering the questions.

Neue E-Mail

Hallo,
wie geht es dir? Danke für deine E-Mail. Du schreibst gut deutsch.
Das ist toll! Wie lange bist du schon in Deutschland? Machst du einen Deutschkurs? Ist Deutsch schwer?
Und arbeitest du? Kennst du schon viele Deutsche?
Tschüs!

……
……
……
……
……
……

16 Definite article, indefinite article, or nothing? Complete the sentences with the words from the box.

— der der die ein eine einen einen einen

1. Hast du …… Laptop? – Nein, ich habe keinen Laptop.
2. a) …… Beamer ist kaputt. Ich hole b) …… neuen Beamer.
3. Kennst du …… Restaurant hier?
4. Seine Schwester ist …… Architektin.
5. Ich sehe a) …… Mann. b) …… Mann hat c) …… Frau. d) …… Frau ist jung.

17 Read the answers below. Then listen to the first question on the CD, pause after the beep and answer. You can hear the correct answer afterwards. Then continue. 1/16

Nein, ich bin Single. Ja, kein Problem. Mir geht es prima.
Mein Vater ist Rechtsanwalt. Meine Mutter ist Architektin.
Ja, ich habe einen Bruder. Ich bin seit 6 Monaten hier.

18 Pierre wrote an e-mail but the verbs are still missing. Read the e-mail and help Pierre fill in the missing verbs in the right form.

machen sein haben sein arbeiten machen gehen
heißen sein kommen kennen

Neue E-Mail

Lieber Michael,
wie .... (1.) es dir? Ich .... (2.) jetzt in Berlin und .... (3.) einen Deutschkurs. Deutsch .... (4.) nicht sehr schwer! Ich .... (5.) viel Spaß!
Eine Freundin aus dem Kurs .... (6.) Iwona. Sie .... (7.) aus Polen.
Mein Praktikum .... (8.) auch toll. Ich .... (9.) schon viele Menschen hier.
Was .... (10.) du? .... (11.) du noch in der Firma?
Viele Grüße
Pierre

19 Listen to the five short dialogues on the CD. Listen to how they say hello or good-bye. Do you know what time these people are meeting? Write the dialogue numbers. 1/17

1. 8 am .... 2. 2 pm .... 3. 10 pm ....

20 Read the phrases. Now say them aloud using the formal *Sie* this time.

1. Du fragst deinen Nachbarn.
2. Woher kommst du?
3. Arbeitest du viel?
4. Kannst du das bitte wiederholen?
5. Du bist aus Deutschland.

Intermediate test 1

1 Which article is right? Strike out the wrong ones.

1. *der* | *die* | *das* Architektin
2. *der* | *die* | *das* Präsentation
3. *der* | *die* | *das* Garten
4. *der* | *die* | *das* Zeit
5. *der* | *die* | *das* Monat
6. *der* | *die* | *das* Restaurant
7. *der* | *die* | *das* Woche
8. *der* | *die* | *das* Dialog

__/8

2 Write the following sentences again but this time use the modal verb given in brackets.

1. Sie holt den Laptop. *(müssen)* ....
2. Ich spreche über meine Familie. *(können)* ....
3. Ihr wiederholt den Satz. *(müssen)* ....
4. Arbeiten Sie sehr viel? *(müssen)* ....

__/4

1/18 **3 Read the following phrases. Then listen to the CD and decide …**

	right	wrong
1. Frau Schneider versteht alles.	☐	☐
2. Martina muss einen falschen Freund wiederholen.	☐	☐
3. Martina ist nicht zufrieden.	☐	☐
4. Yoko hat einen Bruder.	☐	☐
5. Jens ist nicht glücklich.	☐	☐

__/5

4 Either the plural or the singular is missing. Write down the form.

Singular	Plural
1. Land	....
2.	Stunden
3.	Firmen
4. Familie	....
5. Lehrer	....
6.	Söhne
7. Schwester	....
8. Mutter	....
9.	Häuser
10. Restaurant	....

__/10

5 Read the following answers. Then write down appropriate questions using either the formal *Sie* or the informal *Du* as stated.

1. .... (Sie)
Herr Schneider: „Ich komme aus Deutschland."

2. .... (Du)
Claudia: „Ja, ich kann das wiederholen."

3. .... (Du)
Brian: „Ja, ich hole den Beamer."

4. .... (Sie)
Frau Maier: „Ich arbeite in einer Consultingfirma."

__/4

6 Here is a short e-mail from a German friend. After you have read it, mark the right numbers with a cross in the questions below.

Neue E-Mail

An:
Kopie:
Betreff:
Von: Michael

Hallo,
das ist meine Familie: Mein Vater heißt Robert. Er ist Lehrer. Meine Mutter heißt Johanna und arbeitet in einem Kindergarten. Ich habe auch eine Schwester. Ihr Name ist Julia und sie ist zwölf. Ich habe keinen Bruder. Mein Vater hat viele Geschwister: Drei Schwestern und einen Bruder. Aber meine Mutter hat mehr Geschwister: vier Brüder und zwei Schwestern. Meine Eltern kennen sich seit vierzehn Jahren. Und deine Familie?
Tschüs!
Michael

1. Julia ist
   a) ☐ 2 Jahre alt.
   b) ☐ 12 Jahre alt.
   c) ☐ 20 Jahre alt.

2. Michaels Vater hat
   a) ☐ 1 Schwester.
   b) ☐ 2 Schwestern.
   c) ☐ 3 Schwestern.

3. Johanna hat
   a) ☐ 6 Geschwister.
   b) ☐ 7 Geschwister.
   c) ☐ 8 Geschwister.

4. Robert und Johanna haben
   a) ☐ kein Kind.
   b) ☐ 1 Kind.
   c) ☐ 2 Kinder.

5. Roberts Eltern haben
   a) ☐ 5 Kinder.
   b) ☐ 6 Kinder.
   c) ☐ 7 Kinder.

__/5

7 Complete the questions with the correct interrogative pronoun: *Wie, wo, woher.*

1. .... kommst du?
2. .... liegt das?
3. .... lange bist du schon in Berlin?
4. .... heißt du?
5. .... arbeitest du?

__/6 6. .... alt ist deine Mutter?

1/19 **8 Read the three business cards. You can see some information is missing. Now listen to the three short introductions on the CD and fill in the missing information.**

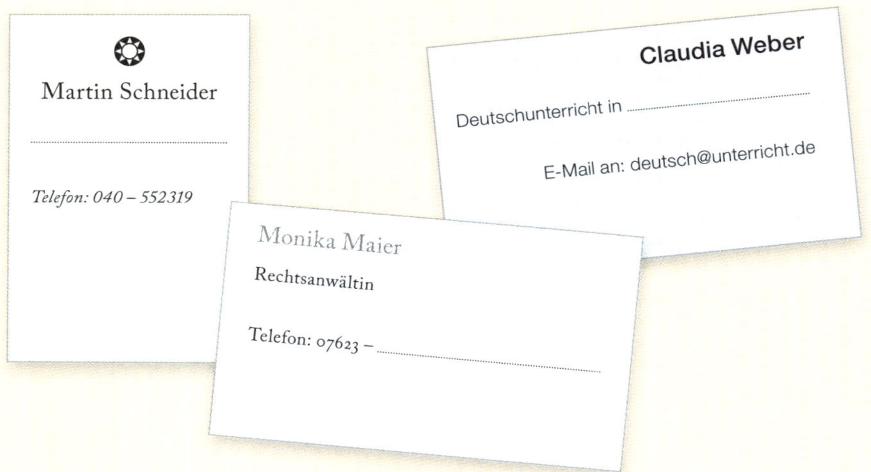

__/3

9 Translate the following sentences.

1. Can you help me? ....
2. I have to get the laptop. ....
3. He has to work a lot. ....
4. Jens can visit his mother often. ....

__/5 5. Can you repeat these words, please? ....

__/50

Shopping Day 7
In a restaurant Day 8
Leisure time in a city Day 9
Sport and hobbies Day 10
Forming new friendships Day 11
Home and chores Day 12
Information and entertainment Day 13
Repeat and practise Day 14

Day 7 Shopping

In this lesson you will learn

- to buy food
- to ask about prices
- to get to know common quantities and packaging

Auf dem Markt

1/20
1/21

Verkäuferin	Na, junger Mann? Was darf's denn sein?
Pierre	Ich möchte Obst kaufen. Was kosten die Pfirsiche?
Verkäuferin	Die Pfirsiche? Ein Kilo kostet 2,60 Euro.
Pierre	O. K., dann bitte vier Pfirsiche. Und noch Weintrauben, bitte. Ein halbes Kilo.
Verkäuferin	Aber gern. Noch etwas?
Pierre	Ja, noch Gemüse. Ich brauche rote Paprika und Zucchini.
Verkäuferin	Wie viel möchten Sie denn?
Pierre	Ich möchte zwei Paprikas und eine Zucchini, bitte.
Verkäuferin	Johannes, gib dem Mann bitte das Gemüse. Ist das dann alles?
Pierre	Ja, vielen Dank.
Verkäuferin	Möchten Sie auch eine Tüte?
Pierre	Oh ja, bitte.
Verkäuferin	Das macht dann zusammen 11,50 Euro. Was gibt es denn zum Essen?
Pierre	Ich möchte Ratatouille kochen.
Verkäuferin	Ah, schön! So, Sie bekommen noch 3 Euro und 50 Cent zurück. Bitte.
Pierre	Danke. Auf Wiedersehen.
Verkäuferin	Auf Wiedersehen.
Pierre	Mal sehen … Ich brauche noch Schinken, eine Flasche Wein, einen Karton Milch und zwei Dosen Tomaten. Aber jetzt treffe ich mich erst mit Iwona. Sie wartet sicher schon auf mich …

Dialog questions

Mark with a cross:

	right	wrong
1. Pierre ist im Supermarkt.	☐	☐
2. Er kauft ein Kilo Pfirsiche.	☐	☐
3. Pierre kauft vier Paprikas.	☐	☐
4. Pierre kauft Zutaten für Ratatouille.	☐	☐
5. Die Waren kosten 3,50 Euro.	☐	☐
6. Pierre braucht noch Zucchinis.	☐	☐

At the market

Saleslady Hello, young man. What would you like to buy?
Pierre I'd like to buy some fruit. How much are the peaches?
Saleslady The peaches? One kilo costs 2,60 Euro.
Pierre OK, then four peaches, please. And grapes, please. Half a kilo.
Saleslady Certainly. Anything else?
Pierre Yes, some vegetables. I need red peppers and courgettes.
Saleslady How much do you want?
Pierre I would like two peppers and one courgette, please.
Saleslady Johannes, give the man the vegetables, please. Is that all then?
Pierre Yes, thank you very much.
Saleslady Would you like a bag?
Pierre Oh yes, please.
Saleslady That's 11,50 Euro altogether. What are you going to cook?
Pierre I'd like to cook Ratatouille.
Saleslady Oh, nice. So, 3 Euro and 50 Cents for you. Here you are.
Pierre Thanks. Good bye.
Saleslady Good bye.
Pierre Let's have a look ... I still need ham, a bottle of wine, a carton of milk and two cans of tomatoes. But now, I'm going to meet Iwona first. She's probably waiting for me already ...

Day 7 Vocabulary

bekommen	get
brauchen	need
Einkaufsliste, -n *f*	shopping list
geben	give
Geld *(only Sg) n*	money
Gemüse *(only Sg) n*	vegetable(-s)
gern, gewiss	certainly
Ich möchte ...	I would like ...
kaufen	buy
kosten	cost
Lebensmittel, – *n (mostly Pl)*	food
Markt, Märkte *m*	market
Milchprodukt, -e *n*	dairy product
Obst *(only Sg) n*	fruit
Preis, -e *m*	price
pro (Kilo)	per (kilo)
Sonderangebot, -e *n*	special offer
Supermarkt, -märkte *m*	supermarket
Verpackung, -en *f*	packaging
warten	wait
Wechselgeld *(only Sg) n*	change
wie viel/viele	how much/many

Weight & packaging	
Kilo, – *n*	kilo (kilogramme)
Gramm, – *n*	gramme/gram
Liter, – *m*	litre
Dose, -n *f*	can
Flasche, -n *f*	bottle
Karton, -s *m*	carton
Packung, -en *f*	package, pack
Stück, -e *n*	piece
Tüte, -n *f*	bag

Food	
Apfel, Äpfel *m*	apple
Birne, -n *f*	pear
Brot, -e *n*	bread
Brötchen, – *n*	bun
Butter *(only Sg) f*	butter
Ei, -er *n*	egg
Fisch, -e *m*	fish
Fleisch *(only Sg) n*	meat
Gurke, -n *f*	cucumber
Hähnchen, – *n*	chicken
Kartoffel, -n *f*	potato
Käse *(only Sg) m*	cheese
Marmelade, -n *f*	jam
Milch *(only Sg) f*	milk
Möhre, -n *f* (*also* Karotte, -n *f*)	carrot
Müsli, -s *n*	muesli
Paprika, -s *m/f*	peppers
Pfirsich, -e *m*	peach
Sahne *(only Sg) f*	cream
Schinken *(only Sg) m*	ham
Tomate, -n *f*	tomato
Wein, -e *m*	wine
Weintraube, -n *f*	grape
Wurst, Würste *f*	sausage
Zucchini, -s *f*	courgette
Zwiebel, -n *f*	onion

Grammar and means of expression

Imperative ► § 8.9

The imperative is the form for commands and requests. The verb goes always to the front of the sentence. Depending on who you address you need one of the following imperative sentences.

Declarative sentence	Rule	Imperative
Du gibst dem Mann das Gemüse.	no pronoun omit ending **-st**	**Gib** dem Mann das Gemüse.
Ihr gebt dem Mann das Gemüse.	no pronoun	**Gebt** dem Mann das Gemüse.
Sie geben dem Mann das Gemüse. *(formal)*	keep the pronoun	**Geben** Sie dem Mann das Gemüse.

Cases: *Dativ* ► § 2.1

The English indirect object is the **Dativ** in German. Certain verbs (like **geben** – see the example for the imperative) and prepositions need an object in the dative. With verbs the dative usually is an object that receives something. A noun in the dative gets an **-n** ending – but only in the plural and when not already there.

Dative of the definite article				
	m	f	n	Pl
Nom.	der	die	das	die
Dat.	dem	der	dem	den (noun+n)

Dative of the indefinite article				
	m	f	n	Pl
Nom.	ein	eine	ein	–
Dat.	einem	einer	einem	– (noun+n)

Remember that the forms of the possessive pronouns and **kein** are similar to the indefinite article. Their plural form is **keinen**, **meinen**, **deinen** ...

Nullartikel ► § 2.2

Nullartikel means you need no article in front of the noun. Like in English, you use nouns of unspecified quantity without any article:
Ich brauche noch Schinken. *I still need ham.*

Day 7 Exercises

1 Take the food table from the vocabulary section and sort the items into the following table.

Obst	Gemüse
....	....
....	....
....	....
....	....
....	....
....	....
....	....

Milchprodukte	Anderes (others)
....	....
....	....
....	....
....	....
....	....
....	....
....	....

2 Connect the questions with the right answers.

1. Was kosten die Orangen?
2. Ist das dann alles?
3. Was darf's denn sein?
4. Wie viele Gurken möchten Sie?

a) Geben Sie mir bitte zwei Stück.
b) Ein Kilo kostet 3 Euro.
c) Nein, ich brauche noch Gemüse.
d) Ich möchte Wurst kaufen.

1/22 **3 Listen to the special offers on the CD. Now write the right prices of the food items.**

1. Kartoffeln: .... pro Kilo
2. Birnen: .... pro Kilo
3. Schinken: .... pro Packung
4. Wein: .... pro Flasche

Kulturtipp Shopping in Germany

If you want to go shopping in Germany keep in mind that, at least in some states (like Bavaria), the opening hours of shops on working days are limited. Bigger supermarkets are at least open till 8 pm. But smaller shops like butchers or bakers normally still close around 6 or 7 pm.

On Saturday some shops close still earlier, some even as early as 1 or 2 pm and on Sunday all shops are closed. All shops? No, there are some exceptions: petrol stations often sell food too and they are mostly open on Sundays and shops at the station (at least in bigger cities) can open on Sundays too.

If you prefer fresh food directly from the farmer go to the **Wochenmärkte** *weekly farmers' markets* like Pierre. They offer a wide variety of food and now a lot of organic products as well. They take place at least once a week, often on two days and usually in central (market) places.

What can you already do?

	☺	😐	☹	
▪ know common food	▫	▫	▫	► Ü1
▪ ask about prices	▫	▫	▫	► Ü2
▪ buy food	▫	▫	▫	► Ü2
▪ understand prices and packaging	▫	▫	▫	► Ü3

So, this was your first lesson in the second part. If you don't understand everything at the beginning, don't let that discourage you. That's normal for everyone! Just listen to the texts on the CD several times and don't forget the appendix – the short grammar section, the complete vocabulary section and the solutions are there to help you!

Day 8

In a restaurant

In this lesson you will learn

- to order something to eat or drink
- to ask for the bill in a restaurant or café
- to speak about food

1/23 1/24

Für mich einen Kuchen

Iwona and Pierre sitzen in einem Café.

Kellner Guten Tag. Was hätten Sie denn gerne?
Iwona Guten Tag. Für mich eine Tasse Kaffee und ein Stück Apfelkuchen, bitte.
Kellner Und für Sie?
Pierre Ich hätte gerne einen Milchkaffee und ein Stück Schokoladen-torte. Könnte ich bitte auch etwas Schlagsahne bekommen?
Kellner Ja, natürlich.
Iwona Kommst du jetzt vom Markt?
Pierre Ja! Und der Markt ist toll – viel besser als ein Supermarkt. Es gibt sogar einen Stand mit französischen Spezialitäten. Das muss ich meiner Mutter erzählen!
Iwona *(etwas später)* Und? Wie ist deine Torte?
Pierre Sehr lecker! Möchtest du sie probieren?
Iwona Gern! Oh ja, sehr lecker! Hier, probier auch von meinem Kuchen.
Pierre Danke. Mmm, schmeckt mir sehr!
Kellner *(noch etwas später)* Darf ich Ihnen noch etwas bringen?
Iwona Nein danke, aber könnten wir bitte die Rechnung bekommen?
Kellner Ja, sehr gern.
Pierre Wie ist das in Deutschland? Geben wir dem Kellner auch Trinkgeld?
Iwona Ja, etwas Trinkgeld ist üblich. Und dann müssen wir gehen. Jens und Martina warten sicher schon.
Pierre Jens und Martina? Treffen wir uns nicht morgen?
Iwona Nein Pierre, wir treffen uns heute!

Dialog questions

Cross out the wrong answer.

1. Iwona isst ein Stück *Apfelkuchen* | *Schokoladentorte*.
2. Pierre möchte *etwas* | *keine* Schlagsahne.
3. Iwona findet Pierres Torte *nicht* | *sehr* lecker.
4. Pierre und Iwona treffen sich *heute* | *morgen* mit Jens und Martina.

A pie for me ...

Iwona and Pierre are in a café.

Waiter Good afternoon. What would you like?

Iwona Good afternoon. A cup of coffee and a slice of apple pie for me, please.

Waiter And for you?

Pierre I'd like a café au lait and a slice of chocolate gateau. Could I have some whipped cream too, please?

Waiter Yes, of course.

Iwona Have you just come from the market?

Pierre Yes! And the market is great – much better than a supermarket. There was even a market stand with French specialties. I have to tell my mother about it!

Iwona *(a bit later)* And? How is your gateau?

Pierre Delicious! Would you like to taste it?

Iwona Yes, please! Oh yes, very tasty! Here, try my pie as well.

Pierre Thanks. Mmm, I like it very much!

Waiter *(later yet)* May I get you anything else?

Iwona No thanks, but could we have the bill please?

Waiter Yes, of course.

Pierre How is it in Germany? Do we tip the waiter?

Iwona Yes, you normally tip. And then we have to go. Jens and Martina for sure are waiting already.

Pierre Jens and Martina? Aren't we meeting them tomorrow?

Iwona No Pierre, today!

Day 8 Vocabulary

Beilage, -n *f*	side dish
bestellen	order
bringen	get, bring
Café, -s *n*	café
erzählen	tell
essen	eat
Essen, – *n*	meal
Gabel, -n *f*	fork
Glas, Gläser *n*	glass
Hauptgericht, -e *n*	main dish
Ich hätte gern...	I'd like (to have)...
ja, natürlich	yes, of course
Könnte ich ...?	Could I...?
Kuchen, – *m*	cake, pie
Löffel, – *m*	spoon
Messer, – *n*	knife
Nachtisch, -e *m*	dessert
probieren	taste, try
Rechnung, -en *f*	bill
schlecht	bad
schmecken	taste
lecker	delicious
Serviette, -n *f*	napkin
sicher	for sure
Tasse, -n *f*	cup
Teller, – *m*	plate, dish
Torte, -n *f*	gateau
trinken	drink
Trinkgeld *(only Sg) n*	tip
üblich	normal, common
warten	wait

Something to drink	
Getränk, -e *n*	beverage, drink
Kaffee, -s *m*	coffee
Tee, -s *m*	tea
(stilles) Wasser, – *n*	(non sparkling) water
Sprudel, – *m*	sparkling water
Bier, -e *n*	beer
Cola, -s *n/f*	coke
Saft, Säfte *m*	juice
Schorle, -n *f*	juice or wine mixed with sparkling water

Popular dishes	
Schnitzel, – *n*	schnitzel
Kartoffeln *f* *(here mostly Pl)*	potatoes
Nudeln *f* *(mostly Pl)*	noodles
Reis *(only Sg) m*	rice
Pommes (frites) *(only Pl)*	chips
Suppe, -n *f*	soup
Salat, -e *m*	salad

Some temporal adverbials	
heute	today
morgen	tomorrow
übermorgen	the day after tomorrow
gestern	yesterday
vorgestern	the day before yesterday
jetzt	now
später	later
früher	earlier

Grammar and means of expression

Polite forms ▸ *§ 8.6*

You've seen in the dialogues from this and the previous lessons what Pierre and Iwona say to get what they want:
Ich möchte zwei Paprikas, bitte. *I would like two peppers, please.*
Ich hätte gerne einen Milchkaffee. *I'd like (to have) a café au lait.*
Könnte ich etwas Schlagsahne bekommen? *Could I have some whipped cream?*
These are the polite forms you can use when you want something.

Personal pronouns ▸ *§ 3.1*

A pronoun usually replaces a noun, like with the nominative (e.g. **er** instead of **Pierre**):
Er kauft Obst. *He buys fruit.*
It's the same with the accusative and the dative.
You've already seen it in the dialogue:
Möchtest du **sie** probieren? *Would you like to taste it?* (accusative)
Darf ich **Ihnen** noch etwas bringen? *May I get you anything else?* (dative)

The personal pronouns in the nominative, accusative and dative						
Nom.	ich	du	er/sie/es	wir	ihr	sie/Sie
Acc.	mich	dich	ihn/sie/es	uns	euch	sie/Sie
Dat.	mir	dir	ihm/ihr/ihm	uns	euch	ihnen/Ihnen

More examples are:
Was hätten **Sie** denn gerne? *What would you like?* (nominative)
Das schmeckt **mir** sehr. *I like it very much.* (dative)
Und für **Sie**? *And for you?* (accusative)
Könnten **wir** die Rechnung bekommen? *Could we have the bill?* (nominative)

Three- and four-digit numbers

200	zweihundert	1000	(ein-)tausend
300	dreihundert	2000	zweitausend
768	siebenhundertachtundsechzig	4179	viertausendeinhundertneun-undsiebzig

Day 8 Exercises

1 Order your lunch. Read the menu and underline what you would like.

Suppen	
Tomatensuppe	2 €
Gemüsesuppe	2 €
Nudelsuppe	1,80 €
Zwiebelsuppe	1,80 €
Beilagen	
Pommes	2 €
Reis	1,80 €
Nudeln	2 €
Kartoffeln	1,50 €
Gemüse	1,80 €
kleiner Salat	1,50 €
großer Salat	3 €

Hauptgerichte	
Schnitzel	5 €
Fisch	5 €
Hähnchen	4,50 €
Ratatouille	3,50 €
Getränke	
Cola	2 €
Wasser	1,50 €
Apfelsaft	2 €
Bier	2,50 €
Tee	1 €
Kaffee	1,80 €

1/25

2 Martina and Jens are in a restaurant. Listen to the short dialogue on the CD and mark who orders what.

	Martina	Jens
Wasser	☐	☐
Bier	☐	☐
Salat	☐	☐
Suppe	☐	☐
Schnitzel mit Pommes	☐	☐
Fisch mit Kartoffeln	☐	☐
Rechnung	☐	☐

3 Imagine you're in a restaurant. What would you say to get the following dishes?

eine Tasse Tee   ein Schnitzel mit Kartoffeln   ein Glas Cola
ein Stück Apfelkuchen   eine Suppe   ein Salat

Kulturtipp Eat and drink

Apart from the common meals throughout the day, **das Frühstück** *breakfast*, **das Mittagessen** *lunch* and **das Abendessen** *supper*, the Germans like to have **Kaffee und Kuchen** *coffee and cake* in the afternoon. Often there's only time for this in the afternoon at weekends. Like Iwona and Pierre, people enjoy meeting in the city to have their coffee and cake in a café.

By the way, coffee is one of the most popular beverages in Germany besides **Bier** *beer* and **Sprudel** *sparkling mineral water.*

When you're in a restaurant or café with other people and you ask for the bill, the waiter may ask if you want to pay **getrennt oder zusammen**. This means he wants to know if each person is paying for her-/himself individually or if the whole sum is going to be paid in one go. Usually it's no problem to divide the sum in other ways: e.g. you pay for the drinks and your friend for the food.

What can you already do?

	☺	😐	☹	
▪ order something to eat or drink	▫	▫	▫	► *Ü2, Ü3*
▪ ask for the bill	▫	▫	▫	► *Ü2*
▪ understand a basic menu	▫	▫	▫	► *Ü1*

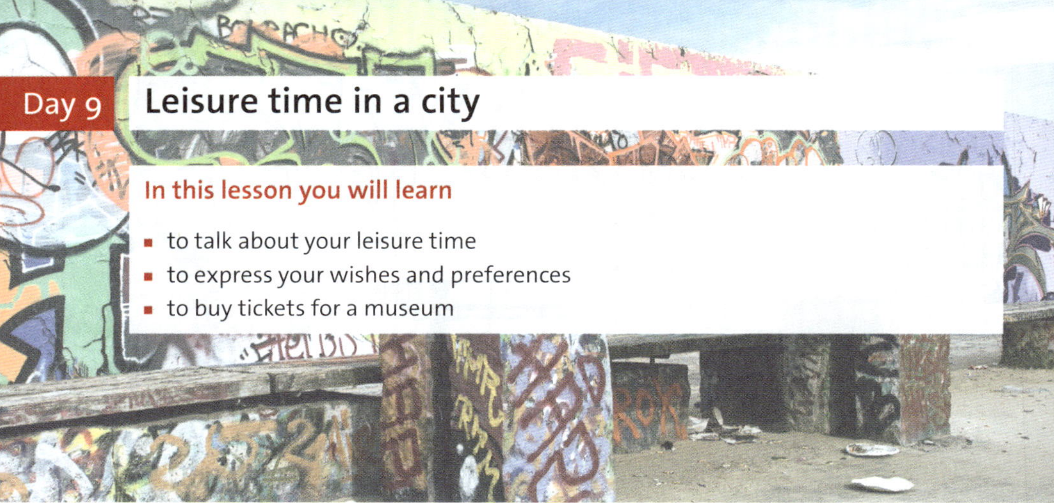

Day 9 Leisure time in a city

In this lesson you will learn

- to talk about your leisure time
- to express your wishes and preferences
- to buy tickets for a museum

1/26
1/27

Berliner Sehenswürdigkeiten

Iwona, Martina, Pierre und Jens treffen sich am Brandenburger Tor.

Jens Hallo Iwona! Hi Pierre. Wie geht's euch?
Iwona Gut, danke.
Pierre Hi. Was unternehmen wir denn heute?
Jens Wart ihr schon auf dem Fernsehturm am Alexanderplatz?
Iwona Nein, aber können wir nicht lieber einen Spaziergang durch die Stadt machen?
Martina Das Wetter ist heute nicht so gut. Am besten finde ich ein Museum!
Pierre Ja, und das ist sicher interessanter als ein Spaziergang.
Iwona O. K, aber welches Museum?
Martina Auf der Museumsinsel sind einige Museen.
Jens Martina, die Museen dort machen alle schon um 18 Uhr zu. Es ist halb vier – das ist zu wenig Zeit. Aber kennt ihr schon das Mauermuseum? Das ist länger offen.
Pierre Nein, was gibt es da zu sehen?
Jens Alles rund um die Berliner Mauer. Wir gehen dann am Abend noch auf den Fernsehturm und sehen Berlin bei Nacht!
Iwona Ja, das hört sich toll an. Das machen wir.

Die vier kommen am Mauermuseum an.

Pierre Bitte vier Eintrittskarten. Gibt es eine Ermäßigung für Studenten?
Verkäuferin Ja. Wie viele Studentenkarten möchten Sie?
Pierre Eine Karte für einen Studenten und drei normale, bitte.
Verkäuferin Darf ich bitte Ihren Studentenausweis sehen? Danke. Das macht dann zusammen 47 Euro ...

Dialogue questions

Mark the right answer.

1. War Iwona schon auf dem Fernsehturm? a) ☐ Ja. b) ☐ Nein.
2. Wer möchte einen Spaziergang machen? a) ☐ Martina. b) ☐ Iwona.
3. Wohin gehen die vier? a) ☐ Museum. b) ☐ Berliner Mauer.
4. Wer bekommt eine Ermäßigung? a) ☐ Pierre. b) ☐ Iwona.

Berlin's sights

Iwona, Martina, Pierre and Jens meet at the Brandenburg Gate.

Jens Hello Iwona! Hi Pierre. How are you?
Iwona Well, thanks.
Pierre Hi. What are we going to do today?
Jens Have you been to the television tower on Alexanderplatz yet?
Iwona No, but can't we go for a walk through the city instead?
Martina The weather's not so good today. I think a museum would be best!
Pierre Yes, and it's certainly more interesting than a walk.
Iwona OK, but which museum?
Martina There are some museums on the museum island.
Jens Martina, the museums there close at 6 pm. It's half past 3 now – that's too little time. But do you know the Wall museum? It closes later.
Pierre No, what's there to see?
Jens Everything about the Berlin Wall. Then we can go up the television tower in the evening and see Berlin by night!
Iwona Yes, that sounds great. Let's do it.

The four arrive at the Wall museum.

Pierre Four tickets please. Is there a discount for students?
Ticket seller Yes. How many tickets for students do you want?
Pierre One ticket for a student and three normal, please.
Ticket seller May I see your student ID? Thanks. That's 47 Euro altogether ...

Day 9 Vocabulary

Abend, -e *m*	evening
alles rund um	all about
ankommen	arrive
bezahlen, zahlen	pay
Das hört sich toll an.	Sounds great.
einige	some
Eintrittskarte, -n *f*	ticket
Ermäßigung, -en *f*	discount
Freizeit *(only Sg) f*	leisure time
geschlossen	closed
groß	big
interessant	interesting
Museum, Museen *n*	museum
Nacht, Nächte *f*	night
normal	normal
offen	open
Öffnungszeit, -en *f*	opening hours
sehen	see
Sehenswürdigkeit, -en *f*	sight
Spaziergang, -gänge *m*	walk
Student, -en *m*	student
Studentenausweis, -e *m*	student ID
Um wie viel Uhr ...?	What time ...?
unternehmen	do, undertake
wann	when
Wetter *(only Sg) n*	weather
zumachen	close

Learning tip

Nouns with the suffixes **-ung** and **-keit** are always feminine – like **die Ermäßigung** and **die Sehenswürdigkeit**.

What to do in your leisure time?

auf ein Konzert gehen	go to a concert
ein Museum besichtigen	visit a museum
eine Stadtrundfahrt machen	go on a sightseeing tour
einkaufen, shoppen	go shopping, shop
faulenzen	do nothing
in eine Ausstellung gehen	go to an exhibition
ins Kino/Theater gehen	go to the cinema/ theatre
spazieren (gehen)	stroll, walk

Grammar and means of expression

Adjective comparison ▸ *§ 6.3*

For most adjectives you simply add ...**-er** for the comparative and **am ...-(e)sten** for the superlative (some adjectives get an umlaut too – see the short grammar!).
Ein Spaziergang ist interessant. *A walk is interesting.*
Das Ägyptische Museum ist interessant**er**. *The Egyptian Museum is more interesting.*
Das Mauermuseum ist **am** interessant**esten**. *The Wall Museum is the most interesting.*

The most important irregular adjectives and adverbs			
	Positive	Comparative	Superlative
good	gut	besser	am besten
gladly	gern	lieber	am liebsten
much	viel	mehr	am meisten

Simple future ▸ *§ 8.4*

An easy and common way to speak about the future is the use of the present tense and a temporal adverbial.
Wir gehen **am Abend** auf den Fernsehturm.
We're going to go up the television tower in the evening.
Wir gehen **morgen** in ein Museum.
Tomorrow we're going to go to a museum.

Time

There are two ways to say what time it is in German. The first is a bit more formal (e.g. as heard at a train station) and it uses the 24 hour clock. The other is less formal and uses the 12 hour clock:

What time is it?		
written	spoken *(formal)*	spoken *(less formal)*
21.00 Uhr	Es ist einundzwanzig Uhr.	Es ist neun (Uhr).
16.30 Uhr	Es ist sechzehn Uhr dreißig.	Es ist halb fünf.
22.45 Uhr	Es ist zweiundzwanzig Uhr fünfundvierzig.	Es ist Viertel vor elf.
02.15 Uhr	Es ist zwei Uhr fünfzehn.	Es ist Viertel nach zwei.

Exercises

1 Complete the sentences. Put the adjective/adverb in the comparative. Use any additional information in brackets for your sentence.

1. Hamburg ist groß. Berlin ....
2. Iwona geht gern in die Stadt. Martina .... (in ein Museum gehen).
3. Ein Spaziergang ist gut. Eine Stadtrundfahrt ....
4. Jens geht gern ins Kino. Martina .... (ins Theater).
5. Das Ägyptische Museum ist interessant. Das Mauermuseum ....
6. Berlin bei Tag ist toll. Berlin bei Nacht ....

2 How would you react in the following situations? Choose the right reply from the box and say it loud.

Ich möchte lieber eine Stadtrundfahrt machen. Ich faulenze lieber.
Gibt es eine Studentenermäßigung? Was kostet eine normale Eintrittskarte?
Ich hätte gerne eine normale Eintrittskarte und zwei für Studenten.
Ich gehe lieber einkaufen als ins Theater. Um wie viel Uhr macht das Museum zu?

1. You want to buy tickets. You need two tickets for students.
2. You'd rather go shopping than to the theatre.
3. You want to know when the museum closes.
4. You need to know if there's a discount for students.
5. You tell your friend that you want to go on a sightseeing tour.
6. You prefer doing nothing.
7. You want to know how much a normal ticket costs.

1/28

3 Listen to the CD. In each sentence you'll hear a time. Write the number of this sentence next to the correct time below. One time has no matching sentence.

1. 11.15 Uhr: ....
2. 14.00 Uhr: ....
3. 9.45 Uhr: ....
4. 8.45 Uhr: ....
5. 19.15 Uhr: ....
6. 15.30 Uhr: ....
7. 18.30 Uhr: ....
8. 15.00 Uhr ....

Kulturtipp
A weekend in Berlin

You want to spend a weekend in Berlin? Berlin has a lot to offer but you'd have to stay a long time there to see everything that's worth seeing.

If you're a fan of museums then you could start with one of the five museums on the **Museumsinsel** *museum island* in the center of the city. You're more interested in recent history? The **Haus am Checkpoint Charlie**, the **Mauermuseum**, tells you all about the history of the Berlin Wall.

But maybe it's a nice day and you don't want to stay inside. You could go to one of the two zoos or take a stroll along the great boulevard **Unter den Linden** and walk through the **Brandenburger Tor** *Brandenburg Gate*. Once there, head over to the **Reichstagsgebäude** *Reichstag building* and enjoy the view from the newly built dome on the roof.

You like shopping too? Then don't miss the **Kaufhaus des Westens** *Department Store of the West*, the **KaDeWe**.

What can you already do?

	☺	😐	☹	
▪ talk about your leisure time	☐	☐	☐	► *Ü1, Ü2*
▪ express your wishes and preferences	☐	☐	☐	► *Ü1, Ü2*
▪ buy tickets for a museum	☐	☐	☐	► *Ü2*
▪ understand time	☐	☐	☐	► *Ü3*

Day 10 Sport and hobbies

In this lesson you will learn

- to give advice
- to talk about your daily routine
- to present your interests, hobbies and favourite sports

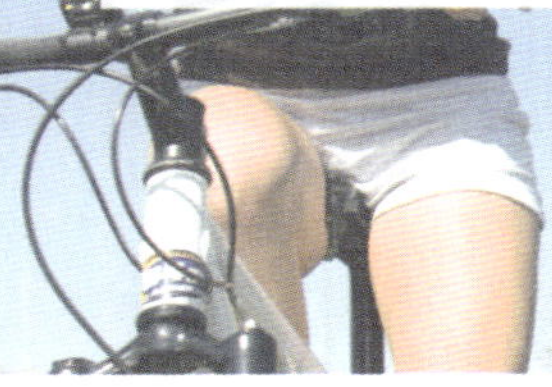

1/29
1/30

Sport in Berlin

Iwona und Martina gehen nach dem Deutschkurs ein Stück zusammen.

Iwona Martina, ich will wieder mehr Sport machen. Kannst du mir ein paar Tipps geben?

Martina Ja, klar. Was machst du denn gerne?

Iwona Am liebsten spiele ich Volleyball. Aber ich gehe auch gern joggen. Wo kann ich das gut machen? Ich laufe nicht gern an der Straße.

Martina Ja, das kann ich verstehen. Du könntest zum Beispiel im Tiergarten laufen. Es gibt auch tolle Laufstrecken außerhalb des Stadtzentrums … Da musst du aber erst hinfahren.

Iwona Ich stehe gerne früh auf und gehe joggen. Danach will ich in Ruhe duschen und frühstücken. Ich habe keine Zeit, noch weit zu fahren. Aber wie ist das mit Volleyball?

Martina Das weiß ich nicht. Aber du solltest mal im Internet suchen – am besten such nach einem Sportverein, vielleicht auch bei der Volkshochschule oder an der Uni.

Iwona Ja, das mache ich. Danke! Welchen Sport machst du denn gerne?

Martina Ich fahre viel Rad in der Stadt. Sonst mache ich keinen Sport. Am Wochenende machen wir manchmal eine Radtour. Wir nehmen dich auch gerne einmal mit!

Iwona Super! Aber ich habe kein Fahrrad …

Martina Das ist kein Problem. Du leihst einfach ein Fahrrad aus!

Dialogue questions

Mark with a cross:

	right	wrong
1. Martina gibt Iwona Tipps.	☐	☐
2. Iwona will nicht in der Stadt joggen.	☐	☐
3. Sie joggt am liebsten nach dem Frühstück.	☐	☐
4. Martina ist in einem Sportverein.	☐	☐
5. Iwona hat ein Fahrrad.	☐	☐

Sport in Berlin

Iwona and Martina walk a short way together after German class.

Iwona Martina, I want to work out more again. Can you give me a few tips?

Martina Yes, of course. What do you like to do?

Iwona I like volleyball the most. But I like to jog too. Where's a good place for this? I don't like running near a street.

Martina Yes, I understand that. You could jog in the Tiergarten park for instance. There are some great running routes out of town too ... But you have to get there first.

Iwona I like to get up early and jog. Afterwards I want to take a shower in peace and eat breakfast. I don't have time for long drives. But what about volleyball?

Martina I don't know. But you should search the internet – the best idea would be to look for a sports club, maybe even at the Volkshochschule or at the university.

Iwona Yes, I will do that. Thanks! What sport do you like?

Martina I cycle a lot in town. Otherwise I don't work out. At weekends we go on a bicycle tour sometimes. We'll gladly take you along some time!

Iwona Super! But I don't have a bike ...

Martina That's no problem. Just borrow one!

Day 10 Vocabulary

ausleihen	borrow
außerhalb	out of
Beispiel, -e *n*	example
danach	afterwards
einmal	once
Fahrrad, -räder *n*	bicycle, bike
früh	early
geben	give
hinfahren	get/drive there
Hobby, -s *n*	hobby
Interessen (*only Pl*)	interests, hobbies
Internet (*only Sg*) *n*	internet
ja, klar	yes, of course
manchmal	sometimes
mitnehmen	take along
oft	often
Park, -s *m*	park
Problem, -e *n*	problem
Radtour, -en *f*	bicycle tour
Ruhe (*only Sg*) *f*	peace
Sport* (*only Sg*) *m*	sport
Sportart**, -en *f*	sport
Sportverein, -e *m*	sports club
Stadt, Städte *f*	town, city
Stadtzentrum, -zentren *n*	city centre
Straße, -n *f*	street
suchen	search
Tipp, -s *m*	tip
vielleicht	maybe
weit	far, long
Wochenende, -n *n*	weekend

* *sport in general*
** *different kinds of sport*

Daily routine	
aufstehen	get up
frühstücken	eat breakfast
etw. zum Frühstück essen	eat sth. for breakfast
duschen	take a shower
Zähne putzen	brush one's teeth
in die Arbeit gehen/fahren	go/drive to work
arbeiten	work
zu Mittag/ Abend essen	have lunch/dinner
nach Hause kommen	return home
fernsehen	watch TV
ins Bett gehen	go to bed
schlafen	sleep

Times of the day	
Morgen *m*	morning
Vormittag *m*	morning
Mittag *m*	noon
Nachmittag *m*	afternoon
Abend *m*	evening
Nacht *f*	night

Sport & hobbies	
joggen, laufen	jog, run
Judo/Karate/ Aikido/... machen	do judo/karate/aikido/...
klettern	climb
Rad fahren	cycle
schwimmen	swim
Volleyball/Fuß-ball/Tennis/ ... spielen	play volleyball/football/ tennis/...

Grammar and means of expression

Trennbare Verben ► *§ 8.7*

Some German verbs have a prefix (usually a preposition) that is **trennbar** *separable*. Let's have a look at the examples from the dialogue:
Wir **nehmen** dich **mit**. *We'll take you along.*
Du **leihst** ein Fahrrad **aus**. *You borrow a bike.*
Their infinitives are **mitnehmen** and **ausleihen**. But when you use them in the present tense the prefix goes to the last position in the sentence.
With a modal verb you use the normal infinitive:
Du musst mich **mitnehmen**. *You have to take me along.*
Sie kann ein Fahrrad **ausleihen**. *She can borrow a bike.*

The modal verbs *wollen* and *sollen* ► *§ 8.6*

sollen shall/are to		wollen want	
ich soll	wir sollen	ich will	wir wollen
du sollst	ihr sollt	du willst	ihr wollt
er/sie/es soll	sie/Sie sollen	er/sie/es will	sie/Sie wollen

Advice ► *§ 8.6*

To give someone advice you can use the imperative (• *Day 7*) or the forms **sollt-** and **könnt-**:
Such im Internet! *Search the internet.*
Lauf im Tiergarten! *Jog in the Tiergarten park.*
... or ...
Du **solltest** im Internet suchen. *You should search the internet.*
Du **könntest** im Tiergarten laufen. *You could jog in the Tiergarten park.*
These forms are more polite than the imperative. And **könnt-** is more like a proposition.
For advice you mainly need the forms of the second person *(Sg/Pl)* and the formal **Sie**:
du sollt**est** ..., ihr sollt**et** ..., Sie sollt**en** ...
du könnt**est** ..., ihr könnt**et** ..., Sie könnt**en** ...

Exercises

1 Connect the phrases with the right advice.

1. Ich will nicht an der Straße joggen.
2. Ich jogge nicht gerne morgens.
3. Ich habe leider kein Fahrrad.
4. Wo finde ich einen Sportverein?
5. Ich spiele gern Fußball.
6. Ich fahre sehr gern Rad.

a) Du könntest eine Radtour mit uns machen.
b) Du solltest im Park laufen.
c) Du solltest mal im Internet suchen.
d) Du könntest ein Rad ausleihen.
e) Du könntest abends joggen.
f) Du solltest einen Sportverein suchen.

1/31

2 Read the sentences below. Then listen to the three short descriptions of daily routines on the CD. Mark them:

	right	wrong
1. Pierre isst nichts zum Frühstück.	☐	☐
2. Nach der Arbeit geht er einkaufen.	☐	☐
3. Martina steht gern früh auf.	☐	☐
4. Sie trinkt nur einen Kaffee zum Frühstück.	☐	☐
5. Iwona kommt oft erst am Abend nach Hause.	☐	☐
6. Am Abend liest sie gern.	☐	☐

3 Iwona posted on an internet forum about sport. Read what she wrote and write a similar text about yourself and your favourite sport.

Hallo,
ich mache gern Sport. Am Morgen gehe ich oft joggen. Am liebsten jogge ich in einem Park. Ich fahre auch gerne Rad, aber ich habe kein Fahrrad in Deutschland. Am liebsten spiele ich Volleyball. Ich bin auch gut. Wo kann ich hier in Berlin Volleyball spielen? Kann mir jemand helfen? Vielen Dank!
Iwona

Kulturtipp Germans and football

Football is one of the most popular sports in Germany – even before the World Cup in Germany in 2006. A lot of Germans spend Saturday afternoon in a football stadium or – after 6 pm – in front of the television watching the **Sportschau** with the results of the **Bundesliga** *German Football League*. The matches of the national football team draw an even greater TV audience or – since 2006 during the World or European Cup – there is **Public Viewing** (yes, that's German!), where the matches are shown on big screens open to the public.

Thanks to the great successes of the women's national football team, women's football has become very popular and is one of the fastest growing sports in Germany.

If you want to play sports actively check out the local **Sportvereine** *sports clubs* where you can participate in your favourite sport for small fees.

What can you already do?

	☺	😐	☹	
▪ give advice	☐	☐	☐	▸ *Ü1*
▪ talk about your daily routine	☐	☐	☐	▸ *Ü2*
▪ present your interests, hobbies and favourite sports	☐	☐	☐	▸ *Ü3*

Learning a foreign language is like sport. You have to stay on the ball. And if you do, you'll get better and better and it's as much fun – but with a lot less sweating! And don't forget that learning a language is a team sport. Sooner or later you're out there "competing" – why not already assemble a team for training?

Day 11

Forming new friendships

In this lesson you will learn

- to introduce others and become introduced
- to welcome guests
- to congratulate someone

1/32
1/33

Jens' Geburtstagsparty

Iwona und Pierre stehen vor der Wohnung von Martina und Jens und klingeln an der Tür ...

Jens Hallo Iwona! Hi Pierre! Kommt herein. Hier könnt ihr eure Jacken aufhängen.

Iwona Hallo Jens. Herzlichen Glückwunsch zum Geburtstag.

Pierre Ja, alles Gute zum Geburtstag. Und vielen Dank für die Einladung.

Iwona Wir haben ein kleines Geschenk für dich. Hier, bitte.

Jens Mensch, vielen Dank! Und willkommen in unserer Wohnung. Martina ist noch in der Küche. Die anderen Gäste sind im Wohnzimmer. Es sind erst zwei da. Ich stelle euch kurz vor: Das ist Kathrin, Martinas Schwester, und ihr Freund Andreas. Und das hier sind Iwona und Pierre. Sie sind aus Martinas Kurs und Pierre ist auch ein Kollege von mir.

Kathrin Hallo! Schön, euch kennenzulernen.

Iwona Hallo.

Pierre Hi, freut mich!

Andreas Hallo, sehr angenehm.

Jens Da hinten auf dem Tisch sind Getränke. Bedient euch einfach.

Einige Zeit später

Kathrin Du kannst echt gut Deutsch. Sprichst du in der Arbeit auch Deutsch?

Iwona Nicht viel. Wir sprechen dort fast nur Englisch. Wir haben viele internationale Kollegen und Kunden.

Kathrin Das ist alles echt interessant! Komm uns doch mal in Potsdam besuchen. Dann reden wir und besichtigen die Stadt.

Dialogue questions

Answer the questions briefly.

1. Wer hat Geburtstag? ....
2. Wer ist Andreas? ....
3. Wo stehen die Getränke? ....
4. Wo wohnt Kathrin? ....

Jens' birthday party

Iwona and Pierre stand in front of Martina's and Jens' flat and ring the doorbell ...

Jens Hello Iwona! Hi Pierre! Come on in. You can put your jackets there.

Iwona Hello Jens. Happy birthday.

Pierre Yes, all the best for your birthday. And thanks a lot for the invitation.

Iwona We have a small present for you. Here you go.

Jens Gosh, thanks a lot! And welcome to our flat. Martina is still in the kitchen. The other guests are in the living room. There are only two at the moment. I'll introduce you briefly: That's Kathrin, Martina's sister, and her boyfriend Andreas. And this is Iwona and Pierre. They are from Martina's class and Pierre is a colleague of mine too.

Kathrin Hello! Nice to meet you.

Iwona Hello.

Pierre Hi, pleased to meet you!

Andreas Hello, pleased to meet you too.

Jens Back there are drinks on the table. Just help yourself.

Some time later

Kathrin You speak German very well. Do you speak German at work too?

Iwona Not much. We speak almost only English. We have a lot of international colleagues and clients.

Kathrin That's really interesting! Come and visit us in Potsdam. We'll be able to talk a lot and visit the city.

Day 11 Vocabulary

aufhängen	put
Einladung, -en *f*	invitation
empfangen	welcome
Freund, -e *m*	(boy-) friend
Freundin, -nen *f*	(girl-) friend
Gast, Gäste *m*	guest
Geburtstag, -e *m*	birthday
Geschenk, -e *n*	present
hereinkommen	come in
international	international
Jacke, -n *f*	jacket
kennenlernen	meet, get to know
Kollege, -n *m*	(male) colleague
Kollegin, -nen *f*	(female) colleague
Kunde, -n *m*	client
Mensch!	Gosh!
noch	still
Raum, Räume *m*	room
sich bedienen	help oneself
Tisch, -e *m*	table
vorstellen	introduce, present
willkommen	welcome
wünschen	wish
Zimmer, – *n*	room

Rooms	
Bad, Bäder *n* (also Badezimmer, – *n*)	bathroom
Flur, -e *m*	corridor
Gästezimmer, – *n*	guest room
Kinderzimmer, – *n*	nursery (children's room)
Küche, -n *f*	kitchen
Schlafzimmer, – *n*	bedroom
Toilette, -n *f*	bathroom, lavatory
Wohnzimmer, – *n*	living room

Learning tip

You'll often see composite nouns in German like **Wohnzimmer** or **Schlafzimmer**. The gender (and the plural) of those nouns is always that of the last noun in the composition (**Zimmer, –** *n* in our example). So **das Wohnzimmer** is also neuter and the plural is **die Wohnzimmer**.

Some adverbs of place	
hier	here
da	here/there
dort	there
oben	above
unten	below
hinten	back
vorne	in front
rechts	right
links	left

Languages	
Chinesisch	Chinese
Deutsch	German
Englisch	English
Französisch	French
Polnisch	Polish
Russisch	Russian
Spanisch	Spanish

Grammar and means of expression

Prepositions of place with the dative ► § 5.1

There are a few prepositions of place that need an object either in the dative or in the accusative.

The prepositions that can have either dative or accusative					
in	in	**über**	over	**zwischen**	between
an	at	**unter**	beneath	**vor**	in front of
auf	on	**neben**	by/next to	**hinter**	behind

There's an easy rule to determine if you need dative or accusative:

If you ask	**where?**	the preposition is followed by a noun in the	**dative.**
	where to?		accusative.

Achtung:
So the dative is used when the preposition specifies a position (and not a direction).

In this lesson's dialogue there were some of those prepositions with the dative. Do you remember?
Da hinten **auf** dem Tisch sind Getränke. *Back there are drinks on the table.*
Sprichst du **in** der Arbeit auch deutsch? *Do you speak German at work?*
Komm uns **in** Potsdam besuchen. *Come and visit us in Potsdam.*

Attention: in + dem ► **im**, an + dem ► **am**
Die anderen Gäste sind **im** Wohnzimmer. *The other guests are in the living room.*

Temporal and local statements ► § 7.1

If you use a temporal and a local statement in your sentence, you normally put the temporal first.
Ich bin **morgen hier**. *I'm here tomorrow.*
Wir sitzen **später im Wohnzimmer**. *We'll sit in the living room later.*
Additionally you can often see the temporal adverb in the first place of the sentence. In this case the personal pronoun comes directly after the verb.
Morgen bin ich **hier**. *Tomorrow I'm here.*
Später sitzen wir **im Wohnzimmer**. *Later we'll sit in the living room.*

Day 11 Exercises

1/34

1 Listen to the short dialogues on the CD. Which dialogue belongs to which situation?

1. Gäste vorstellen ☐
2. Small Talk ☐
3. etwas zu trinken holen ☐
4. zum Geburtstag gratulieren ☐
5. Gäste empfangen ☐

2 Who is in which room? Read the text and mark.

Auf der Party von Jens sind viele Gäste. Jens ist gerade im Flur und spricht mit Martinas Schwester Kathrin. Kathrin wartet auf ihren Freund Andreas.
Andreas ist auf der Toilette. Iwona sucht Martina. Martina ist nicht in der Küche. Iwona findet sie im Wohnzimmer. Die anderen Gäste sind auch im Wohnzimmer und reden. Aber wo ist Pierre? Er ist nicht im Wohnzimmer.
Er ist im Bad.

	Bad	Flur	Küche	Toilette	Wohnzimmer
Andreas	☐	☐	☐	☐	☐
Jens	☐	☐	☐	☐	☐
Kathrin	☐	☐	☐	☐	☐
Martina	☐	☐	☐	☐	☐
Pierre	☐	☐	☐	☐	☐

3 Can you put the mixed up sentences back in their right order?

1. kennenzulernen / Sie / freut / sehr / mich.

....

2. alles Gute / dir / ich / zum Geburtstag / wünsche /.

....

3. vorstellen / möchte / euch / kurz / ich /.

....

4. in / willkommen / unserer / herzlich / Wohnung /.

....

5. mein / Paul / Kollege / das / ist /.

....

Kulturtipp Happy birthday!

The most important personal holiday is one's **Geburtstag** *birthday*. Formerly, **der Namenstag** *the name day* was a popular holiday in Catholic regions, but is now rarely celebrated. On a birthday the person celebrating her/his birthday is **das Geburtstagkind** *the birthday child* and usually gets **Geburtstagsgeschenke** *birthday presents* and **einen Geburtstagskuchen** *a birthday cake* with one candle for each year.

Herzlichen Glückwunsch (**zum Geburtstag**) *best wishes / happy birthday* and **Alles Gute** (**zum Geburtstag**) *all the best* are the standard congratulations – but beware: congratulating before the actual birthday is said to bring bad luck in Germany! There's often **eine Geburtstagsparty** *a birthday party* for family and/or friends too on that day or one of the following weekends.

Attaining full age (with 18) or a so called **runder Geburtstag** *literally a round birthday* (30, 40, 50 ...) are often specially celebrated. But no matter how old you've become, your friends might consider it necessary to sing you a birthday song. The most popular in Germany is probably **Happy Birthday to You**. It's often sung in English, but there's a German translation too and that often causes funny moments when the singers sing different versions.

What can you already do?

	☺	😐	☹	
▪ introduce others and become introduced	☐	☐	☐	► Ü1, Ü3
▪ welcome guests	☐	☐	☐	► Ü1, Ü3
▪ congratulate someone on her/his birthday	☐	☐	☐	► Ü1, Ü3
▪ give a present	☐	☐	☐	► Ü1, Ü3
▪ name basic rooms in a flat/house	☐	☐	☐	► Ü2

Day 12

Home and chores

In this lesson you will learn

- to say what you like to do and what you don't
- to apologize
- about the home, furniture and chores

1/35
1/36

Aufräumen nach der Party

Die Party ist zu Ende und die meisten Gäste sind weg. Nur Iwona und Pierre sind noch da.

Iwona Die Party war toll! Wir hatten wirklich viel Spaß!

Martina Und ihr wollt uns jetzt sicher beim Aufräumen helfen?

Pierre Klar! Das ist ja nicht viel Arbeit! Was sollen wir denn machen?

Martina Pierre, auf der Kommode im Wohnzimmer stehen noch saubere Gläser. Kannst du diese Gläser bitte ins Regal stellen?

Pierre Ja, mache ich.

Martina Und trägst du bitte das dreckige Geschirr in die Küche, Iwona? Stell die Sachen dort einfach auf den Tisch.

Jens Und was darf ich machen?

Martina Das darfst du dir aussuchen: abspülen oder kehren.

Jens Kehren mag ich nicht! Ich spüle lieber ab. Wir brauchen dringend einen Geschirrspüler …

Martina Das ist gut. Kehren ist in Ordnung. Aber ich spüle nicht gern ab. Bringst du dann später Iwona und Pierre zur Tür? … Und nimmst den Müll mit?

Jens Na ja …

Pierre Oh nein!

Martina Was ist los?

Pierre Entschuldigung, zwei Weingläser sind kaputt. Das tut mir leid!

Martina Das macht nichts. Die Gläser waren nicht teuer. Ich mache gleich die Scherben weg.

Dialogue questions

Cross out the wrong answer.

1. Pierre räumt *im Wohnzimmer* | *in der Küche* auf.
2. Jens *kehrt gerne* | *spült gerne ab.*
3. *Iwona* | *Pierre* macht die Weingläser kaputt.
4. Die Weingläser waren *sehr* | *nicht* teuer.

Cleaning up after the party ...

The party is over and most of the guests are gone. Only Iwona and Pierre are still there.

Iwona The party was great! We really had a lot of fun!

Martina And you really want to help us clean up now?

Pierre Sure! There's not much to do! What should we do?

Martina Pierre, there are still some clean glasses on the chest of drawers in the living room. Can you put those glasses on the shelf please?

Pierre OK, I can do that.

Martina And would you please carry the dirty dishes into the kitchen, Iwona? Just put them on the table.

Jens And what may I do?

Martina You may choose: washing-up or sweeping.

Jens I don't like sweeping! I'd rather do the washing-up. We badly need a dishwasher ...

Martina That's good. Sweeping is fine. But I don't like doing the washing-up. Will you show Iwona and Pierre to the door later? ... And take the rubbish with you?

Jens Oh well ...

Pierre Oh no!

Martina What's the matter?

Pierre Sorry, two wine glasses are in pieces. I'm really sorry!

Martina Never mind. The glasses weren't expensive. I'll clear the shards away.

Day 12 Vocabulary

aussuchen	choose
brauchen	need
bringen	bring
Das ist in Ordnung.	That's fine/OK.
Das macht nichts.	Never mind.
Das tut mir leid!	I'm (really) sorry!/My apologies!
dreckig	dirty
Entschuldigung, -en *f*	apology
Geschirr *(only Sg) n*	dishes
Glas, Gläser *n*	glass
Hausarbeit, -en *f*	chore
Ich mag ...	I like ...
Klar!	Sure!
legen	lay
liegen	lie
Möbel, – *(mostly Pl) n*	furniture
Müll *(only Sg) m*	rubbish
Ordnung *f*	order
Party, -s *f*	party
Sache, -n *f*	thing
sauber	clean
setzen	put
sitzen	sit
Spaß *m*	fun
stehen	stand
stellen	put
teuer	expensive
tragen	carry
Was ist los?	What's the matter?
Weinglas, -gläser *n*	wine glass

Chores	
abspülen	wash up
aufräumen	clean up
bügeln	iron
fegen, kehren	sweep
Müll wegbringen	take the rubbish out
staubsaugen	hoover
Wäsche waschen	do one's laundry

Furniture	
Kommode, -n *f*	chest of drawers
Lampe, -n *f*	lamp
Regal, -e *n*	shelf
Schrank, Schränke *m*	cupboard
Sofa, -s *n*	couch
Stuhl, Stühle *m*	chair
Tisch, -e *m*	table

Grammar and means of expression

Local prepositions with the accusative ► *§ 5.1*

Look at the examples from the dialogue first:
Kannst du die Gläser **in** den Schrank stellen? *Can you put the glasses in the cupboard?*
Stell die Sachen **auf** den Tisch. *Put the things on the table.*

These are the very same prepositions you learned about in the previous lesson's grammar. However, now they don't specify a point but a direction!

Let's repeat the rule. Now the second line is highlighted:

If you ask	where?	the preposition is followed by a noun in the	dative.
	where to?		**accusative.**

Attention: in + das ► **ins**, an + das ► **ans**
Kannst du diese Gläser **ins** Regal stellen? *Can you put these glasses on the shelf?*

Certain verbs indicate **where** an object is. These are for example **sein**, **stehen**, **sitzen**, **liegen**.
Other verbs indicate **where** an object moves/is moved **to**, like **stellen**, **setzen**, **legen**, **bringen**, **tragen**.

haben and *sein* in the simple past ► *§ 8.5*

Die Party **war** toll! Wir **hatten** wirklich viel Spaß!
The simple past is called **Präteritum** in German. It's mainly used in written German like in novels or reports. But **haben**, **sein** and the modal verbs are used in the **Präteritum** in spoken German as well.
Let's have a look now at the **Präteritum** forms of **haben** and **sein** – we'll show you the forms of the modal verbs in the next lesson.

haben		sein	
ich hatte	wir hatten	ich war	wir waren
du hattest	ihr hattet	du warst	ihr wart
er/sie/es hatte	sie/Sie hatten	er/sie/es war	sie/Sie waren

Day 12 Exercises

1/37  **1 Listen to the dialogue on the CD. Iwona and Pierre are talking about chores. If you hear a chore, decide who does it and if she/he likes (☺) it or not (☹) and fill it in the table.**

	☺	☹
Iwona	....	....
Pierre	....	....

 **2 How would you react in the following situations? Choose the right reply from the box and say it out loud.**

Das macht nichts. Abspülen ist in Ordnung. Das tut mir leid!
Was ist los? Was soll ich machen? Kehren mag ich nicht.
Stell das dreckige Geschirr in den Geschirrspüler.

1. Say that washing the dishes is OK.
2. The sound of breaking glass can be heard. You want to know what happened.
3. Ask your friend to put the dirty dishes in the dishwasher.
4. Someone stepped on your toe and apologizes – but it didn't hurt.
5. You want to help clean up but you don't know what to do.
6. You broke a plate while cleaning up.
7. You don't like sweeping.

 **3 Fill the gaps with the furniture given in brackets and it's article. Be careful to use the appropriate form (accusative or dative).**

1. Die Gläser stehen im .... (shelf)
2. Pierre legt seine Jacke auf .... (couch)
3. Iwona sitzt auf .... (chair)
4. Der Stuhl steht unter .... (table)
5. Jens stellt die Teller in .... (cupboard)
6. Martina steht vor .... (chest of drawers)
7. Die Flasche ist neben .... (lamp)
8. Das Messer und die Gabel liegen neben .... (plate)

Kulturtipp Living and waste separation

For some Germans, having a house of their own is their life's goal. But nevertheless renting a flat (or house) is popular. Among young people and students **Wohngemeinschaften** *flat share*, so called **WGs**, are quite common. If you need to find an accommodation for a longer stay check the internet but don't forget the local newspaper. There's often a special day during the week for **Wohnungsanzeigen** *flat advertisements*.

"Could you please take out the rubbish?" Maybe not one of the most loved chores but it sounds quite easy, doesn't it? You might want to change your mind after being asked that question during your stay in Germany. The Germans segregate their rubbish. Most households have at least two rubbish bins and maybe up to five! The city councils issue leaflets with long lists of all kinds of waste and the appropriate way to dispose of it. You'll have to separate glass and paper, organic waste, different kinds of plastic, metal and other recyclable materials...

What can you already do?

	☺ ☹ ☹	
▪ say what you like doing and what you don't	▫ ▫ ▫	► *Ü1, Ü2*
▪ apologize	▫ ▫ ▫	► *Ü1*
▪ name basic furniture and chores	▫ ▫ ▫	► *Ü1, Ü2, Ü3*

Day 13 Information and entertainment

In this lesson you will learn

- to talk about TV programs
- to search and present short information about mass media

1/38
1/39

Ein Fernsehabend

Von der Party ist noch Essen übrig. Martina und Jens laden Iwona und Pierre noch einmal ein.

Iwona Das Essen war sehr lecker! Danke.

Martina Kein Problem! Ihr wolltet gestern auf der Party ja nicht alles essen. Also war noch viel Essen übrig.

Pierre Ich wollte ja, aber ich konnte nicht noch mehr essen! Du kochst fantastisch!

Martina Danke!

Jens Sehen wir uns vielleicht noch einen Film an? Habt ihr Lust?

Pierre Ja. Was kommt denn heute Abend im Fernsehen?

Jens Moment, ich hole die Fernsehzeitschrift. Also ... es gibt eine Komödie auf einem Privatsender. Eine Quizsendung ... Oh, im Ersten kommt ein Tatort!

Iwona Was ist Tatort?

Jens Das ist eine Krimiserie. Normalerweise kommt jeden Sonntag ein Fall aus einem anderen Bundesland ...

Martina Wo spielt er denn heute?

Jens So ein Zufall! Heute ermitteln die Kommissare aus Berlin!

Pierre Das hört sich gut an. Was meinst du, Iwona?

Iwona Ja, gerne.

Jens Gut, ihr könnt euch schon auf das Sofa setzen. Trinken wir einen Wein?

Pierre Natürlich!

Jens Rot oder weiß?

Iwona Rotwein, bitte.

Pierre Ja, für mich auch.

Dialogue questions

Mark with a cross:

	right	wrong
1. Martina kann gut kochen.	☐	☐
2. Pierre hat keine Lust auf einen Film.	☐	☐
3. Iwona möchte eine Krimiserie ansehen.	☐	☐
4. Iwona und Pierre trinken beide Rotwein.	☐	☐

An evening in front of the TV

There's still food left from the party. Martina and Jens invite Iwona and Pierre once again.

Iwona The meal was delicious! Thank you.

Martina No problem! You didn't want to eat everything at the party yesterday. So there was a lot of food left over.

Pierre I wanted to, but I couldn't eat any more. You're a great cook!

Martina Thanks!

Jens What about watching a film? Are you up for it?

Pierre Yes. What's on TV tonight?

Jens Wait a moment, I'll go get the TV guide. Let's see ... there's a comedy on a private station. A quiz show ... Oh, there's a "Tatort" on the first channel!

Iwona What is a "Tatort"?

Jens It's a crime series. Each Sunday a case from another German state is shown ...

Martina Where does it take place today?

Jens What are the odds! Today the Berlin detectives are investigating!

Pierre Sounds good. What do you think, Iwona?

Iwona Yes, sure.

Jens Well, you can go and sit on the couch already. Shall we have some wine?

Pierre Of course!

Jens Red or white?

Iwona Red wine, please.

Pierre Yes, for me too.

Day 13 Vocabulary

essen	eat
Fall, Fälle *m*	case
fantastisch	great, fantastic
Fernseher, – *m*	television
Film, -e *m*	film, movie
im Fernsehen kommen	be on TV
kochen	cook
Kommissar, -e *m*	detective
lecker	delicious, tasty
Lust haben	be up for sth.
meinen	think, mean
Moment, -e *m*	moment
Natürlich!	Of course!
normalerweise	usually
Programm, -e *n*	programme, channel
Radio, -s *n*	radio
Sender, – *m*	channel, station
Sendung, -en *f*	broadcast, show, programme
So ein Zufall!	What are the odds!
Zufall, Zufälle *m*	coincidence, chance

Media	
DVD, DVDs *f*	DVD
Fernsehen *(only Sg) n*	television, TV
Radio *(only Sg) n*	radio
Zeitschrift, -en *f*	magazine, journal
Zeitung, -en *f*	newspaper

Colours	
blau	blue
braun	brown
gelb	yellow
grün	green
rot	red
schwarz	black
weiß	white

Genres	
Actionfilm, -e *m*	action movie
Drama, Dramen *n*	drama
Komödie, -n *f*	comedy
Krimi, -s *m*	crime series, detective story
Nachrichten *(only Pl)*	news
Quizsendung, -en *f*	quiz show
Serie, -n *f*	series
Thriller, – *m*	thriller

Grammar and means of expression

Modal verbs in present and past tense ► § 8.6

Modal verbs change the sense of a sentence to a certain mode: These modes are, for example, duty, advice, order and so on.

The first table is a repetition of all the modal verbs you already know.
And the second table shows all new **Präteritum** forms.

Modal verbs in the present tense					
	müssen must/ have to	sollen shall/are to	wollen want	können can	dürfen may/might
ich	muss	soll	will	kann	darf
du	musst	sollst	willst	kannst	darfst
er/sie/es	muss	soll	will	kann	darf
wir	müssen	sollen	wollen	können	dürfen
ihr	müsst	sollt	wollt	könnt	dürft
sie/Sie	müssen	sollen	wollen	können	dürfen

Modal verbs in the Präteritum					
	müssen must/ have to	sollen shall/are to	wollen want	können can	dürfen may
ich	musste	sollte	wollte	konnte	durfte
du	musstest	solltest	wolltest	konntest	durftest
er/sie/es	musste	sollte	wollte	konnte	durfte
wir	mussten	sollten	wollten	konnten	durften
ihr	musstet	solltet	wolltet	konntet	durftet
sie/Sie	mussten	sollten	wollten	konnten	durften

Be careful with the negation:
Du musst nicht ... means *You needn't .../you don't have to ...*
Du darfst nicht ... means *You mustn't ...*

Day 13 Exercises

1/40 **1 Listen to the dialogue on the CD and answer the questions.**

	a)	b)
1. Wer will ins Kino?	a) ☐ Martina	b) ☐ Jens
2. Was ist „Insomnia"?	a) ☐ Thriller	b) ☐ Komödie
3. Wo kommt „Insomnia"?	a) ☐ Fernsehen	b) ☐ Kino
4. Kommt eine Komödie im Fernsehen?	a) ☐ Ja	b) ☐ Nein
5. Wer sucht den Film „Rush Hour 3" aus?	a) ☐ Martina	b) ☐ Jens
6. Wie findet Jens „Rush Hour 3"?	a) ☐ Gut	b) ☐ Schlecht

2 Go to the websites listed below (or maybe you have a printed TV guide) and search for the information you need to answer the questions.

ARD (www.daserste.de):

1. Welche Sendung kommt normalerweise um 20 Uhr?

....

2. Um wie viel Uhr beginnt der Tatort?

....

ZDF (www.zdf.de):

3. Um wie viel Uhr kommt normalerweise das „heute journal"?

....

4. Und welches Genre ist das „heute journal"?

....

Deutsche Welle (www.dw.com):

5. Wie lange sendet der Kanal DW Deutsch täglich?

....

1/41  **3 Listen to the questions on the CD and reply after the beep with one of the answers from the box. Afterwards you'll hear the right answer.**

Heute spielt er in Hamburg. Heute Abend gibt es einen Actionfilm.
Um 19 Uhr. Nein, ich will lieber lesen.

Kulturtipp Media

A good approach to German media is **Deutsche Welle** or **DW**. They offer radio and TV (both via internet too – either live or as podcasts) and plenty of additional services (like German lessons, information about Germany) on the internet – often suitable even for beginners. **DW** is a part of the **öffentlich-rechtliche Rundfunkanstalten** *broadcasting corporations regulated by public law* (e.g. like the BBC), their prominent members being **ARD** (**das Erste** *the first channel*) and **ZDF** (**das Zweite** *the second (channel)*. Additionally there are a lot of private broadcasting corporations on the radio and TV.

There are some nationwide newspapers. Maybe you've already seen or heard of **Frankfurter Allgemeine Zeitung**, **Süddeutsche Zeitung**, **Die Welt** or **Bild**. If you need local information like the cinema program or flat advertisements then look for the town's local newspaper.

What can you already do?

	☺ 😐 ☹	
▪ talk about TV programme	▪ ▪ ▪	► *Ü1, Ü2, Ü3*
▪ search and present short information	▪ ▪ ▪	► *Ü2*
▪ talk about mass media	▪ ▪ ▪	► *Ü1*

One more part is nearly finished now and you've even left the confines of this book to gather information. Now that you know the websites of ARD and ZDF: check their programme guide! You'll find something interesting or a film you'd like to see, for sure. Watch TV and listen to the radio to get the German language in your ear! And now have fun with more exercises in the next lesson ...

Day 14 Repeat and practise

Here you repeat

- numbers and time
- sports, hobbies and leisure time
- daily routine

1 Fill the missing verb forms in the table. Be careful with the second and third person in the singular, they conjugate irregularly. Use the short grammar in the appendix for help.

	fahren	essen	schlafen	fernsehen	geben
ich	....	....	....	*sehe fern*	....
du	....	*isst*	....	....	....
er/sie/es	....	....	....	....	*gibt*
wir	....	....	....	....	....
ihr	....	....	*schlaft*	....	....
sie/Sie	*fahren*	....	....	....	....

2 A typical day in the life of Jens. You can see the times below and what he does at that time. Write his daily routine in a few easy sentences. Use the less formal time where possible.

1. 7.30 (*aufstehen*) ....
2. 8.00 (*in die Arbeit fahren*) ....
3. 12.45 (*zu Mittag essen*) ....
4. 18.15 (*nach Hause kommen*) ....

....

 2/1

3 Listen to the CD. Now fill in the gaps on your shopping list.

Markt:
1. .... *Tomaten*
2. *1* ....
3. .... *Kilo* ....
4. .... *Bananen*
5. *0,5 kg* ....

Supermarkt:
6. *400 g* ....
7. .... *Flaschen* ....
8. *1* .... *Milch*

4 One word is missing in each line. Choose the right one from the box. Be careful, there are two extra words which you don't need.

unten Zucchini Brot Tüte Wasser faulenzen
Fleisch rot Zeitschrift joggen

1. Tomate, Paprika, Gurke, ……………
2. klettern, schwimmen, spielen, ……………
3. Schinken, Wurst, Hähnchen, ……………
4. Dose, Becher, Packung, ……………
5. vorne, hinten, oben, ……………
6. Radio, Fernsehen, Zeitung, ……………
7. braun, gelb, blau, ……………
8. Cola, Saft, Bier, ……………

5 Transform the advice into imperative sentences.

1. Du könntest dein Zimmer aufräumen.

   ……………
2. Ihr solltet mehr Sport machen.

   ……………
3. Sie sollten mit dem Kunden reden.

   ……………
4. Sie könnten einen Kaffee trinken gehen.

   ……………
5. Du solltest deinen Freund besuchen.

   ……………
6. Ihr könntet eine Stadtrundfahrt machen.

   ……………

6 Complete the sentences with a personal pronoun in the right form.

1. Gib der Frau bitte das Obst.	Gib …………… bitte das Obst.
2. Martina ist Lehrerin.	…………… ist Lehrerin.
3. Ich bringe dem Kunden einen Kaffee.	Ich bringe …………… dem Kunden.
4. Ich bringe dem Kunden einen Kaffee.	Ich bringe …………… einen Kaffee.
5. Pierre gibt Iwona eine Orange.	…………… gibt Iwona eine Orange.
6. Pierre gibt Iwona eine Orange.	Pierre gibt …………… Iwona.

7 One word does not match the others. Find it and cross it out.

1. Krimi, Fernsehen, Thriller, Komödie, Drama
2. abspülen, aufräumen, fegen, aufstehen, staubsaugen
3. Orange, Apfel, Pfirsich, Banane, Gurke
4. Stuhl, Schrank, Tisch, Zimmer, Regal
5. Salat, Saft, Nudeln, Reis, Suppe
6. Rad fahren, Tennis spielen, Müll wegbringen, Judo machen, schwimmen

8 Read the following text. Choose the right article from the box and fill in the gaps. (— is the *Nullartikel*).

ein eine dem — einen — den — einen — das ein

Iwona ist auf .... (1.) Markt. Sie möchte .... (2.) Obst und .... (3.) Gemüse kaufen. Nach dem Einkauf will Iwona etwas essen. Sie geht in .... (4.) Café. Dort isst sie .... (5.) Stück Kuchen und trinkt .... (6.) Kaffee. Später will sie noch in .... (7.) Supermarkt gehen. Dort muss sie .... (8.) Flasche Wein und .... (9.) Brot kaufen. Am Nachmittag möchte sie .... (10.) Freunde treffen. Mit .... (11.) Freunden geht sie dann in .... (12.) Mauermuseum.

2/2 **9** Listen to the CD and complete the sentences with the information you hear.

1. Klaus ist ....
2. Sie waren zusammen ....
3. Klaus' Eltern wohnen ....
4. Klaus wohnt ....
5. Martina und Klaus gehen ....
6. Aber lieber machen sie ....
7. Klaus spielt ....
8. Am Abend .... und ....

10 Write the following numbers as words.

1. 357 ....
2. 812 ....
3. 1001 ....
4. 2010 ....
5. 9999 ....

11 *Trennbare Verben.* **Read the text and write down the verbs with separable prefixes in their infinitive.**

Was unternimmt Iwona am Wochenende? Am Wochenende leiht sie ein Fahrrad aus. Martina und Jens nehmen sie auf eine Radtour mit. Sie fahren an den Wannsee außerhalb von Berlin. Dort schwimmen sie auch. Nach der Radtour kauft Iwona im Supermarkt ein. Am Abend geht sie auf eine Party. Vor der Party räumt sie auf und spült ab. Danach kommt sie nach Hause und sieht noch fern. Um halb eins in der Nacht geht sie ins Bett und schläft.

1. ....
3. ....
5. ....
2. ....
4. ....
6. ....

12 Now write the text from the previous exercise again using modal verbs. Use the modal verbs in brackets but put them in the appropriate present tense form.

Was *soll Iwona am Wochenende unternehmen?* (sollen)
1. Am Wochenende .... (können)
2. Martina und Jens .... (wollen)
3. Sie .... (wollen)
4. Dort .... (können)
5. Nach der Radtour .... (müssen)
6. Am Abend .... (wollen)
7. Vor der Party .... (müssen)
8. Danach kommt sie nach Hause und .... (wollen)
9. Um halb eins in der Nacht .... (möcht-)

13 Read the shopping list. How would you tell a salesman what you want?

Einkaufen:
3 Paprika, 0,5 kg Tomaten, 1 kg Weintrauben, 2 Gurken,
1 Flasche Saft, 2 Gläser Honig, 1 Becher Sahne, 200 g Wurst

14 Transform the sentences into Präteritum

1. Iwona will nicht an der Straße joggen.

....

2. Ich soll etwas im Internet suchen.

....

3. Wir haben viel Freizeit.

....

4. Ihr könnt alles auf dem Markt kaufen.

....

5. Du musst den Müll wegbringen.

....

6. Das Museum ist interessant.

....

2/3

15 Read the times below and listen to the CD. Repeat each time of day after the beep. Then search for it in the list and put the correct number in the box. Two times are extra.

☐ 0.40 Uhr ☐ 4.30 Uhr ☐ 5.15 Uhr ☐ 9.15 Uhr ☐ 13.00 Uhr ☐ 13.15 Uhr
☐ 15.30 Uhr ☐ 15.45 Uhr ☐ 16.30 Uhr ☐ 16.45 Uhr ☐ 21.20 Uhr ☐ 23.30 Uhr

16 Complete the sentences. Use the preposition and object given in brackets but put the object in the appropriate form (accusative/dative). Be careful with the article!

1. Pierre geht .... (vor – das Haus)
2. Die Lampe steht .... (auf – der Tisch)
3. Die Orangen liegen ....
   (hinter – die Pfirsiche *(plural!)*)
4. Der Teller liegt ....
   (zwischen – das Messer und die Gabel)
5. Jens stellt einen Stuhl .... (an – der Tisch)
6. Die Jacke ist .... (in – der Schrank)
7. Pierre sitzt .... (neben – seine Schwestern *(plural!)*)
8. Martina setzt sich .... (auf – das Sofa)
9. Iwona stellt die Gläser .... (in – das Regal)

17 How are you? Fill in the missing dative pronouns. Look who answers and use the appropriate pronouns.

1. Wie geht es a) .... ? – Iwona und Pierre: b) .... geht es gut!
2. Wie geht es a) .... ? – Martina: b) Danke, es geht .... gut.
3. Wie geht es a) .... ? – Frau Schneider: b) Na ja, ... geht es nicht so gut.

18 Read the sentences and questions. Listen to the dialogue on the CD and complete or answer them. 2/4

1. Wo war Pierre gestern?
   a) ☐ Auf einer Präsentation. b) ☐ In der Arbeit. c) ☐ Im Deutschkurs.
2. Der Deutschkurs gestern war ...
   a) ☐ sehr interessant. b) ☐ schlecht. c) ☐ cool.
3. Martina hatte eine Präsentation über ...
   a) ☐ Goethe. b) ☐ Freizeit. c) ☐ Partys.
4. Wann ist die Party?
   a) ☐ Heute. b) ☐ Morgen. c) ☐ Übermorgen.
5. Und um wie viel Uhr beginnt sie?
   a) ☐ 18 Uhr. b) ☐ 19 Uhr. c) ☐ 20 Uhr.
6. Was macht Pierre heute noch?
   a) ☐ Arbeiten. b) ☐ Freunde treffen. c) ☐ Schlafen.

19 Complete the crossword. The letters show the solution.

1. spoon
2. plate
3. eat
4. main dish
5. cup
6. glass
7. drink
8. fork
9. side dish
10. knife
11. napkin
12. dessert

Solution (a–j): ....

Intermediate test 2

1 Fill in the gaps with the words from the box.

nach Hause   Tschüs   möchten   Kartoffeln   Ermäßigung
ihnen   Glas   lecker   einem   muss   Spaziergang   kauft
Apfelschorle   interessanter   Wurst   aufräumen

Iwona und Pierre sind in ………………… (1.) Restaurant. Der Kellner gibt ………………… (2.) die Speisekarten. Später kommt er und fragt: „Was ………………… (3.) Sie bestellen?" Iwona bestellt ein Schnitzel mit Pommes frites und eine ………………… (4.). Pierre möchte den Fisch mit Gemüse und ………………… (5.). Zu trinken bestellt er ein ………………… (6.) Wasser. Das Essen ist sehr ………………… (7.). Nach dem Essen machen die beiden einen ………………… (8.) in der Stadt. Sie gehen in eine Ausstellung. Iwona ………………… (9.) die Eintrittskarten. Es gibt keine ………………… (10.) für Studenten und die Ausstellung ist nicht interessant! Das Museum gestern war ………………… (11.) … Pierre braucht jetzt noch Lebensmittel und Iwona ………………… (12.) auch etwas einkaufen. Sie gehen in einen Supermarkt. Pierre kauft Milchprodukte und ………………… (13.), Iwona kauft Getränke. „Was machst du jetzt, Pierre?", fragt Iwona. Pierre sagt: „Ich gehe ………………… (14.). Ich muss noch ………………… (15.)." „O. K. ………………… (16.)!", sagt Iwona. Iwona geht noch nicht nach Hause. Sie trifft sich noch mit Kollegen.

__/16

2 Connect the English phrases with their German translations. One has no translation – add it please.

1. Never mind.
2. My apologies.
3. The bill, please.
4. What's the matter?
5. Sorry!
6. Happy birthday!
7. Have fun!
8. Welcome.

a) Viel Spaß!
b) Das macht nichts.
c) Herzlichen Glückwunsch!
d) Das tut mir leid.
e) Herzlich willkommen.
f) Was ist los?
g) Entschuldigung!
h) …………………………

__/8

3 Listen to the short messages on your voicemail. Who does what and when? Complete the table. 2/5

	What?	When?
Iwona	....	....
Kathrin	....	....
Pierre	....	....

__/6

4 Look at the table in the picture and fill in the gaps using prepositions and articles.

1. Der Teller ist .... Gabel und .... Messer.
2. Die Gabel liegt links .... Teller.
3. Der Löffel liegt .... Teller.
4. Die Serviette ist .... Teller.
5. Die Speisekarte steht .... Flasche. __/5

5 Complete the answers using a personal pronoun in the correct form.

1. Gibt Claudia ihrem Vater ein Stück Kuchen? – Ja, sie gibt .... ein Stück Kuchen.
2. Leiht Iwona ein Fahrrad aus? – Ja, sie leiht .... am Wochenende aus.
3. Wie geht es deiner Mutter? – Es geht .... gut!
4. Besucht dich dein Onkel? Nein, ... besucht mich nicht.
5. Wohin stellt Jens den Stuhl? – Er stellt .... an den Tisch. __/5

6 Which announcement matches who? There is one extra person.

a)

KinoMaxx
Tipp: Der neue Thriller mit **Robert DeNiro**.
Heute um **20 Uhr** im **KinoMaxx**.

b)

Heute im Sonderangebot:
Frische Schnitzel, 100 g nur **1,99 Euro**

c)

Stadtrundfahrten.
Jeden Tag um 15 Uhr am Alexanderplatz.
Anmelden unter **030/235**...

d)

Wer will mit uns joggen?
Wer hat Lust? Schick eine
E-Mail an **joggen@**...

1. Pierre möchte die Stadt sehen. ☐
2. Martina muss Fleisch einkaufen. ☐
3. Jens geht auf eine Geburtstagsparty. ☐
4. Kathrin möchte wieder mehr Sport machen. ☐
5. Iwona will einen Film sehen. ☐

__/4

7 Fill in the gaps with the verbs from the first sentences. Decide whether you need the present or past tense.

1. Gestern wollte ich schwimmen. Heute .... ich klettern.
2. Pierre ist Student. Jens und Martina .... Studenten.
3. Pierre, Iwona und Martina haben Geschwister. Jens .... keine Geschwister.
4. Wir müssen jetzt einkaufen. Gestern .... wir aufräumen.
5. Du hattest gestern keine Lust! Und heute .... du auch keine Lust?!
6. Gestern durftest du nicht fernsehen. Aber heute .... du.

__/6

__/50

Plan a journey Day 15
Means of transport Day 16
Where is ...? Ask the way Day 17
In the hotel Day 18
At the Oktoberfest Day 19
In case of an emergency Day 20
Report on the journey Day 21
Repeat and practise Day 22

Day 15 Plan a journey

In this lesson you will learn

- to make suggestions and to talk about plans
- to gather information about a hotel and to book a room online
- ordinal numbers, dates and months

2/6 Wohin wollen wir fahren?

Iwona und Pierre machen Pläne für ein freies Wochenende.

Iwona Pierre, der 3. Oktober ist ein Feiertag in Deutschland und wir haben ein langes Wochenende. Wollen wir wegfahren?

Pierre Gern! Ich wollte immer mal nach Köln. Wir können dort zum Beispiel den Dom besichtigen oder in ein Museum gehen ...
Was hältst du davon?

Iwona Tut mir leid, Pierre, aber ich war schon in Köln. Ich habe eine bessere Idee: Wir fahren nach München und gehen auf das Oktoberfest.
Was meinst du dazu?

Pierre Ja, die Idee ist toll! München wollte ich mir auch ansehen.

Iwona Am besten fahren wir am 2. Oktober am Nachmittag, denn dann haben wir fast drei ganze Tage Zeit für München.

Pierre Gut. Wo wollen wir übernachten? In einer Jugendherberge?

Iwona Eine Jugendherberge ist billiger, aber nicht sehr komfortabel.
Wir suchen erst im Internet nach einem günstigen Hotel.
Wie findest du den Vorschlag?

Pierre Der Vorschlag gefällt mir. Das machen wir so. Im Notfall können wir immer noch in der Jugendherberge übernachten ... Also, dann sind wir vom 2. bis 5. Oktober in München, ja?

Iwona Genau.

Pierre Gut. Ich suche mal ein paar Angebote und wir können uns dann für ein Hotel entscheiden.

Dialogue questions

Mark with a cross:

	right	wrong
1. Pierre will am 3. Oktober in Berlin sein.	☐	☐
2. Iwona war schon in Köln.	☐	☐
3. Die Fahrt nach München ist Iwonas Idee.	☐	☐
4. Iwona will in einer Jugendherberge übernachten.	☐	☐

Where do we want to go to?

Iwona and Pierre make plans for a free weekend.

Iwona Pierre, 3 October is a holiday in Germany and we have a long weekend. Shall we go away on a trip?

Pierre Sure! I've always wanted to go to Cologne. We could visit the cathedral for instance or a museum ... What do you think?

Iwona I'm sorry, Pierre, but I've already been to Cologne. I have a better idea: Let's go to Munich and, to the Oktoberfest. What do you think?

Pierre Yes, that's a great idea! I wanted to see Munich too.

Iwona Best we go on 2 October in the afternoon, because then we have almost three full days for Munich.

Pierre Fine. Where do you think we should stay? In a youth hostel?

Iwona A youth hostel is cheaper, but not very comfortable. Let's search for an inexpensive hotel on the internet first. What do you think?

Pierre Sounds good. Let's do it. If need be we can always stay in a youth hostel ... Well, then we're in Munich from 2 to 5 October, right?

Iwona Exactly.

Pierre Good. I'll look for a few offers and then we can decide about the hotel.

Day 15 Vocabulary

Angebot, -e *n*	offer
ansehen	see, view
billig	cheap, inexpensive
bleiben	stay
Dom, -e *m*	cathedral
ein paar	(a) few
entscheiden	decide
fahren	go, ride, drive
fast	almost, nearly
Feiertag, -e *m*	holiday
finden	here: think
gefallen	appeal, please
günstig	low priced
Hotel, -s *n*	hotel
Idee, -n *f*	idea
im Notfall	if need be
Jugend-herberge, -n *f*	youth hostel
komfortabel	comfortable
Notfall, -fälle *m*	emergency
Plan, Pläne *m*	plan
planen	plan
Reise, -n *f*	journey, trip, tour
übernachten	stay/spend the night
Vorschlag, Vor-schläge *m*	proposition, suggestion
vorschlagen	propose, suggest
Was hältst du davon?	What do you think?
wegfahren	go away (on a trip)

Hotel	
Anreise (*mostly Sg*) *f*	arrival
Abreise (*mostly Sg*) *f*	departure
Übernachtung, -en *f*	overnight stay
inklusive (*short* inkl.)	inclusive
Doppelzimmer (*short* DZ), – *n*	double room
Einzelzimmer (*short* EZ), – *n*	single room
Dusche, -n *f*	shower
WC, WCs *n*	WC, toilet
Rezeption, -en *f*	reception, front desk
Bett, -en *n*	bed
Doppelbett, -en *n*	double bed

Months	
Januar *m*	January
Februar *m*	February
März *m*	March
April *m*	April
Mai *m*	May
Juni *m*	June
Juli *m*	July
August *m*	August
September *m*	September
Oktober *m*	October
November *m*	November
Dezember *m*	December

Seasons	
Frühling *m*	spring
Sommer *m*	summer
Herbst *m*	autumn
Winter *m*	winter

Grammar and means of expression

Coordinating conjunctions ► *§ 9*

With the coordinating conjunctions **und** *and*, **oder** *or*, **aber** *but*, **denn** *for/because* you can connect two or more main clauses. The word order in both connected sentences stays the same: verb in the second position (the conjunction does not count!). If the subject and/or verb are the same in both sentences you can omit them (not possible with **denn**!).
Der 3. Oktober ist ein Feiertag **und** wir haben ein langes Wochenende.
3 October is a holiday in Germany and we have a long weekend.
Wir können den Dom besichtigen **oder** (wir können) in ein Museum gehen.
We could visit the cathedral for instance or a museum.

Temporal prepositions ► *§ 5.4*

Check the following table for the most common temporal prepositions and when you need them.

um at	**am** in, on	**im** in
Time: **Wir treffen uns um 14 Uhr.** We meet at 2 p.m.	Daytime: **Am Morgen frühstücke ich.** In the morning I eat breakfast.	Months: **Das Oktoberfest ist im September.** The Oktoberfest is in September.
	Weekdays and dates: **Ich fahre am Dienstag nach München.** I go to Munich on Tuesday. **Wir fahren am 2. Oktober.** We go on 2 October.	Seasons: **Das Oktoberfest ist im Herbst.** The Oktoberfest is in autumn.

Ordinal numbers

When talking about dates you need ordinal numbers. In German, when written as a number, they always have a full stop.
Up to 19. you just add **-te** as an ending (with the exceptions: 1. erste, 3. dritte, 7. siebte, 8. achte). All numbers above (when the cardinal number ends with -**zig**) get the ending -**ste**: 110. – hundert**zehn** + **te** = hunderzehnte; 93. – dreiundneun**zig** + **ste** = dreiundneunzigste.

Exercises

2/7

1 Listen to the dates on the CD. The months are written below but the day is missing. Write the ordinal numbers in the gaps.

1. .... Januar	4. .... April	7. .... Juli	10. .... Oktober
2. .... Februar	5. .... Mai	8. .... August	11. .... November
3. .... März	6. .... Juni	9. .... September	12. .... Dezember

2 Read the sentences and find the appropriate replies in the box. Say them loud.

Nein, ich muss an dem Tag arbeiten.
Mir gefällt dein Vorschlag. Ich finde Ihre Idee gut.

1. Wohin fahren wir? Mein Vorschlag ist Hamburg.
2. Was halten Sie von einer Reise nach Frankreich?
3. Können wir am 6. Oktober fahren?

3 Read the short information about a hotel and answer the questions.

Verbringen Sie Ihren Urlaub in unserem komfortablen Hotel. Wir bieten Ihnen 18 Doppelzimmer und 6 Einzelzimmer mit Dusche und WC und zusätzlich TV und Radio. Pro Person und Nacht kostet das Einzelzimmer 55 Euro, das Doppelzimmer 45 Euro. Das Frühstück ist inklusive. Sie können erst am Abend anreisen? Kein Problem! Die Rezeption ist immer offen und eine Anreise auch nach 20 Uhr ist möglich!

1. Wie viel kosten zwei Nächte in einem Einzelzimmer? .... Euro.
2. Gibt es eine Dusche im Zimmer? ☐ Ja. ☐ Nein.
3. Ist eine Anreise um 21 Uhr möglich? ☐ Ja. ☐ Nein.
4. Wie viele Zimmer hat das Hotel? .... Zimmer.

2/8

4 Look at the booking form and listen to the short dialogue on the CD to gather the information needed. Then fill in the form.

Anreise: .... – Abreise: ....

Erwachsene: .... – Kinder: ....

Einzelzimmer ☐ Doppelzimmer ☐

Inkl. Frühstück? Nein ☐ Ja ☐ (+ 7,00 EUR)

Kulturtipp The Oktoberfest in Munich

You've probably heard of the Oktoberfest already and that's no big surprise, because it's one of the events Germany is famous for. It takes place from late September to early October and is the travelling destination for lots of tourists from all over the world.

In the first years from 1810 on it was more of a sporting event with a big horse race. That changed in the late 19th century and the Oktoberfest became what it is today when they started to sell beer in 1880. And today it's most famous attraction is still beer. Over 6 million people come to the Oktoberfest and consume almost 7 million litres of beer in the big **Festzelte** *festival tents*.

Other culinary delicacies are **Hendl** *roast chicken*, **Haxn** *pork knuckle*, **Würstl** *sausage* and **Brezn** *pretzel* and many more...

In the 20th century more and more rides were added to the Oktoberfest. Today's attractions are the big wheel with its height of 48 metres or the world's largest portable roller coaster with five loops, among others.

What can you already do?

	☺	😐	☹	
▪ make suggestions and talk about plans	☐	☐	☐	▸ *Ü2*
▪ gather information about a hotel	☐	☐	☐	▸ *Ü3*
▪ book a room	☐	☐	☐	▸ *Ü4*
▪ understand dates, months and ordinal numbers	☐	☐	☐	▸ *Ü1*

Day 16

Means of transport

In this lesson you will learn

- to read a timetable
- to look for a train connection on the internet
- about means of transport, especially trains

2/9 Wie kommen wir nach München?

Jetzt müssen die beiden nur noch das geeignete Verkehrsmittel finden.

Pierre Gut. Die Zimmer sind gebucht. Aber wie kommen wir nach München? Mit dem Flugzeug?

Iwona Ich glaube nicht, dass wir einen guten Flug bekommen, aber wir prüfen das im Internet. Ich denke, dass wir am besten mit dem Auto oder dem Zug fahren.

Pierre Dann bin ich für den Zug! Das ist besser, weil wir dann nicht im Stau stehen und auch keine Parkplätze suchen müssen.

Iwona Ja, du hast recht. Aber lass uns erst noch nach einem Flug suchen.

Pierre O. K. Hmm ... Nein, die Flüge sind zu teuer und die Zeit passt nicht. Wir fahren also mit dem Zug!

Iwona Ja, dann geh auf die Webseite der Bahn und such uns eine Verbindung nach München!

Pierre In Ordnung. Also: Von Berlin ... nach München. Hinfahrt ... am 2.10. und Rückfahrt ... am 5.10. Zweite Klasse ... zwei Erwachsene. Um wie viel Uhr wollen wir am Donnerstag hier abfahren?

Iwona Vielleicht starten wir so, dass wir um 20 Uhr in München ankommen. Wie lange dauert die Fahrt?

Pierre Moment ... die Fahrt dauert ungefähr 6 Stunden. Dann müssen wir um 14 Uhr hier abfahren.

Iwona Das ist O. K.

Pierre Gut, das passt mir auch. Oh, sieh mal: Wir können die Fahrkarten gleich online buchen und auch noch ausdrucken. Soll ich uns Sitzplätze reservieren? Das kostet zwei Euro mehr ... Hast du eine Kreditkarte?

Dialogue questions

Cross out the wrong answer.

1. Pierre und Iwona *fahren* | *fliegen* nach München.
2. Sie reisen in der *ersten* | *zweiten* Klasse.
3. Die Fahrt nach München dauert *sechs* | *vierzehn* Stunden.
4. Pierre kauft die Fahrkarten *am Schalter* | *online.*

How to get to Munich?

Now the two just have to find the right means of transport.

Pierre OK. The rooms are booked. But how do we get to Munich? By plane?

Iwona I don't think that we will be able to get a good flight, but we can check it on the internet. I think, the best would be we driving by car or taking the train.

Pierre Then I prefer the train! It's better because we won't get caught up in a traffic jam and won't have to look for parking spaces.

Iwona Yes, you're right. But let's still look for a flight first.

Pierre OK. Hmm ... No, the flights are too expensive and the time is wrong. We'll go by train then!

Iwona Yes, so go to the website of the railway company and look for a connection to Munich!

Pierre All right. Well: From Berlin ... to Munich. Journey there ... on 2.10. and return journey ... on 5.10. Second class ... two adults. When do you want to depart?

Iwona Maybe we should set off in order to arrive in Munich at 8 p.m. How long does the journey take?

Pierre Just a moment ... the journey takes about 6 hours. So we have to leave here at 2 p.m.

Iwona That's OK.

Pierre Good, fine by me. Oh, look: We can book the tickets immediately online and print them too. Should I book seats for us? That costs two Euro more ... Do you have a credit card?

Day 16 Vocabulary

(aus)drucken	print
Auto, -s *n*	car
Bahn, -en *f*	train, railway
buchen	book
Das passt mir!	Fine by me!
dauern	take
denken	think
erst	first
Erwachsene, -n *f+m*	adult, grown-up
Fahrt, -en *f*	journey, trip, drive
Flug, Flüge *m*	flight
Flugzeug, -e *n*	plane
für etwas sein	favour, prefer
gleich	immediately
im Stau stehen	get caught up in a traffic jam
In Ordnung!	All right!
kommen	here: get to
Kreditkarte, -n *f*	credit card
lass uns	let's
Moment!	Just a moment!
nach	to
still	noch
Parkplatz, -plätze *m*	parking space
prüfen	check
recht haben	be right
reisen	travel
reservieren	book, retain
Sieh mal!	Look!
Sitzplatz, -plätze *m*	seat
Stau, -s *m*	traffic jam
suchen	search, look for
Verkehrsmittel, – *n*	means of transport
von	from
Zug, Züge *m*	train

Around the station	
Bahnhof, -höfe *m*	station
Gleis, -e *n*	rails
Bahnsteig, -e *m*	platform
Abfahrt (*mostly Sg*) *f*	departure
abfahren	depart
Ankunft (*mostly Sg*) *f*	arrival
ankommen	arrive
2. Klasse (*only Sg*) *f*	second class
Regionalzug, -züge *m*	regional train
einsteigen	board, get on
umsteigen	change
aussteigen	alight, get off
Fahrplan, -pläne *m*	timetable
Fahrkarte, -n *f*	ticket
(Fahrkarten-) Schalter, – *m*	ticket office
einfache Fahrt	one-way (ticket)
Hinfahrt, -en *f*	journey there
Rückfahrt, -en *f*	return journey
pünktlich	punctual
Verspätung, -en *f*	delay

Grammar and means of expression

Subordinate clauses with *dass* and *weil* ► *§ 9*

Dass *that* and **weil** *because* are subordinating conjunctions – unlike the coordinating conjunctions you've learned in the previous lesson. The big difference is the word order in the subordinate clause:
It's always conjunction first and (conjugated) verb last.

Dass usually stands after certain verbs like **glauben** *believe*, **denken** *think*, **meinen** *mean*, **sagen** *say*, **wissen** *know*:
Ich **glaube** nicht, **dass** wir einen guten Flug bekommen.
I don't think that we will be able to get a good flight.

If you want to give a reason or a cause you can use **weil**. You can use **denn** for the same purpose and you've noticed already that the translation for **denn** and **weil** is both "because".
But be careful: First, the word order is different! And second, you can always use **weil** (much like with "because", you can, for example, say or write the subordinate clause first), but **denn** is only possible **between** two coordinated main clauses.

Day 16 Exercises

1 Read the extract from the timetable of Berlin Hbf and answer the questions below.

Abfahrt	Zug	Reiseziel	Gleis
16:29	EC 47	Frankfurt (Oder) 17:30 – Warszawa Centralna 22:06 – **Warszawa Wschodnia 22:18**	11
16:32	ICE 875	Göttingen 18:53 – Frankfurt (Main) Hbf 20:44 – Freiburg (Breisgau) Hbf 23:09 – **Basel SBB 23:55**	14
16:36	EC 179	Dresden Hbf 18:52 – Praha-Holesovice 21:16 – **Praha hl. n. 21:27**	2

1. Auf welchem Gleis fährt der Zug nach Freiburg ab? Gleis ……………
2. Wann fährt der EC nach Frankfurt ab? ……………
3. Wohin fährt der ICE? ……………
4. Wann ist der EC 179 in Dresden? ……………

2 Pierre wants to look up the train connection on the internet. Help him fill in the form. Find the information needed in this lesson's dialogue.

☐ Einfache Fahrt ☐ Hin- und Rückfahrt
Von: ……………, Nach: ……………
Hinfahrt am: ……………, Uhrzeit: …………… ☐ Abfahrt ☐ Ankunft
Rückfahrt am: ……………, Uhrzeit: 15.30 ☒ Abfahrt ☐ Ankunft

3 Bring the sentences in the correct order. Be careful with the subordinated clauses.

1. lieber / weil / Ich / schneller / fahre / er / mit dem ICE / ist / .

……………

2. die Regionalbahn / Ich / dass / zu langsam / denke / ist / .

……………

3. fahren / Iwona / wollen / Pierre / nach München / und / .

……………

4. ist / Pierre / ein Flug / dass / zu teuer / sagt / .

……………

Kulturtipp Travelling in Germany

The (mostly) well built **Autobahnen** *motorways* allow for fast travel throughout Germany. But often you have to cope with traffic jams, especially at the beginning and end of holidays and on long weekends (keep in mind that different **Bundesländer** can have different dates for holidays). An alternative are **Billigflieger** *no-frills airlines* between the big cities – be careful, because not all fly to the main airports but to other ones often quite a distance away from the city.

Travelling by train is often considered more expensive, but **die Deutsche Bahn** (**DB** and often simply **die Bahn**, the German railway company) has some special offers worth considering: e.g. the **Schönes-Wochenende-Ticket** allows up to 5 persons to travel on Saturday or Sunday throughout Germany, but limited to **Nahverkehrszüge** *commuter trains*. Check the **Bahn**'s web page for other offers!

Abbreviations around the train		
RB	Regionalbahn *f*	a regional train that stops at every station
RE	Regional-Express *m*	a regional train that stops at most stations
ICE	Intercity-Express *m*	high-speed train in Germany
IC	Intercity *m*	fast train between major German cities
EC	Eurocity *m*	fast train between major European cities
Hbf	Hauptbahnhof *m*	main station
Bf	Bahnhof *m*	station

What can you already do?

	☺ ☹ ☹	
▪ read a timetable	■ ■ ■	► *Ü1*
▪ look for train connections	■ ■ ■	► *Ü2*
▪ know means of transport	■ ■ ■	► *Ü3*

Day 17 Where is ...? Ask the way

In this lesson you will learn

- to approach strangers and ask for help
- to ask the way
- to give and understand directions

2/10 Zum Hotel

Iwona und Pierre sind am Bahnhof in München angekommen.

Pierre	Hurra! Endlich in München. Jetzt müssen wir nur noch den Weg zum Hotel finden.
Iwona	Auf der Webseite steht ja „nur 10 Minuten vom Bahnhof". Wir fragen einfach jemanden. Entschuldigen Sie bitte.
Passantin	Ja?
Iwona	Können Sie uns vielleicht sagen, wo wir das Hotel München finden?
Passantin	In welcher Straße ist das denn?
Pierre	In der Schillerstraße.
Passantin	Ah ja, das ist ganz einfach. Gehen Sie dort vorne rechts, am Bahnhof vorbei bis zu der Kreuzung und geradeaus über die Kreuzung. Dann sind Sie schon in der Schillerstraße. Am Ende der Straße ist das Hotel.
Iwona	Also hier rechts und dann immer geradeaus?
Passantin	Ja, genau!
Pierre	Das finden wir! Vielen Dank.
Passantin	Gern geschehen. Schönen Aufenthalt in München!
Iwona	Danke. Auf Wiedersehen.
Pierre	Na, das ist wirklich einfach und nicht weit.
Iwona	Stimmt, lass uns gehen. Sieh mal, das dort ist sicher die Kreuzung ...

Dialogue questions

Mark the right answer.

1. Wen fragt Iwona?
   a) ☐ Einen Mann. b) ☐ Eine Frau.
2. Wie heißt das Hotel?
   a) ☐ München. b) ☐ Schiller.
3. Wo ist das Hotel?
   a) ☐ Direkt am Bahnhof. b) ☐ 10 Minuten vom Bahnhof.
4. Wie erreichen Iwona und Pierre das Hotel?
   a) ☐ Sie fahren mit dem Bus. b) ☐ Sie gehen.

To the hotel

Iwona and Pierre have arrived at the station in Munich.

Pierre Hooray! Finally in Munich. Now we just have to find the hotel.

Iwona On the website it said “only 10 minutes from the station”. Let’s just ask someone. Excuse me, please.

Passerby Yes?

Iwona Could you tell us where we can find the hotel München?

Passerby What street is it on?

Pierre On Schiller street.

Passerby Ah yes, that’s quite easy. There, up ahead, turn right, go past the station to the crossroads and straight on over the crossroads. Then you’re already in Schiller street. The hotel’s at the end of the street.

Iwona So here right and then just straight on?

Passerby Yes, exactly!

Pierre We’ll find it! Thank you very much.

Passerby You’re welcome. Have a nice stay in Munich!

Iwona Thanks. Goodbye.

Pierre Well, that’s really easy and not far.

Iwona True, let’s go. Look, there, that’s surely the crossroads ...

Day 17

Vocabulary

Aufenthalt, -e *m*	stay
einfach	just, simply
einmal	once
Ende, -n *n*	end
endlich	finally
entschuldigen	excuse
Entschuldigen Sie.	Excuse me.
Entschuldigung.	Sorry./Excuse me.
helfen	help
Hurra!	Hooray!
keinmal	not once, never
Passant *m*/ Passantin *f*, Passanten	passerby
schön	nice, beautiful
Stimmt!	True!
weit	far
welcher, welche, welches	which, what
wirklich	really

Basic buildings and landmarks	
Ampel, -n *f*	traffic light
Baustelle, -n *f*	road works, construction site
Bushaltestelle, -n *f*	bus stop
Einbahnstraße, -n *f*	one-way street
Haltestelle, -n *f*	stop
Hochhaus, -häuser *n*	high-rise building
Kirche, -n *f*	church
Kreuzung, -en *f*	crossroads
Post (*only Sg*) *f*	post (office)
Straßenbahn-haltestelle, -n *f*	tram stop
Zebrastreifen, – *m*	zebra crossing

Directions	
abbiegen	turn
die nächste/erste Straße	the next/first street/road
die zweite/dritte/... Straße	the second/third/... street/road
dort	there
dort hinten	back there
dort vorne	there up ahead
geradeaus	straight on
hier	(right) here
Kurve, -n *f*	turn
links	left
nehmen	take
rechts	right
sich halten	keep
vorbeigehen	pass

Grammar and means of expression

Subordinate clauses with interrogative pronouns ► *§ 9*

All interrogative pronouns that you used until now for 'wh' questions only, can also be used as subordinating conjunctions. The rules are the same as for subordinate clauses with **dass** *that* and **weil** *because*: the conjunctions come first and the verb last.
It's a way to transform a question into a subordinate clause, used after certain verbs like:

sagen	say
wissen	know
fragen	ask
schreiben	write

Wo finden wir das Hotel? *Where can we find the hotel?*
Können Sie uns sagen, **wo** wir das Hotel finden?
Could you tell us, where we can find the hotel?

Prepositions with the dative ► *§ 5.2*

In part 2 of this book you learned the prepositions that can have either dative or accusative. But there are also prepositions that always have the following noun in the same case. Nouns after the prepositions in the table are always in the dative case – like in the dialogue:
Wir müssen den Weg **zum** Hotel finden. *We have to find the way to the hotel.*
Das sind 10 Minuten **vom** Bahnhof. *It's 10 minutes from the station.*

aus	from
von	from, of
nach	to, toward, past, after
zu	to, toward
bei	at, by, next to
mit	with
seit	since, for

Here again the prepositions **von**, **zu** and **bei** are merged with the article **dem** of masculine and neuter nouns to **vom**, **zum** and **beim**. Additionally **zu** merges with **der** of feminine dative nouns to **zur**.

Day 17 Exercises

1 Read the situations below. Then find the appropriate sentences in the box and say them out loud.

Können Sie mir bitte sagen, wo der Bahnhof ist?
Entschuldigen Sie, ich suche das Theater. Entschuldigen Sie bitte.
Wissen Sie, wo die Schillerstraße ist? Können Sie mir vielleicht helfen?

1. You want to stop a passerby politely.
2. You ask a passerby if he could help you.
3. Your train is leaving soon, but you can't remember the way to the station.
4. You need directions to a certain street.
5. You're going to see "Romeo and Juliet". If only you knew the way ...

2 Look at the pictures and then write short directions. Start at the arrow and go to the X.

1.
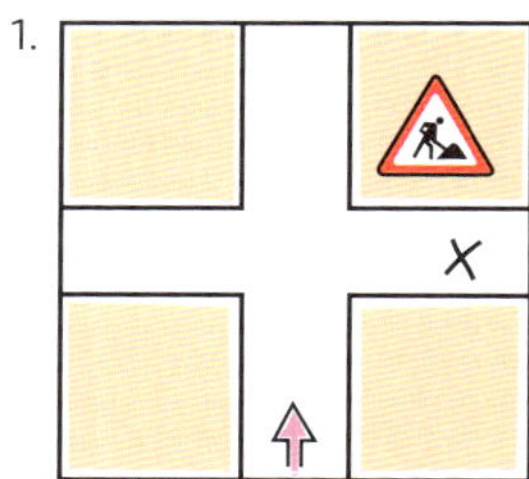

3.
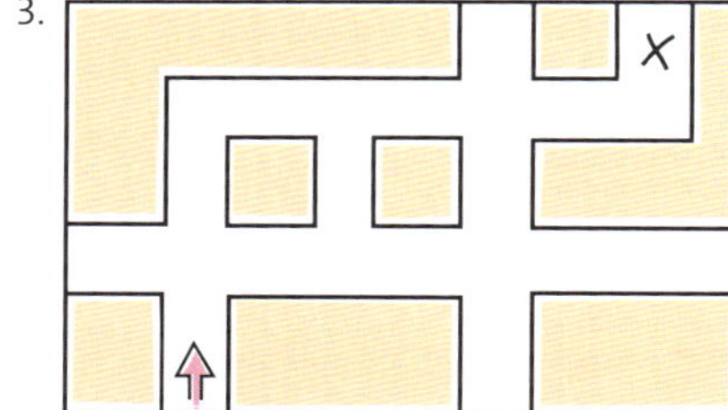

2.
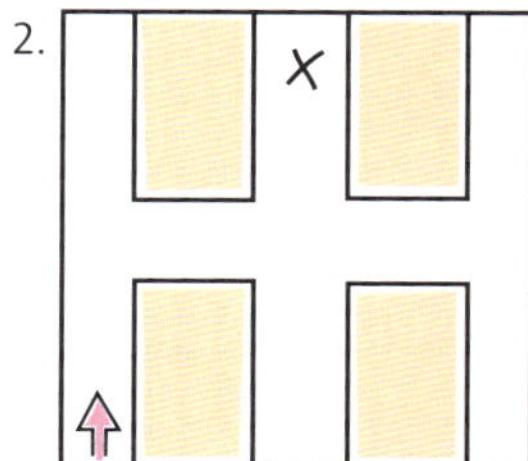

4.
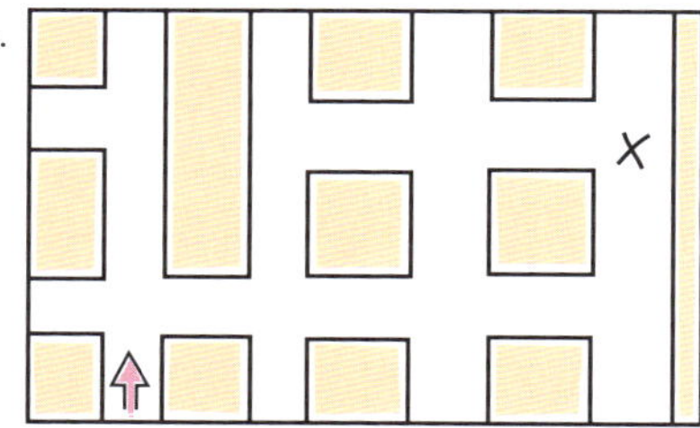

1. ....
2. ....
3. ....
4. ....

Kulturtipp
Munich's sights

Like Berlin, Munich has so much to offer but time is short:

In the historic city centre is **der Marienplatz**, the central square, and not far from it **die Frauenkirche**, its full name "Cathedral of Our Blessed Lady" and considered the town's greatest landmark.

Still in the city centre you can visit the **Viktualienmarkt**, a huge market with a wide variety of all kinds of food, which is constantly open (except for Sundays and holidays).

On a sunny day **der Englische Garten** *the English Garden*, one of the world's biggest parks, is good for walks, sport or just sitting in a **Biergarten** *beer garden* to enjoy a **Weißbier** *wheat beer* (literally *white beer*) and a **Brezn** *pretzel.*

And if you're a museum fan then don't forget to pay a visit to **das Deutsche Museum** *the German Museum*, the world's biggest museum of technology and science with a lot of interactive exhibits for children and grown-up children.

What can you already do?

	☺	😐	☹	
▪ approach strangers and passersby and ask for help	▪	▪	▪	► *Ü1*
▪ ask the way	▪	▪	▪	► *Ü1*
▪ give directions	▪	▪	▪	► *Ü2*

So, now you're more than halfway through the book. How's it going? Good, we hope. If you have the feeling that it's getting more difficult now, don't get discouraged. If you can't solve an exercise, repeat the lesson and have a look in the solution in the appendix – you'll learn a lot in that way too!

Day 18

In the hotel

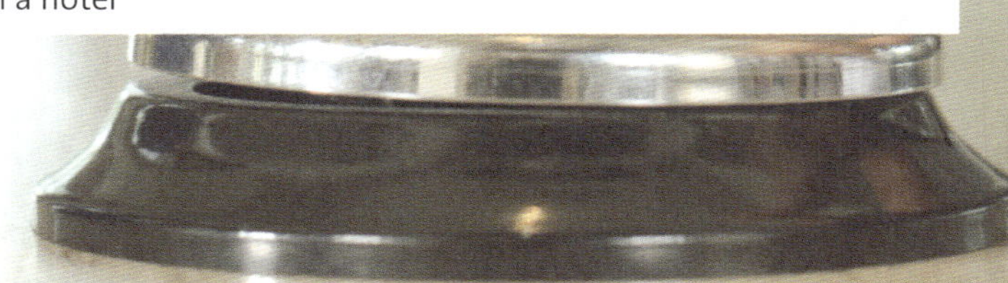

In this lesson you will learn

- to deal with the check-in at a hotel
- to fill in forms with your personal data
- about services in a hotel

2/11 Beim Einchecken

Nach der Ankunft im Hotel müssen die beiden einchecken.

Hotelangestellter Grüß Gott, wie kann ich Ihnen helfen?

Pierre Mein Name ist Pierre Dupont und das ist Iwona Nowak. Wir haben online zwei Zimmer reserviert.

Hotelangestellter Haben Sie die Bestätigung der Buchung dabei?

Pierre Ja. Hier bitte.

Hotelangestellter Vielen Dank. Einen Moment bitte ... Nowak und Dupont ... ah ja, hier. Wir haben die Zimmer 211 und 212 für Sie hergerichtet. Ich bräuchte noch Ihre Personalausweise oder Reisepässe, bitte.

Iwona Bitte schön.

Hotelangestellter Danke. Hier sind Ihre Schlüssel. Ihre Zimmer sind im zweiten Stock. Dort links ist der Aufzug und die Treppe. Der Speiseraum ist dort rechts. Frühstück gibt es von 6.30 Uhr bis 10 Uhr. Haben Sie noch irgendwelche Fragen?

Iwona Ja, wann müssen wir am Sonntag das Zimmer verlassen?

Hotelangestellter Sie haben bis 12 Uhr mittags Zeit auszuchecken. Ah, und ich möchte Sie bitten, dass Sie noch diese Formulare ausfüllen. Sie können das auf dem Zimmer machen und sie später hier abgeben.

Iwona Gut. Auf Wiedersehen. Ich möchte mich kurz waschen und frisch machen. Ich beeile mich. Gehen wir dann in die Stadt?

Pierre Ja, gern!

Dialogue questions

Mark with a cross:

	right	wrong
1. Pierre hat die Buchungsbestätigung dabei.	☐	☐
2. Der Speiseraum ist rechts von der Rezeption.	☐	☐
3. Um 9 Uhr gibt es noch Frühstück.	☐	☐
4. Pierre möchte nicht mehr in die Stadt.	☐	☐

Checking in

After arriving at the hotel, the two have to check in.

Hotel clerk Good evening, how may I help you?

Pierre My name is Pierre Dupont and this is Iwona Nowak. We booked two rooms online.

Hotel clerk Do you have the booking confirmation with you?

Pierre Yes. Here you are.

Hotel clerk Thank you. Just a moment, please ... Nowak and Dupont ... ah yes, here. We've prepared rooms 211 and 212 for you. I need your ID cards or passports, please.

Iwona Here you go.

Hotel clerk Thanks. Here are your keys. Your rooms are on the second floor. There on the left are the elevator and the stairs. The dining room is there on the right. Breakfast is from 6.30 to 10 o'clock. Do you have any questions?

Iwona Yes, when do we have to leave the rooms on Sunday?

Hotel clerk You have time to check out until noon. Ah, and I'd like to ask you to fill in these forms. You can do it in your rooms and return them later.

Iwona Fine. Goodbye. I'd like to wash myself and freshen up. I'll hurry. Shall we go to the city then?

Pierre Yes, I'd love to!

Day 18 Vocabulary

abgeben	deliver
angenehm	pleasant
Aufzug, Aufzüge *m*	elevator
auschecken	check out
ausfüllen	fill in
Bestätigung, -en *f*	confirmation
Buchung, -en *f*	booking
einchecken	check in
Formular, -e *n*	form
herrichten	prepare
irgendwelche	any
kostenlos	(for) free
Personalausweis, -e *m*	ID card
Reisepass, -pässe *m*	passport
Schlüssel, – *m*	key
sich beeilen	hurry
sich frisch machen	freshen up
sich waschen	wash (oneself)
Stock, – *m*/ Stockwerk, -e *n*/ Etage, -n *f*	floor, level
Treppe, -n *f*	stairs
verlassen	leave

Hotel services	
(Mini)Bar, -s *f*	bar
Schwimmbad, -bäder *n*	swimming pool
Radverleih, -e *m*	bike rental
Zimmerservice, -s *m*	room service
Sauna, Saunen *f*	sauna
Filmverleih, -e *m*	film rental

Personal data	
Nachname, -n *m*	last name
Titel, – *m*	(academic) title
Postleitzahl, -en *f* (*often short* PLZ)	postal code
Telefon, -e *n* (*often short* Tel.)	telephone
geschäftlich	business
Geburtsdatum, -daten *n*	date of birth
Anrede, -n *f*	title (Herr Mr or Frau Ms)
Hausnummer, -n *f* (*often short* Haus-Nr.)	house number
Wohnort, -e *m*	residence
privat	private
Mobiltelefon, -e *n*	mobile phone
Staats-angehörigkeit, -en *f*	nationality

Grammar and means of expression

Reflexive verbs ▸ § 8.8

Maybe you wondered why some verbs in the vocabulary sections in the previous lessons had the word **sich**. **Sich** means *oneself* and indicates that the subject and the object are the same ("reflexive"). In German reflexive verbs are used much more frequently than in English and often the English translation is not reflexive – as in the following example:
Ich beeile **mich**. *I'll hurry.*
Iwona macht **sich** frisch. *Iwona will freshen up.*
Often the same verb can be used reflexively and not reflexively. (In this case **sich** is put in brackets in the vocabulary.)
Take the verb **waschen** *wash* for example:
You can wash yourself:
Ich wasche **mich**. *I wash myself.*
Or you can wash another person or something:
Ich wasche **meinen Bruder/ihn/mein Kind/das Gemüse**.
I wash my brother/him/my child/the vegetables.
In all cases we have an accusative object, that in the first example is identical to the subject (I – myself).

The reflexive pronouns in nominative, accusative						
	Sg			Pl		
Nom.	ich	du	er/sie/es	wir	ihr	sie/Sie
Acc.	mich	dich	sich	uns	euch	sich

Nationalities

We introduced a few languages in Day 11 (• Day 11). The nationalities are generally the same like the languages – but since they are adjectives, they start with a lowercase letter. You'll see they most often end with **-isch** – but there is no general rule as how to build the form. Best is, you look up the German word for your own nationality and language and remember it! Some commonly used nationalities are in the table below.

deutsch	German	**britisch**	British
polnisch	Polish	**US-amerikanisch**	American
russisch	Russian	**japanisch**	Japanese

Day 18 **Exercises**

1 Fill in the form with your personal data.

Anrede: .... ☐ Herr ☐ Frau
Titel: ...., Vorname: ...., Nachname: ....
Straße, Haus-Nr.: ....
PLZ: ...., Wohnort: ....
Land: ...., Staatsangehörigkeit: ....
Tel.: ...., Mobiltelefon: ....

2 Martina and Jens arrived at their hotel, but the dialogue at the reception got mixed up. Can you put it back in its original order?

1. **Hotelangestellter**	Darf ich bitte noch Ihren Personalausweis sehen?
2. **Hotelangestellter**	Und wie ist Ihr Name?
3. **Hotelangestellter**	Danke. Sie haben Zimmer 103, im ersten Stock. Hier ist Ihr Schlüssel. Haben Sie noch Fragen?
4. **Hotelangestellter**	Guten Tag, was kann ich für Sie tun?
5. **Hotelangestellter**	Ich wünsche Ihnen einen angenehmen Aufenthalt. Auf Wiedersehen.
6. **Jens**	Guten Tag, wir haben ein Zimmer reserviert.
7. **Jens**	Ja, hier ist er, bitte.
8. **Jens**	Nein. Auf Wiedersehen.
9. **Jens**	Schubert, Jens Schubert.

Correct order: ....

2/12 **3 Jens discovered a leaflet with additional hotel services. Read the questions below and listen to his conversation with Martina. Then briefly answer the questions.**

1. Wie viel kostet die Sauna? ....
2. Wo kann man etwas trinken? ....
3. Was kann man in dem Hotel ausleihen? ....
4. Welche kostenlosen Services gibt es? ....

Kulturtipp Bread

Even in smaller villages with no other shops you'll probably find a **Bäckerei** *baker's shop*. Those shops often open as early as 6 a.m. and close again at 6 p.m. – some are closed for a lunch break and some are even open on Sunday morning.

Entering a **Bäckerei** you might be overwhelmed with the choice of bread and other bakery products. Most German breads are rather dark and made from rye and sourdough instead of wheat and yeast. But it's also possible to get your favourite French baguette or Italian ciabatta.

Besides bread you can choose from a wide variety of **Brötchen** *bread rolls* (all with different names and forms in different regions: **die Semmel** in Bavaria, **die Schrippe** in Northern Germany and many, many more) and sweet pastries and cakes.

What can you already do?

	☺	😐	☹	
▪ deal with the check in	☐	☐	☐	► *Ü2*
▪ fill in a form	☐	☐	☐	► *Ü1*
▪ know about hotel services	☐	☐	☐	► *Ü3*

Day 19 At the Oktoberfest

In this lesson you will learn

- to talk about the weather
- to understand short weather forecasts
- to write a simple SMS

2/13 Auf zum Riesenrad!

Dann kommen Iwona und Pierre endlich auch auf dem Oktoberfest an.

Iwona Wir haben echt Glück mit dem Wetter! Es ist richtig warm und sonnig!

Pierre Ja! Komm, wir fahren erst einmal mit dem Riesenrad ... dann können wir alles von oben sehen.

Iwona Das ist eine gute Idee! Aber mit der Achterbahn möchte ich auch fahren.

Pierre Na klar! Dann auf zum Riesenrad!

Einige Zeit später

Iwona Das war großartig.

Pierre Das stimmt! Iwona, es ist jetzt schon nach vier und ich habe Hunger. Wollen wir etwas essen gehen?

Iwona Ja, gern, ich habe auch Hunger. Schau mal, dort gibt es Bratwurst. Hast du darauf Lust?

Pierre Hmm, ich weiß noch nicht. Lass uns vielleicht schauen, was es sonst noch gibt.

Iwona Möchtest du in eins dieser großen Festzelte?

Pierre Nein, lieber nicht. Da ist es zu voll!

Iwona Du hast recht. Lass uns hier draußen etwas Leckeres suchen. Ich schreibe nur noch schnell Martina eine SMS.

Kurze Zeit später in Berlin

Martina Jens, hör mal. Iwona schreibt vom Oktoberfest: „Liebe Martina. Die Sonne scheint, es ist warm. Uns geht es gut, das Oktoberfest ist toll! LG Iwona & Pierre".

Jens Na toll ... und hier regnet es!

Dialogue questions

Cross out the wrong answer.

1. Das Wetter in München ist *gut* | *schlecht*.
2. Pierre und Iwona fahren zuerst mit *dem Riesenrad* | *der Achterbahn*.
3. Pierre möchte *sehr gern* | *lieber nicht* in ein Festzelt.
4. *Iwona* | *Pierre* schreibt eine SMS an *Martina* | *Jens*.

To the big wheel!

Then Iwona and Pierre finally arrive at the Oktoberfest as well.

Iwona We're quite lucky with the weather! It's really warm and sunny!

Pierre Yes! Come on, let's ride the big wheel first ... then we can see everything from above.

Iwona That's a good idea! But I want to ride the roller coaster too.

Pierre Of course! Then to the big wheel!

Some time later

Iwona That was awesome.

Pierre True! Iwona, it's already past four and I'm hungry. Are we going to eat something?

Iwona I'd like that, I'm hungry too. Look, they're selling bratwurst there. Are you up for that?

Pierre Hmm, I don't know yet. Maybe let's look first, what else there is.

Iwona Do you want to go in one of those big festival tents?

Pierre No, rather not. It's too crowded in there!

Iwona You're right. Let's find something delicious out here. I'm just writing quickly an SMS to Martina.

A short time later in Berlin

Martina Jens, listen. Iwona writes from the Oktoberfest: „Dear Martina. The sun's shining, it's warm. We're fine, the Oktoberfest is great! Love Iwona & Pierre".

Jens Well great ... and here it's raining!

Day 19 Vocabulary

Achterbahn, -en *f*	roller coaster
Bratwurst, -würste *f*	bratwurst
es gibt	there is/are
Fahrgeschäft, -e *n*	ride
Festzelt, -e *n*	festival tent
Hör mal!	Listen!
hungrig	hungry
Karussell, -e/-s *n*	roundabout
Komm!	Come on!
Leute (*only Pl*)	people
lieber nicht	rather not
Riesenrad, -räder *n*	big wheel
schreiben	write
simsen	text
SMS, – *f*	SMS, text (message)
sonst	else
Wetter (*only Sg*) *n*	weather
Zelt, -e *n*	tent

Common abbreviations for farewells in SMS	
hdl (hab dich lieb)	I like/love you (not necessarily for lovers but for good friends too)
bb (bye, bye/bis bald)	see you (later)
cu (see you)	see you
lg (liebe Grüße)	love, regards (common among friends)

Weather	
bewölkt	cloudy, overcast
Eis (*only Sg*) *n*	ice
eisig	icy
Gewitter, – *n*	thunderstorm
heiß	hot
kalt	cold
kühl	chilly, cool
Nebel (*mostly Sg*) *m*	fog
neblig	foggy
Regen (*only Sg*) *m*	rain
regnen	rain
scheinen	shine
Schnee (*only Sg*) *m*	snow
schneien	snow
Sonne, -n *f*	sun
sonnig	sunny
stürmen	storm
Sturm, Stürme *m*	storm
verschneit	snowy
warm	warm
Wind, -e *m*	wind
winden	blow
Wolke, -n *f*	cloud

Grammar and means of expression

The impersonal *es* ► *§ 3.1.1*

Each sentence has to have a subject. If there's no person (or animal or thing) that acts as a subject you normally use **es** *it*.
It's like in English and you can use it – as you already know – when talking about time.
Es ist jetzt schon nach vier. *It's already after four.*
Another use is when talking about the weather – which we will show you below.

Weather

Let's have a look at an example from the dialogue:
Es ist richtig sonnig und warm. *It's really sunny and warm.*
Most expressions around the weather are similar to English expressions.
A question often asked is **"Wie ist das Wetter?"** *"How's the weather?"*. But how do you answer? You can say for example:
Das Wetter ist gut/schlecht. *The weather's fine/bad.*
Es regnet/schneit/stürmt. *It's raining/snowing/stormy.*
Es ist regnerisch/verschneit/stürmisch. *It's rainy/snowy/stormy.*
Die Sonne scheint. *The sun's shining.*
Es ist kalt/warm/heiß. *It's cold/warm/hot.*

Tips for writing SMS to your friends

Your space for a SMS is limited: But with friends, you normally know who sends and gets an SMS, so you can omit the names and use the abbreviations from the vocabulary:
Hi, bin auf dem Oktoberfest. Es ist toll! LG *Hi, I'm on the Oktoberfest. It's great! Love*
When Germans send you SMS, you'll also see that they omit from time to time certain verbs or pronouns or articles. There are no general rules as long as the message makes still sense. So, in the above example, the personal pronoun **ich** is missing, because **bin** states clearly the first person. And, lastly, it's also no problem to write the whole SMS in lowercase.

Day 19 Exercises

◉ 2/14

1 Listen to the short weather forecasts on the CD. Then write the number of each forecast next to the appropriate weather icon. One icon remains.

1. .... 3. .... 5. ....

2. .... 4. .... 6. ....

2 Write a short SMS to your friends. Try to stay under 160 characters!

1. You're at the Oktoberfest. It's great, the sun is shining and there are lots of people.

   ....

2. Your friend's on holiday. Ask her/him, how she/he is and how the weather is.

   ....

3. You're meeting your friend at the Oktoberfest. Tell her/him that you've arrived and will wait by the rollercoaster.

   ....

4. Your friend sent you an SMS asking about the weather. Tell her/him that it's overcast and chilly, but you like that.

   ....

3 Connect the sentences below with the appropriate replies.

1. Wie ist das Wetter in Hamburg?
2. Schneit es bei euch?
3. Nimm einen Regenschirm mit!
4. Ist es heute kalt?
5. Windet es?

a) Wieso? Heute regnet es nicht!
b) Ja, es stürmt sogar!
c) In Hamburg regnet es und es ist kalt.
d) Nein, es gibt keinen Schnee. Bei uns scheint die Sonne.
e) Ja, es ist bewölkt und richtig kalt.

Kulturtipp
Snack specialties

You're in Germany and you're hungry? You don't want to sit in a restaurant and you've already checked out all kinds of bread and bread rolls your bakery offers? Then it's time to taste one of the many German snacks!

There is for example **die Currywurst**. It's a hot pork sausage with curry sauce (usually ketchup with curry) that often comes with chips. It's said that it was invented in 1949 in Berlin. Additionally, there are a lot of different regional sausage specialties in the different German regions – often available for takeaway too. For example **die Thüringer Rostbratwurst** *Thuringian sausage* from Thuringia or **die Weißwurst** *weisswurst* (literally *white sausage*) from Bavaria.

Another snack is **der Döner** or **der Kebab** or **der Dönerkebab**. Brought to Berlin by Turkish immigrants, the German version in a flatbread with different salads, cabbages and sauces quickly became one of the most popular snacks in Germany.

Especially in the northern coastal region, bread rolls with fish (often **Bismarckhering** *pickled herring* with salad and onion) are common snacks too.

What can you already do?

	☺	😐	☹	
▪ talk about the weather	◻	◻	◻	► *Ü2, Ü3*
▪ understand weather forecasts	◻	◻	◻	► *Ü1*
▪ write an SMS in German	◻	◻	◻	► *Ü2*

Day 20 In case of an emergency

In this lesson you will learn

- to talk about illness and health
- to give a short accident report
- about body parts

 2/15

Pierre beim Arzt

Krankenschwester	Herr Dupont. Waren Sie schon einmal bei uns in Behandlung?
Pierre	Nein, das ist das erste Mal.
Krankenschwester	Gut, dann brauche ich Ihre Versicherungskarte, bitte. Und füllen Sie bitte diesen kurzen Fragebogen mit Ihren persönlichen Daten und Informationen zu Allergien und so weiter aus.
Pierre	O. K., hier ist meine Karte.
Krankenschwester	Danke, dann können Sie dort im Wartebereich Platz nehmen und den Fragebogen ausfüllen. Wir rufen Sie dann auf.
Arzt	*(im Behandlungsraum)* Herr Dupont, was tut Ihnen denn weh?
Pierre	Hier am Knöchel schmerzt es beim Auftreten. Ich kann kaum gehen.
Arzt	Was haben Sie denn gemacht? Wie haben Sie sich verletzt?
Pierre	Wir haben ein Museum besichtigt. Auf der Treppe beim Ausgang habe ich eine Stufe übersehen. Dann bin ich ausgerutscht, hingefallen und mit dem Fuß umgeknickt. Zuerst konnte ich noch gehen, aber dann hat es nach ein paar Minuten so wehgetan, dass ich nicht mehr gehen konnte.
Arzt	Hmm ... ja, da ist eine starke Schwellung am Knöchel. Zuerst müssen wir den Fuß röntgen. Dann sehen wir, ob sie ihn gebrochen haben oder nicht. Sonst ist aber alles in Ordnung?
Pierre	Ja.
Arzt	Das ist gut. Warten Sie hier, ich hole einen Pfleger, der Sie zum Röntgen bringt.

Dialogue questions

Mark the right answer.

1. Wie oft war Pierre schon in diesem Krankenhaus?
   a) ☐ Keinmal. b) ☐ Einmal.
2. Wo hat Pierre Schmerzen?
   a) ☐ Am Fuß. b) ☐ An der Hand.
3. Wo ist der Unfall passiert?
   a) ☐ Im Krankenhaus. b) ☐ Im Museum.
4. Wer bringt Pierre zum Röntgen?
   a) ☐ Eine Krankenschwester. b) ☐ Ein Pfleger.

Pierre goes to see the doctor

Nurse Mister Dupont. Have you already been treated here before?

Pierre No, it's the first time.

Nurse Well, then I need your health insurance card, please. And please fill in this short questionnaire with your personal data and information about allergies and so on.

Pierre OK, here's my card.

Nurse Thank you, you can take a seat in the waiting area then and fill in the questionnaire. We'll call you when the doctor will see you.

Doctor *(in the surgery)* Mister Dupont, where does it hurt?

Pierre It hurts here in my ankle when I tread on it. I can hardly walk.

Doctor What have you done? How did you harm yourself?

Pierre We visited a museum. On the stairs at the exit I missed a step. Then I slipped, fell over and twisted my ankle. At first I still could walk, but then after a few minutes it hurt so much, that I couldn't walk anymore.

Doctor Hmm ... yes, there's a heavy swelling around your ankle. We'll have to x-ray the foot first. Then we'll see, whether you've broken it or not. But everything else is OK?

Pierre Yes.

Doctor That's good. Wait here, I'll get a male nurse, who'll take you for the X-ray.

Day 20 Vocabulary

sich verletzen	hurt (oneself), injure
Arzt, Ärzte *m*	(male) doctor
Ärztin, -nen *f*	(female) doctor
aufrufen	call
auftreten	tread
ausrutschen	slip
behandeln	treat
Behandlung, -en *f*	treatment
einmal	once
Fragebogen, – *m*	questionnaire
hinfallen	fall over
kaum	hardly
Krankenhaus, -häuser *n*	hospital
Kranken-schwester, -n *f*	nurse
Mal, -e *n*	time
umknicken	twist
nicht mehr	not anymore
Pfleger, – *m*	male nurse
Platz nehmen	have a seat
röntgen	x-ray
schon	already, yet
sonst	else
Stufe, -n *f*	stair step
übersehen	overlook
Wartebereich, -e *m*	waiting area
Wartezimmer, – *n*	waiting room
wehtun, schmerzen	hurt

Body parts	
Arm, -e *m*	arm
Bauch, Bäuche *m*	stomach, belly
Bein, -e *n*	leg
Fuß, Füße *m*	foot
Gelenk, -e *n*	joint
Hals, Hälse *m*	neck, throat
Hand, Hände *f*	hand
Knöchel, – *m*	ankle
Knochen, – *m*	bone
Kopf, Köpfe *m*	head
Nase, -n *f*	nose
Ohr, -en *n*	ear
Rücken, – *m*	back

Health and illness	
(sich) etwas brechen	break
Allergie, -n *f*	allergy
Erkältung, -en *f*	cold
Fieber (*only Sg*) *n*	fever
gesund	healthy
Gesundheit (*only Sg*) *f*	health
Grippe (*only Sg*) *f*	flu
husten	cough
krank	ill
Krankheit, -en *f*	illness
niesen	sneeze
Schmerz, -en *m*	pain
sich gut/schlecht fühlen	feel good/bad
Verletzung, -en *f*	injury

Grammar and means of expression

Perfekt – haben or *sein*? ▸ *§ 8.2*

You've learned a past tense (the **Präteritum**) already and now it's time to learn another one: the **Perfekt**.
If you're talking about the past you use mostly the **Perfekt** in spoken language. However, as we've already said in the lessons with the **Präteritum**, **haben** and **sein** (as main verbs!) and the modal verbs are still used in **Präteritum**, even in spoken language.
The **Perfekt** is a compound tense built similar to the English present perfect, i.e. you have an auxiliary verb (**haben** or **sein** in present tense • *Day 4*) and the past participle of the main verb. Be careful, though, because the use of German **Perfekt** and the English present perfect differs!
Now, grammatical questions get a bit philosophical, for the question is: to have or to be?
Most German verbs build their **Perfekt** with **haben**:
Was **haben** Sie denn gemacht? *What have you done?*
Wir **haben** ein Museum besichtigt. *We have visited a museum.*
But some verbs have **sein**:
Dann **bin** ich ausgerutscht. *Then I've slipped.*

As a general rule most verbs of movement (like **gehen** *go*, **fahren** *drive*, **ausrutschen** *slip*, **hinfallen** *fall over*) and change of state (like **einschlafen** *fall asleep*, **werden** *become*) build the **Perfekt** with **sein**.

As for the word order: the auxiliary verb (i.e. **haben** or **sein**) is the conjugated verb and therefore stands in the second position. The past participle stands in the last position in the sentence.
Dann **bin** ich ausgerutscht. *Then I slipped.*
Es **hat** so wehgetan. *It hurt so much.*

Day 20 Exercises

1 If a certain part of your body hurts, you can sometimes use a composite noun of this part and *-schmerzen* or *-weh*. Write a short sentence about what hurts.

die Gelenkschmerzen – *Meine Gelenke tun weh./Meine Gelenke schmerzen.*

1. das Bauchweh – ....
2. die Zahnschmerzen – ....
3. das Halsweh – ....
4. die Ohrenschmerzen – ....
5. die Kopfschmerzen – ....

2/16

2 Listen to the CD. You hear some statements about health that help you fill in the gaps. One term from the box is not used.

Rückenschmerzen gesund eine Verletzung eine Erkältung
eine Allergie eine Grippe gebrochen krank

1. Martina hat ....
2. Jens hat ....
3. Johannes' Fuß ist ....
4. Pierre hat ....
5. Iwona hat ....
6. Peter hat .... am Arm.
7. Claudia ist ....

3 Read the short text. Then give a short accident report as if that had happened to you. Where needed, use Perfekt with the past participles from the box.

ausgewichen gehört umgedreht hingefallen gefahren
bewegt wehgetan gesehen gegangen ausgerutscht

Heute ist Freitag, der 13. März. Julia geht im Park spazieren. Julia hört ein Fahrrad kommen und dreht sich um. Ein Mann auf einem Fahrrad fährt sehr schnell in ihre Richtung. Er sieht Julia nicht. Im letzten Moment kann der Mann ausweichen*. Aber Julia rutscht aus und fällt hin. Ihre rechte Hand tut weh und sie kann sie nicht mehr bewegen.

* ausweichen *dodge*

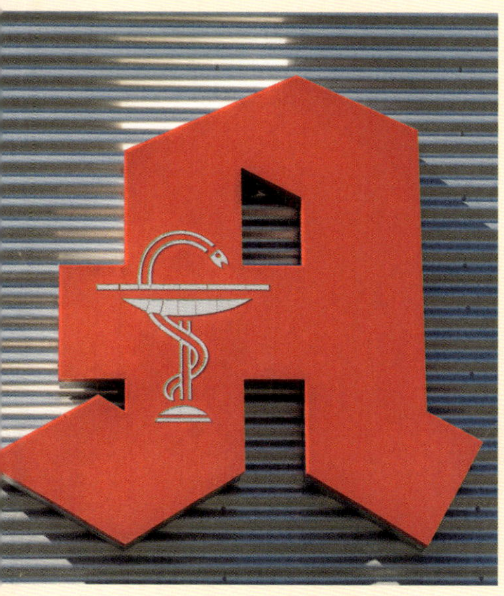

Kulturtipp German health care system

If you're in Germany for a short stay you probably have travel health insurance. If you stay longer to work or study in Germany, you must have health insurance. Usually, as an employee, you and your employer share the cost for health insurance in one of the **gesetzliche Krankenkassen** *government health insurance companies*. If you're self-employed, you have to choose a private insurance company.

You get your medicine in one of the many **Apotheken** *pharmacies*, usually marked with a big red, gothic type A.

What can you already do?

	☺ ☹ ☹	
▪ talk about illness and health	☐ ☐ ☐	▸ Ü1, Ü2
▪ give a short accident report	☐ ☐ ☐	▸ Ü3
▪ know body parts	☐ ☐ ☐	▸ Ü1, Ü2

Have you been to Germany already? Not yet? Could we whet your appetite to visit Munich for instance or one of the other cities worth seeing? From the language point of view you should be perfectly able to enjoy your stay there!
If you're going to work in Germany or with Germans, just complete this part of the book and then we'll teach you the basics concerning work and business.

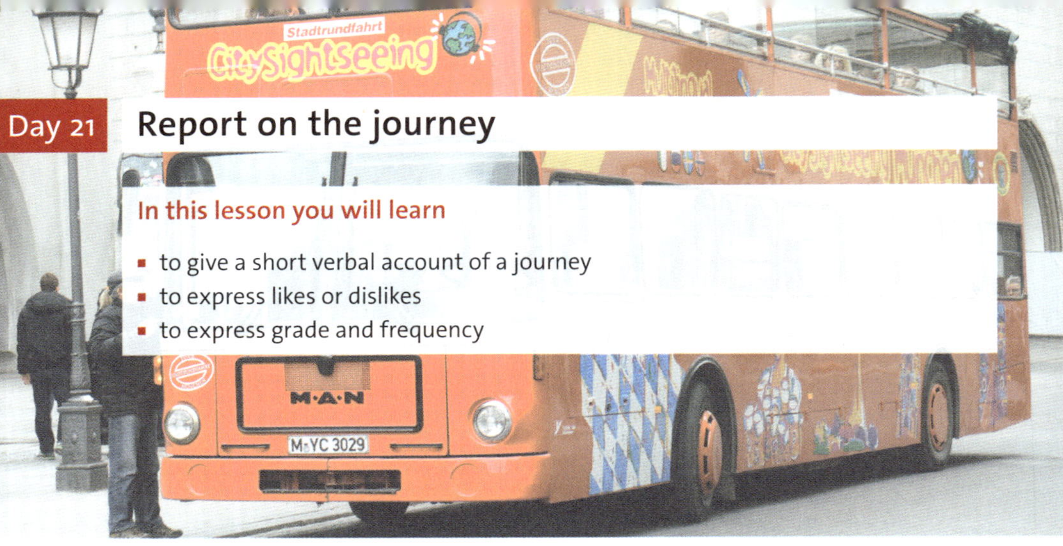

Day 21 Report on the journey

In this lesson you will learn

- to give a short verbal account of a journey
- to express likes or dislikes
- to express grade and frequency

2/17 Zurück in Berlin

Zurück in Berlin treffen sich Iwona und Pierre mit Martina und Jens in einem Café.

Martina Mensch, Pierre ... Was ist denn mit deinem Fuß passiert?

Pierre Ich bin ausgerutscht, als ich aus dem Museum gegangen bin. Wenn es wieder besser ist, muss ich hier wieder zum Arzt zur Kontrolle.

Jens Oje, das ist schlimm. Aber wie war euer Ausflug? Hattet ihr trotzdem schöne Tage?

Martina Erzählt doch bitte!

Iwona Ja, wir hatten schöne Tage in München und Pierres Unfall war erst am Samstag. Wir sind am Donnerstag mit dem Zug nach München gefahren. Aber die Fahrt war etwas langweilig.

Pierre Als wir dann in München waren, sind wir zuerst zum Hotel gegangen und haben eingecheckt. Dann haben wir noch etwas im Stadtzentrum gegessen und sind früh ins Bett gegangen.

Iwona Und am Freitag sind wir früh aufgestanden. Zuerst haben wir eine kleine Stadtrundfahrt gemacht. Das hat mir sehr gefallen. Nach dem Mittagessen sind wir dann auf das Oktoberfest gegangen.

Pierre Das war echt toll. So ein großes Volksfest habe ich noch nicht erlebt!

Iwona Ja, ich auch nicht. Aber es war sehr voll. Das hat mir nicht so gefallen. Am Samstag waren wir im Englischen Garten und in einem Museum und – nach Pierres Unfall – im Krankenhaus!

Dialogue questions

Answer the questions briefly.

1. An welchem Tag war Pierres Unfall?

2. Was haben Iwona und Pierre in München zuerst gemacht?

3. Was hat Iwona in München gefallen?

4. Wann waren Pierre und Iwona auf dem Oktoberfest? Am Vormittag oder Nachmittag?

Back in Berlin

Back in Berlin Iwona and Pierre meet Martina and Jens in a café.

Martina Blimey, Pierre ... What has happened to your foot?

Pierre I slipped, when leaving the museum. When it's better again, I'll have to see the doctor here for checkup.

Jens Oh dear, that's bad. But how was your trip? Did you have nice days anyway?

Martina Tell us, please!

Iwona Yes, we've had nice days in Munich and Pierre's accident was not until Saturday. We went to Munich by train on Thursday. But the journey was a bit boring.

Pierre When we were in Munich, we went to the hotel first and checked in. Then we ate something in the city centre and went to bed early.

Iwona And on Friday we got up early. First we went on a short sightseeing tour. I liked that very much. After lunch we went to the Oktoberfest.

Pierre That was really terrific. I haven't experienced such a big fair in my life!

Iwona Yes, neither have I. But it was very crowded. I didn't like that very much. On Saturday we were in the English Garden and in a museum and – after Pierre's accident – in the hospital!

Day 21 Vocabulary

Das finde ich gut/ schlecht.	I think that's good/bad.
Das gefällt mir (nicht).	I (don't) like that.
eintönig	monotonous
erzählen	tell
gefallen	like
informativ	informative
interessant	interesting
Kontrolle, -n *f*	checkup
langweilig	boring
Mensch!/ Meine Güte!	Blimey!
Oje!	Oh dear!
passieren	happen
schlimm	bad
spannend	fascinating
trotzdem	anyway
Unfall, Unfälle *m*	accident
Volksfest, -e *n*	fair
voll	crowded

Adverbs of grade	
gar nicht/ überhaupt nicht	not at all
nicht so (sehr)	not that much, not very much
etwas	somewhat, a little
total	totally
wenig	little
ein bisschen	a bit
sehr	very

Temporal adverbs of order	
zuerst	(at) first
zuletzt, zum Schluss	lastly
dann, danach	then

Temporal adverbs of frequency	
immer	always
manchmal, ab und zu	sometimes
nie	never
oft, häufig	often
selten	rarely

Grammar and means of expression

Perfekt – the past participle ▸ *§ 8.2*

How to build the past participle? For most verbs it's easy, because you have the infinitive as a base for the participle. This is the case with the so called regular verbs. With the irregular verbs, you have to learn the forms with the verb tables in the appendix.

For a general overview over the regular verbs look at the following table:

verb type	infinitive	transfor-mation	past participle	rule
"normal"	machen	**ge** + mach~~en~~ + **t**	gemacht	For regular verbs without a prefix you add **ge**- prefix, omit -**en** ending and put -**t** instead (-**et** if it ends on **t** or **d**)
	warten	**ge** + wart~~en~~ + **et**	gewartet	
non-separable prefix	verletzen	verletz~~en~~ + **t**	verletzt	Just keep the prefix, ending the same as above.
separable prefix	einchecken	ein + **ge** + check~~en~~ + **t**	eingecheckt	-**ge**- is put in between, right after the prefix, ending the same as above.

The rules regarding the prefixes are also valid for the irregular forms! The past participle of regular verbs always ends with **-t**, that of irregular verbs always with -**en**!

Temporal subordinate clauses with *wenn* and *als* ▸ *§ 9*

Both conjunctions are translated as "when" in English. You use them, when you want to specify a certain point in time. If referring to a one-time event in the past, you use **als**, in all other cases **wenn**.
Ich bin ausgerutscht, **als** ich aus dem Museum gegangen bin.
I slipped, when leaving the museum.
Wenn es wieder besser ist, muss ich hier wieder zum Arzt.
When it's better again, I'll have to see the doctor here.

Day 21 **Exercises**

1 Put the adverbs from the box on the scales. Decide which word belongs to which scale and sort them accordingly starting with the least.

ein bisschen immer sehr total wenig nie
gar nicht etwas oft manchmal nicht so selten

Grade: 1. .... 5. ....
2. .... 6. ....
3. .... 7. ....
4. ....

Frequency: 1. .... 4. ....
2. .... 5. ....
3. ....

2/18

2 Listen to the account of Martina's and Jens' journey. Who liked (☺) and who didn't like (☹) what? Write the names on the appropriate line.

	☺	☹
1. Prag	....	....
2. die Fahrt	....	....
3. die Innenstadt	....	....
4. die Kirchen	....	....
5. die Burg	....	....
6. die Läden	....	....
7. der Urlaub	....	....

3 Tell your friend what you've seen on your weekend trip and whether you liked it or not. Use the past tense.

Museum: *Ich war im Museum. Das hat mir nicht so gefallen. Das war langweilig.*
1. Ausstellung: ....
2. Kirche: ....
3. Spaziergang: ....
4. Zugfahrt: ....
5. Markt: ....
6. Restaurant: ....

Kulturtipp
Tourism in Germany

Over 50% of the foreigners that come to Germany each year, come on holiday. Most visitors are from Europe, but a great number are from the U.S.A. and a growing number from the far east, especially China.

City breaks are very popular, with Berlin and Munich being the top destinations. Another common way to spend the holidays in Germany are round trips through the country. It's no surprise that, for most, the main reason to come to Germany are the country's sights. But there are also travellers who come to Germany for holidays in the countryside, to relax and enjoy the nature. And Germany has a lot to offer: A lot of interesting cities with a long history, castles and palaces, mountains, big forests and nature reserves, lakes, the northern coastal region and much more ... So everyone can find their favourite spot!

What can you already do?

	☺	😐	☹	
▪ give an account of a journey	■	■	■	► Ü3
▪ express likes or dislikes	■	■	■	► Ü2, Ü3
▪ express grade and frequency	■	■	■	► Ü1

Day 22 Repeat and practise

Here you repeat

- talking about the weather
- understanding directions
- talking about plans
- the topic of health and illnesses

1 Build the past participles of the verbs in the box and then sort them into the table depending on their auxiliary verb used in *Perfekt*.

regnen ansehen ausfüllen ausrutschen einchecken fahren finden gefallen gehen hinfallen husten machen niesen planen sagen schmerzen übernachten übersehen verletzen wegfahren wehtun schneien

haben	sein
....	....
....	....
....	....
....	....
....	....
....	....
....	....
....	....
....	....
....	....
....	....

2 Which word does not belong here? Cross out the wrong one.

1. Nase, Bauch, Kopf, Halsweh, Rücken
2. Bahnhof, Gleis, Bahnsteig, Fahrkarte, Baustelle
3. Kopfweh, Grippe, Gesundheit, Verletzung, Allergie
4. Zug, Sitzplatz, Flugzeug, Auto, Straßenbahn
5. Bratwurst, Riesenrad, Karussell, Fahrgeschäft, Achterbahn
6. eisig, wenig, sonnig, neblig, windig

3 Fill in the gaps with the appropriate forms of *haben* or *sein*.

Gestern .... (1.) ich einkaufen gegangen. Im Supermarkt .... (2.) ich einen Freund getroffen. Ich .... (3.) meine Einkäufe bezahlt und wir .... (4.) zusammen in ein Café gegangen. Im Café .... (5.) ich ein Stück Torte bestellt und eine große Tasse Cappuccino. Mein Freund .... (6.) Apfelkuchen bestellt und ein Glas Cola. Wir .... (7.) viel geredet. Danach .... (8.) wir noch einen Spaziergang durch die Stadt gemacht. Wir .... (9.) auch auf den Marktplatz gegangen. Dort .... (10.) gerade Wochenmarkt. Mein Freund .... (11.) noch frisches Obst gekauft. Dann .... (12.) wir uns verabschiedet und ich .... (13.) die Straßenbahn genommen und .... (14.) nach Hause gefahren.

4 Listen to the CD. You'll hear five people giving directions. Follow the directions and write down what building is at the end of each route.

2/19

1. ....
2. ....
3. ....
4. ....
5. ....

5 Fill in the gaps with the correct prepositions.

1. .... Sommer ist es oft sehr heiß.
2. Wir treffen uns .... 14 Uhr im Café am Marktplatz.
3. .... 4. Mai habe ich Geburtstag.
4. Ich habe .... Mai Geburtstag.
5. Wann treffen wir uns? – .... a) Donnerstag, ... b) 17 Uhr.
6. .... a) Vormittag arbeite ich und .... b) Nachmittag lerne ich Deutsch.

6 Put the sentences in the Perfekt in the correct order.

1. Iwona / sind / einkaufen / Pierre / und / gestern / gegangen / .

   ....

2. du / gemacht / die Aufgabe / richtig / hast / !

   ....

3. Martina / wann / eingecheckt / im Hotel / hat / ?

   ....

4. gesehen / hast / in München / was / du / ?

   ....

5. ich / nach Hamburg / gefahren / bin / gestern / .

   ....

2/20

7 Read the phrases in the box and then listen to the CD. You will hear some questions. Choose the correct answer from the box (one is not used) and say it out loud after the beep. You can hear the correct answer after the next beep.

Nicht direkt. Wir müssen noch 5 Minuten laufen. Am besten nehmen wir den Bus.
Nein, am Samstag wollen wir eine Radtour machen. Um 19.30 Uhr.
Im Sommer fahren wir Fahrrad. Am Mittwoch, den 3. Juli.

8 Read the sentences and insert the missing reflexive pronouns.

1. Es ist 13 Uhr und der Zug fährt um 13.14 Uhr ab. Wir müssen .... beeilen!
2. Frau Gerber, wie fühlen Sie .... ? a) – Ach, heute fühle ich .... b) nicht gut!
3. Möchtest du noch etwas trinken? Dort stehen Getränke und du darfst .... einfach bedienen.
4. Iwona und Pierre gehen noch in die Stadt. Aber zuerst will Iwona .... waschen.
5. Mensch, was ist passiert? Wie habt ihr .... verletzt?

2/21

9 Read the sentences below and then listen to the weather reports. Mark:

	right	wrong
1. In Köln regnet es.	☐	☐
2. Das Wetter in Hamburg ist schön.	☐	☐
3. In München regnet es am Vormittag.	☐	☐
4. In Berlin ist es warm.	☐	☐
5. In Stuttgart ist es kalt.	☐	☐

10 Complete the sentences with *und, oder, aber* or *denn*.

1. Ich gehe gern ins Kino, ... ich mag Filme.
2. Pierre hat zwei Schwestern, ... keinen Bruder.
3. Iwonas Eltern haben eine Tochter .... einen Sohn.
4. Fahren Iwona und Pierre nach München .... nach Köln?
5. Martina ist Deutschlehrerin .... Jens ist Informatiker.
6. Ich bin krank, ... ich gehe nicht zum Arzt!
7. Martina geht zum Arzt, ... sie ist krank.

11 Read the questions below. Then listen to the announcements at the station and answer the questions. 2/22

1. Wie viel Verspätung hat der Zug nach München?

....

2. Woher kommt der Zug an Gleis 3?

....

3. Wohin fährt der Regionalexpress?

....

4. Welcher Zug fährt nach Hamburg?

....

5. Auf welchem Gleis fährt der Zug nach Potsdam ab?

....

6. Wohin fährt der ICE?

....

12 Describe the typical German weather for each season. Use adverbs of frequency too.

Frühling: ....

....

Sommer: ....

....

Herbst: ....

....

Winter: ....

....

13 Read about Iwona's plans for next summer. Write down your own plans in 5 or 6 sentences following her example. Then present your plans to a friend.

Im Sommer möchte ich nach Italien fahren, am liebsten nach Rom. Dort will ich das Kolosseum* sehen und den Petersdom** besichtigen. Aber zuerst will ich eine Stadtrundfahrt machen. Und dann möchte ich in ein Café gehen und Espresso trinken. Ich mache auch einen Spaziergang in der Stadt. Das finde ich toll!

* das Kolosseum *Colosseum*
** der Petersdom *St. Peter's Basilica*

....

....

....

....

....

....

....

....

14 Find the generic term for the lexical fields below.

1. .... : Ohren, Beine, Hände
2. .... : Karussell, Achterbahn, Riesenrad
3. .... : ICE, Regionalbahn, Intercity
4. .... : Sonne, Regen, Schnee
5. .... : Schalter, Gleis, Fahrplan
6. .... : Röntgen, Pfleger, Behandlungsraum
7. .... : Grippe, Erkältung, Halsschmerzen

15 Complete the sentences with *wenn* or *als*.

1. .... ich auf dem Oktoberfest war, bin ich Karussell gefahren.
2. Im Sommer stehe ich morgens auf, ... die Sonne aufgeht.
3. .... a) ich ein Kind war, habe ich immer eine Schokolade bekommen,
   .... b) ich mit meiner Mutter einkaufen war.
4. .... ich auf dem Oktoberfest bin, will ich mit der Achterbahn fahren.
5. Ich muss wieder zum Arzt, ... mein Fieber bleibt.

16 Imagine you have the following illnesses. Describe the symptoms or how you feel briefly. Exercise 2 in lesson 20 can help you.

Grippe Allergie Erkältung Halsweh Verletzung am Knöchel

....

....

....

....

....

....

....

....

....

....

17 Complete the crossword. The grey fields show the solution.

1. flu
2. sneeze
3. sore throat
4. stomach
5. cold
6. hand
7. bone
8. illness
9. fever
10. cough

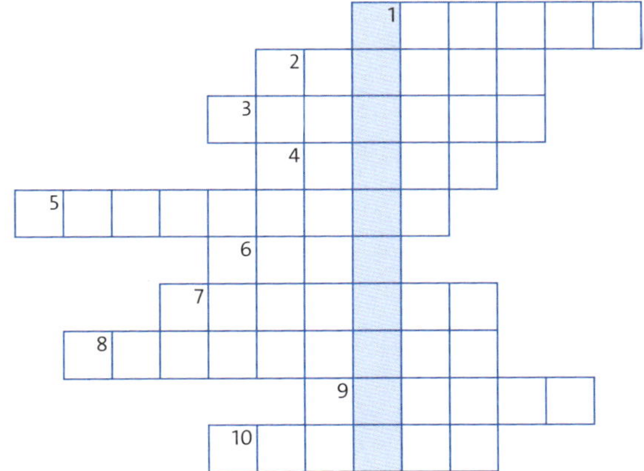

Solution: ....

Intermediate test 3

1 Read the text and fill in the gaps with the correct word from the box. Make sure to use the appropriate forms (e.g. plural).

immer Englisch Jugendherberge ein Fahrradverleih sind für
haben sich Stockwerk Bett morgens wir Doppelzimmer
wollen Sehenswürdigkeit sprechen denn fragen

Willkommen in unserer .... (1.)!
Suchen Sie eine günstige Übernachtung? Dann .... (2.) Sie hier genau richtig! Wir .... (3.) 10 Einzelzimmer und 20 .... (4.).
Und für Gruppen haben wir auch Zimmer mit 4–10 .... (5.). Duschen und WCs finden Sie auf jedem .... (6.).
.... (7.) gibt es Frühstück und Sie können auch ein kleines Essen .... (8.) den Tag mitnehmen.
.... (9.) haben auch verschiedene Sportangebote: einen Fußballplatz, Tischtennisplatten*, ... (10.).
.... (11.) Sie die Stadt besichtigen? Unser Team hilft Ihnen .... (12.) gerne: .... (13.) Sie nach dem Weg, nach .... (14.), nach Verkehrsmitteln ... Sie sprechen nicht Deutsch? Das ist kein Problem, ... (15.) mit uns können Sie .... (16.), Französisch, Spanisch und Italienisch .... (17.)!
Wir freuen .... (18.) auf Ihren Besuch!

__/18 * die Tischtennisplatte *table tennis table*

2 Read the text from the previous exercise again and mark if the following phrases are right or wrong.

	right	wrong
1. Übernachten in der Jugendherberge ist teuer.	☐	☐
2. In der Jugendherberge gibt es mehr als 30 Zimmer.	☐	☐
3. Es gibt auch Zimmer für 10 Personen.	☐	☐
4. In jedem Zimmer gibt es eine Dusche.	☐	☐
5. Es gibt auch Abendessen in der Jugendherberge.	☐	☐
6. Es gibt einen Sportplatz und ein Schwimmbad.	☐	☐
7. Das Team hilft gerne bei Fragen.	☐	☐
__/8 8. Die Leute dort sprechen auch Spanisch.	☐	☐

3 Listen to the short dialogues on the CD and find the matching situations. ⊙ 2/23

1. Beim Arzt: ....
2. Auf dem Bahnhof: ....
3. Im Hotel: ....
4. Auf dem Oktoberfest: ....
5. Auf der Straße: .... __/5

4 Fill in the gaps with the missing prepositions and articles. But be careful, not all words in the box are used!

beim zur bei nach zu mit dem
nach seit dem mit aus mit der

1. Ich bin .... England.
2. Ich fahre morgen .... Berlin.
3. Können Sie mir sagen, wie ich .... Frauenkirche komme?
4. Wie fahren wir .... a) München? .... b) Auto oder .... c) Bahn?
5. .... Unfall habe ich oft Kopfweh.
6. Das Hotel ist direkt .... Bahnhof. __/8

5 Read the questions and listen to David's plans for the summer. Then mark the right answer. ⊙ 2/24

1. Wann geht David nach England?
   a) ☐ Am 14. Juni. b) ☐ Am 4. Juli. c) ☐ Am 14. Juli.
2. Wie lange bleibt David in London?
   a) ☐ 4 Tage. b) ☐ 8 Tage. c) ☐ 14 Tage.
3. Wohin geht David zuletzt?
   a) ☐ Nach London. b) ☐ Nach Oxford. c) ☐ Nach Brighton.
4. Was will David in London nicht sehen?
   a) ☐ Den Hyde Park. b) ☐ Das British Museum. c) ☐ Madame Tussauds.
5. Was macht David dann in Brighton?
   a) ☐ Etwas besichtigen. b) ☐ Einkaufen. c) ☐ Faulenzen. __/5

6 Transform the questions into subordinate clauses.

1. Was hast du in Prag besichtigt?

   Erzähl doch mal, ...

2. Wo ist das Hotel „Seeblick“?

   Können Sie mir bitte sagen, ... ?

3. Wie haben Sie sich verletzt?

   Sagen Sie mir bitte, ...

4. Wer hat dir geschrieben?

   Weißt du, ... ?

5. Wann warst du im Urlaub?

   Ich möchte gern wissen, ...

6. Warum hast du das gemacht?

   __/6 Kannst du mir sagen, ... ?

__/50

On the phone Day 23
E-mails Day 24
Making appointments Day 25
Making contacts Day 26
Meetings Day 27
Draw the balance Day 28
Job-related plans Day 29
Repeat and practise Day 30

Day 23

On the phone

In this lesson you will learn

- to say hello and goodbye on the phone
- to leave messages
- to ask about people

2/25 Iwona am Telefon

Iwona muss zur Vorbereitung einer Präsentation für ihre Firma einige Anrufe machen.

Frau List Firma Steigmann, List am Apparat.

Iwona Guten Tag, Iwona Nowak von der Firma Consult hier in Berlin. Kann ich bitte mit Herrn Steigmann sprechen?

Frau List Tut mir leid, aber Herr Steigmann ist heute nicht im Büro. Kann ich Ihnen vielleicht weiterhelfen?

Iwona Ja, vielleicht: Am Donnerstag nächste Woche findet bei Ihnen eine Besprechung statt. Ich bereite die Präsentation vor und habe noch ein paar Fragen. Haben Sie einen Beamer und könnten wir ihn am Donnerstag benutzen?

Frau List Ja, wir haben einen. Ich werde sicherstellen, dass niemand ihn an dem Tag benutzt. Brauchen Sie auch einen Laptop?

Iwona Nein, ich bringe selbst einen mit. Aber haben Sie vielleicht ein Whiteboard?

Frau List Nein, wir haben keins, tut mir leid. Aber wir haben ein Flipchart im Besprechungszimmer. Reicht das?

Iwona Ja, das reicht auch, vielen Dank. Gut, dann ist alles vorbereitet. Ich muss aber Herrn Steigmann persönlich auch noch einige Fragen stellen ... Können Sie ihm bitte ausrichten, dass er mich zurückrufen soll? Meine Telefonnummer ist 0154 223456678.

Frau List Gut, ich schreibe ihm eine Notiz.

Iwona Vielen Dank. Auf Wiederhören.

Frau List Auf Wiederhören.

Dialogue questions

Mark with a cross:

	right	wrong
1. Iwona ruft bei der Firma Consult an.	☐	☐
2. Herr Steigmann ist im Büro.	☐	☐
3. Iwona hat einen eigenen Laptop.	☐	☐
4. Iwona muss noch mit Herrn Steigmann sprechen.	☐	☐

Iwona on the phone

Iwona has to make a few phone calls for her company in connexion with her preparation of a presentation.

Frau List Steigmann company, List speaking.

Iwona Good morning, Iwona Nowak of Consult company here in Berlin. Could I speak to Mr Steigmann, please?

Frau List I'm sorry, but Mr Steigmann is not in the office today. Maybe I can help you with something?

Iwona Yes, please. Next Thursday in your office a meeting is taking place. I'm preparing the presentation and I have a few questions. Do you have a video projector and could I use it on Thursday?

Frau List Yes, we have one. I will make sure that nobody's going to use it on that day. Do you need a laptop too?

Iwona No, I'll bring my own. But do you have a whiteboard?

Frau List No, we haven't , I'm sorry. But we have a flip chart in the meeting room. Is that enough?

Iwona Yes, that's enough of course, thank you. Well, all's set then. But I still have to ask Mr Steigmann a few questions personally ... Could you leave him a message if he could call me back, please? My phone number is 0154 223456678.

Frau List Very well, I'll make a note.

Iwona Thank you very much. Goodbye.

Frau List Goodbye.

Day 23 Vocabulary

Anruf, -e *m*	(telephone) call
Anrufbeantworter, – *m*	answering machine
anrufen	call, phone
Anschluss, Anschlüsse *m*	line, telephone connection
Apparat, -e *m*	here: telephone, phone
Auf Wiederhören. *(only phone)*	Goodbye.
ausrichten	leave/deliver a message
benutzen	use
Besprechung, -en *f*	meeting
Besprechungszimmer, – *n*	meeting room
Büro, -s *n*	office
erreichen	reach
Festnetzanschluss, -anschlüsse *m*	landline
Flipchart, -s *n*	flip chart
hinterlassen	leave
mitbringen	bring along
Nachricht, -en *f*	message
Notiz, -en *f*	note
Null, -en *f*	zero
Nummer, -n *f*	number
persönlich	personally
Piepston, -töne *m*	beep, pip
reichen	be enough
Rufnummer, -n *f*	phone number
sicherstellen	make sure
stattfinden	take place
Telefon, -e *n*	phone/telephone
telefonieren	call, phone, talk over the phone
Telefonnummer, -n *f*	phone number
verbinden	put through
verwählen	dial the wrong number
vorbereiten	prepare
Vorbereitung, -en *f*	preparation
wählen	dial
Whiteboard, -s *n*	whiteboard
weiterhelfen	help
zurückrufen	call back

Grammar and means of expression

Indefinite pronouns I – *einer, keiner* ▸ *§ 3.5.1*

You already know the indefinite article **ein** and the negation article **kein**. These pronouns look almost identical to the articles, but they are not articles because they stand alone, instead of a noun!
You saw in the dialogue that Iwona asks about a video projector.
Haben Sie einen Beamer? *Do you have a video projector?*
And Ms List answers without repeating the noun using the pronoun instead.
Ja, wir haben **einen**. *Yes, we have one.*
Iwona asks for a whiteboard too which they don't have. That's why Frau List answers:
Nein, wir haben **keins**. *No, we haven't.*

Look at the following table with the forms of the indefinite pronouns and notice differences to the articles highlighted bold.

	m	f	n	Pl
Nom.	ein**er**/keiner	eine/kein	ein**s**/keins	–/keine
Acc.	einen/keinen	eine/keine	ein**s**/keins	–/keine
Dat.	einem/keinem	einer/keiner	einem/keinem	–/keinen

Indefinite pronouns II – *alles, alle, etwas, jemand, nichts, niemand* ▸ *§ 3.5.3*

These indefinite pronouns are easy to use, they are like their English counterparts. Normally they don't change because of gender or case (while not often used in spoken language, there are accusative and dative forms for **jemand** and **niemand** – see the grammar in the back). These pronouns either refer to people (**alle** *everybody*, **jemand** *someone/somebody*, **niemand** *no one/nobody*) or things (**alles** *everything*, **etwas** *something*, **nichts** *nothing*).
Be careful: If you use **alle** as a subject you need the verb in the third person plural – for all others (including **alles**) use the third person singular.

Day 23 Exercises

⊙2/26  **1 Listen to the short phone calls and answering machine messages and write down the phone numbers you hear.**

1. .... 3. .... 5. ....

2. .... 4. .... 6. ....

2 Read the situations. Then choose the right German phrase from the box and say it loud.

Kann ich etwas ausrichten? Meine Telefonnummer ist 030 998766.
Kann ich bitte mit Frau Meisner sprechen? Auf Wiederhören.
Bleiben Sie bitte am Apparat. Rufen Sie mich bitte zurück.
Entschuldigung, ich habe mich verwählt. Am Apparat.
Sagen Sie ihm bitte, dass ich angerufen habe.

1. Ask someone to call you back.
2. Say your phone number.
3. Ask for the person you want to talk with.
4. A caller asked if he could talk to you. Say that it's you speaking.
5. Ask the other to hold the line.
6. Apologise for dialing the wrong number.
7. Ask if you should deliver a message.
8. Ask to convey the message that you've called.
9. Say goodbye on the phone.

3 Fill in the gaps using indefinite pronouns.

1. Hast du einen Festnetzanschluss? – Nein, ich habe .... Ich habe nur ein Handy.
2. Ich bestelle einen Kuchen. Willst du auch a) .... ? – Nein, danke. Ich will b) ....
3. Ich habe das nicht verstanden – .... konnte es für mich übersetzen.
4. Leider habe ich .... verstanden.
5. Kommt a) .... mit? – Ja, b) .... kommen mit!
6. Ist dort ein Beamer? – Nein, dort ist ....

Kulturtipp
Phoning home

Before mobile phones and smartphones took over the world, there used to be **öffentliche Fernsprecher** *public phones* or **Telefonzellen** *phone boxes* in many places in towns and on country roads. In Germany, these phone booths were yellow and offered a more or less quiet and dry place to make phone calls, providing you had **Kleingeld** *small change*. They were also quite popular as meeting points. Nowadays almost everyone has their own phone in their pocket, so most of the phone boxes have vanished. However, some are now being used as **öffenliche Bücherregale** *public bookshelves*, where you can take books home or leave books for others to take.

If you need to use a phone, you can of course use your own mobile in Germany. If your stay is longer, you might want to consider getting a German prepaid **SIM-Karte** *SIM* card. There are plenty of different providers and you can even buy SIM cards in discount supermarkets. Before you make your first call, the law requires providers to record your name and address and only then can the card be activated.

What can you already do?

	☺	😐	☹	
▪ say hello and goodbye on the phone	☐	☐	☐	► *Ü1, Ü2*
▪ leave messages	☐	☐	☐	► *Ü1, Ü2*
▪ ask about people	☐	☐	☐	► *Ü1, Ü2*

Well, the last part of this book has begun. You have made it this far and now you can understand and say a lot. Congratulations! The rest is now a piece of cake ... enjoy the last part!

Day 24

E-mails

In this lesson you will learn

- to write formal e-mails
- to understand a formal e-mail
- common salutations and valedictions

2/27 Pierres Pläne

Pierre besucht Jens in seinem Büro.

Pierre Hi, Jens. Hast du kurz Zeit?

Jens Hi, Pierre. Klar, komm rein! Was gibt's denn?

Pierre Mein Praktikum ist ja bald zu Ende. Ich möchte nach meinem Abschluss gerne in Deutschland weiterarbeiten. Aber wenn ich hier bleiben will, dann muss ich mich jetzt bewerben. Kannst du mir da ein paar Tipps geben?

Jens Ja, natürlich! Was willst du denn wissen?

Pierre Eine Firma will zum Beispiel, dass ich die Bewerbung per E-Mail verschicke. Meine Bewerbung hier war per Post. Muss ich da noch etwas beachten?

Jens Eigentlich nicht. Für eine Online-Bewerbung gilt das Gleiche wie für eine auf Papier.

Pierre Aha, dann scanne ich einfach meine Zeugnisse ein und schicke sie als Anhang mit?

Jens Ja, aber es ist wichtig, dass alle deine Dateien lesen können. Wenn ein Personalchef eine Datei nicht öffnen kann, bekommst du die Stelle sicher nicht!

Pierre Stimmt, das merke ich mir!

Jens Und schau genau, was die Firma wirklich braucht. Schick keine unnötigen Dokumente! Am besten du machst eine einzelne PDF-Datei aus deinen Bewerbungsunterlagen – dann ist die E-Mail auch nicht zu groß. Hast du noch eine Frage?

Pierre Nein, das ist alles. Vielen Dank.

Jens Aber klar!

Dialogue questions

Answer the questions briefly.

1. Was will Pierre von Jens? ....
2. Was will Pierre nach dem Abschluss machen? ....
3. Wie kann Pierre seine Bewerbung verschicken? ....
4. Was macht Pierre mit seinen Zeugnissen? ....

Pierre's plans

Pierre visits Jens in his office.

Pierre Hi, Jens. Have you got a moment?

Jens Hi, Pierre. Sure, come on in! What's the matter?

Pierre My internship is going to end soon. After my degree, I'd like to continue working in Germany. But if I want to stay, I have to apply for a job now. Could you give me a few tips?

Jens Yes, of course! What do you want to know?

Pierre One company, for instance, wants me to send my application by e-mail. My application here was by mail. Do I have to pay attention to something?

Jens Actually, no. The same applies for an online application as for one on paper.

Pierre I see. Then I just need to scan my certificates and send them as an attachment?

Jens Yes, but it's important that everybody could read your files. If the personnel manager can't open a file, you won't get the job for sure!

Pierre True, I'll keep that in mind!

Jens And pay attention to what the company really needs. Don't send unnecessary documents! The best way is to make one single PDF file from your application documents – then also the e-mail isn't too big. Do you have some more questions?

Pierre No, that's all. Thanks a lot.

Jens You're welcome!

Day 24 Vocabulary

Abschluss, Abschlüsse *m*	degree
arbeiten	work
Arbeitgeber, – *m*	employer
Arbeitnehmer, – *m*	employee
Arbeitsplatz, -plätze *m*	job, position
beachten	pay attention to
bewerben	apply
Bewerbung, -en *f*	job application
bleiben	stay
das Gleiche	the same
Dokument, -e *n*	document
einzeln	single
gelten	apply
öffnen	open
per	by
Personalchef, -s *m*	personnel manager
Planung, -en *f*	planning
Post *(only Sg) f*	mail
scannen	scan
Stelle, -n *f*	job
Stellenanzeige, -n *f*	job advertisement
unnötig	unnecessary
Unterlagen *(only Pl)*	documents
weiterarbeiten	continue working
wichtig	important
Zeugnis, -se *n*	certificate
zu Ende sein	to end

E-mails	
Absender, – *m*	sender
an	to
Anhang, Anhänge *m*	attachment
Antwort, -en *f*	reply, answer
antworten	reply, answer
Betreff, -e *m*	subject
E-Mail-Adresse, -n *f*	e-mail address
Empfänger, – *m*	recipient
Posteingang, -eingänge *m*	in-box
schicken	send
senden	send
verschicken	send
von	from
weiterleiten	forward

Grammar and means of expression

Conditional clauses ► § 9

Conditional clauses are subordinate clauses that usually begin with **wenn** *if* and state a condition. The main clause contains the outcome if the condition comes true.
For the word order let's look at the example:
Wenn ich hier bleiben will, (dann) muss ich mich jetzt bewerben.
If I want to stay, I have to apply for a job now.

You can swap the order of main and subordinate clause:
Ich muss mich bewerben, **wenn** ich hier bleiben will.
The word order in the conditional clause is clear: conjunction first and verb last.
In the first example the subordinate clause (including the optional **dann**) takes the first position in the main clause – that's why the verb is now positioned before the subject.

Writing a formal e-mail (or letter)

If you don't know who will receive the e-mail you use the salutation
Sehr geehrte Damen und Herren, ... *Dear Madam or Sir, ...*
You can also write **Guten Tag** or even **Hallo**, but that's already less formal.
However, for formal correspondence it's always better to address the recipient personally by name:
Sehr geehrte Frau Nowak, ... *Dear Ms Nowak, ...*
Guten Tag, Herr Dupont, ...
Not limited to private mails is the use of **Liebe/r Frau/Herr** ... *Dear Ms/Mr* or **Hallo Frau/Herr ...**, but you should use it only if there's a friendly relationship between you and the recipient.
The valediction does not differ whether you know the recipient's name or not.
The formal standard for all kinds of formal correspondence is:
Mit freundlichen Grüßen *Yours sincerely/faithfully*
A more familiar valediction (for all recipients you address with **Liebe/r**) can be the following:
Es grüßt Sie herzlich
Herzliche/Liebe Grüße *Best/Kind regards*

Day 24 Exercises

1 Read Iwona's e-mail and fill in the gaps with the words/phrases from the box. Not all words/phrases are used!

anrufen Besprechung Fragen geplant Hallo Liebe mich mir
Mit freundlichen Grüßen schicken Sehr geehrte Sie telefoniert
Tschüs weil wenn wir zwei

Neue E-Mail

An:
Kopie:
Betreff: Planung der ....(1.) am Donnerstag, 23.4
Von:

.... (2.) Frau List,
wir haben ja vor ein paar Tagen .... (3.). Gestern habe ich mit Herrn Steigmann gesprochen und ich soll Ihnen noch die Details zur Besprechung .... (4.). Ich komme mit .... (5.) Kollegen. Wir haben zwei Präsentationen .... (6.): eine Präsentation dauert etwa 30 Minuten, die andere etwa 60. Am Schluss ist noch Zeit für .... (7.) und Antworten. Wenn Sie noch Fragen zur Planung haben, dann schicken .... (8.) mir eine E-Mail oder rufen Sie .... (9.) an.
.... (10.)
Iwona Nowak

2 Read the e-mail above again and answer the questions.

1. Was soll Iwona Frau List schicken? ....
2. Wie viele Personen von Consult gehen zur Firma Steigmann? ....
3. Was soll Frau List machen, wenn sie Fragen hat? ....

3 Write the following sentences in one using *wenn*.

1. Ich esse etwas. Ich habe Hunger.
   ....
2. Wir fahren nach München. Wir gehen auf das Oktoberfest.
   ....
3. Ich rufe dich an. Du gibst mir deine Telefonnummer.
   ....

Kulturtipp German (formal) e-mail style

Regarding form and orthography, Germans can be quite picky – and that concerns e-mails too (or at least formal and business e-mails). So even brief e-mails normally have the formal salutation and valediction. Just think about an e-mail like a letter and write it with equal care.

And give the e-mail's subject a thought or two, too! If the recipient gets hundred or more e-mails a day a concise subject is more than important.

Before you send your German e-mail, don't forget to run a spell check or – for important e-mails like a job application – give it to a German native speaker to read it.

Since e-mail is a form of communication not unlike a personal talk, more or less the same rules apply. If you're writing your first formal e-mails and you don't know the recipients yet, it's never a problem if you're rather formal in the beginning. If the correspondence continues you'll see how the others write and you can adapt to their style and formulations.

As long as you don't yet know the habits, it's better not to use acronyms (like ASAP or BTW – yes, those can be used in Germany too) or smiles and emoticons.

What can you already do?

	☺ 😐 ☹	
▪ write formal e-mails	▫ ▫ ▫	► Ü1
▪ understand formal e-mails	▫ ▫ ▫	► Ü2
▪ know common salutations and valedictions	▫ ▫ ▫	► Ü1

Day 25 **Making appointments**

In this lesson you will learn

- to make appointments
- to agree to appointments and to decline
- date, time, days

2/28 Wann haben Sie denn Zeit?

Pierre sitzt in seinem Büro als auf einmal sein Handy klingelt ...

Pierre	Pierre Dupont.
Herr Maler	Maler, von der Firma Gleisser, Hamburg. Tag, Herr Dupont. Sie haben sich bei uns beworben – ist das richtig?
Pierre	Ja, das stimmt.
Herr Maler	Vor mir liegt Ihre Bewerbung, die mir sehr gut gefallen hat. Wir möchten Sie gerne zu einem persönlichen Gespräch einladen.
Pierre	Oh, das ist toll!
Herr Maler	Herr Dupont, wann haben Sie denn Zeit, zu uns zu kommen? Welcher Tag passt Ihnen denn am besten?
Pierre	Hmm ... am besten passt mir Donnerstag oder Freitag. Da habe ich nachmittags fast immer Zeit.
Herr Maler	Gut. Wie ist dann Donnerstag, der 18.5.?
Pierre	Der 18. Mai? Einen Moment, bitte ... Nein, tut mir leid, ausgerechnet da habe ich schon einen Zahnarzttermin ...
Herr Maler	Und einen Tag später, am Freitag?
Pierre	Ja, Freitag, der 19., ist gut. Da habe ich keine Termine!
Herr Maler	Wunderbar! Geht 15 Uhr?
Pierre	Ja, das ist kein Problem!
Herr Maler	Gut, kommen sie dann direkt in mein Büro, das im ersten Stock liegt. Sie können aber auch an der Rezeption fragen. Dort sind Mitarbeiter, die Ihnen gern den Weg erklären! Wir sehen uns in zwei Wochen, Herr Dupont.
Pierre	Ja, ich freue mich darauf. Auf Wiederhören.

Dialogue questions

Cross out the wrong answer.

1. Die Firma *Maler* | *Gleisser* ruft Pierre an.
2. Herr Maler lädt Pierre zu *Kaffee und Kuchen* | *einem Bewerbungsgespräch* ein.
3. Am 18.5. hat Pierre *ein Bewerbungsgespräch* | *einen Zahnarzttermin*.
4. Pierre soll *an der Rezeption warten* | *direkt ins Büro gehen*.

When do you have time?

Pierre is sitting in his office when his mobile suddenly rings ...

Pierre Pierre Dupont.

Mr Maler Maler, of Gleisser company, Hamburg. Good morning, Mr Dupont. You did apply for a job with us – is that correct?

Pierre Yes, that's correct.

Mr Maler Your job application, which I liked very much, is lying in front of me. We would like to invite you to a personal interview.

Pierre Oh, that's great!

Mr Maler Mr Dupont, when do you have time to come to us? Which day suits you best?

Pierre Hmm ... Thursday or Friday suits me best. Then I have nearly always time in the afternoon.

Mr Maler Well. How about Thursday, on 18th May then?

Pierre On 18th May? One moment, please ... No, I'm sorry, I have an appointment with my dentist then.

Mr Maler And one day later, on Friday?

Pierre Yes, Friday 19th is good. I have no appointments on that day!

Mr Maler Marvelous! Will 3 p.m. be fine?

Pierre Yes, that'll be fine!

Mr Maler Great. Please come directly to my office then, which is on the first floor. You can ask at the reception too. There is personnel who will gladly give you directions! We'll meet in two weeks, Mr Dupont.

Pierre Yes, I'm looking forward to it. Goodbye.

Day 25 Vocabulary

anbieten	offer
Bewerbungs-gespräch, -e *n*	job interview
Buch, Bücher *n*	book
Büro, -s *n*	office
direkt	directly
einen Termin vereinbaren	make an appointment
einladen	invite
frei halten	keep free
frei	free
Freitagnach-mittag, -e *m*	Friday afternoon
Ich freue mich darauf.	I'm looking forward to it.
Jahreszeit, -en *f*	season
Kein Problem!	No Problem!
leider	unfortunately
Mitarbeiter *Pl*	personnel
nachmittags	in the afternoon
passen	fit, suit
persönlich	personal
plötzlich	suddenly
richtig	correct, right
Termin, -e *m*	appointment
Terminkalender, – *m*	diary
Verabredung, -en *f*	appointment, date, rendezvous
Zahnarzt, -ärzte *m*	dentist
Zeit haben	have time

Learning tip I

When saying the year in German you don't use a preposition:
2012 fahre ich nach Frankreich.
In 2012 I'm going to go to France.

Learning tip II

To specify a time of day (like afternoon) on a certain day of the week (like Friday), you build a compound noun: **der Freitagnachmittag** or **der Montagmorgen.**

Days	
Montag *m*	Monday
Dienstag *m*	Tuesday
Mittwoch *m*	Wednesday
Donnerstag *m*	Thursday
Freitag *m*	Friday
Samstag/ Sonnabend *m*	Saturday
Sonntag *m*	Sunday

Grammar and means of expression

Relative clauses ► § 3.4

Relative clauses are subordinate clauses that specify a noun. The relative pronouns are **der**, **die**, **das** *who/which/that* – they replace the noun in the subordinate clause. Thereby, their number and gender match the related noun:
Vor mir liegt **Ihre Bewerbung**, **die** mir sehr gut gefallen hat.
Your job application, which I liked very much, is lying in front of me.
Here, the relative pronoun is the subject in the subordinate clause and therefore its case is nominative.

The forms of the relative pronouns are the same as of the definite articles – with one exception: the dative plural relative pronoun is **denen** (whereas the article is **den**)!
Wir geben **den** Kindern Bonbons.
We give the children sweets.
Da sind die Kinder, **denen** wir Bonbons geben.
There are the children, whom we give sweets.

These examples show that the relative pronoun isn't always the subject. In fact, a relative pronoun can be any kind of object in the subordinate clause.
Die Wohnung, **in der** ich wohne, ist klein.
The flat, in which I live, is small.
In the previous two examples the relative pronoun is not the subject, but a dative object or an object with a preposition that requires dative.

Interrogative articles ► § 6.2

Welcher Tag passt Ihnen am besten? *Which day suits you best?*
With **welcher**, **welche**, **welches** (*Pl* **welche**) *which/what* you can ask about a person or thing from a group. If you want to ask about the type of a thing or the nature of a person you use **was für ein/eine** *what* (*Pl* **was für**). See the difference in the examples:
Was für ein Buch kaufst du? – Einen Thriller.
What (kind of) book are you buying? – A thriller.
Welches Buch kaufst du? – Harry Potter.
Which book are you buying? – Harry Potter.

Exercises

2/29

1 Read the questions below. Then listen to the short dialogues on the CD and answer the questions.

1. An welchem Tag hat die Frau Zeit? ☐ Am 4.3. ☐ Am 4.5. ☐ Am 14.5.
2. a) In welchem Monat liegt der Termin? ....
   b) Um wie viel Uhr ist der Termin? ....
3. a) Um wie viel Uhr soll der Mann kommen? ☐ Um 4 Uhr. ☐ Um 16 Uhr.
   b) Hat er zu diesem Termin Zeit? ....
4. An welchem Tag, in welchem Monat und Jahr und um wie viel Uhr ist der Termin?
   ....
5. Um wie viel Uhr fährt der Zug ab? ....

2 Answer each question with one possible answer from the box. Some questions may have multiple answers and some answers fit to more than one question.

An diesem Tag habe ich keine Zeit. Ja, das passt mir gut.
Am Montag. Tut mir leid. Leider nicht. Im Juli. Am Mittwoch um 16 Uhr.
Ich habe meinen Terminkalender leider nicht hier.

1. Wann haben Sie Zeit? ....
2. Haben Sie am Freitag einen freien Termin? ....
3. Können Sie am Dienstag zu mir kommen? ....
4. Haben Sie am 17.8. Zeit? ....
5. Wann können wir uns treffen? ....
6. An welchem Tag passt es Ihnen? ....

3 Fill in the gaps using the appropriate relative pronoun.

1. Meine Schwester, ... in Berlin studiert, hat einen Sohn.
2. Gibst du mir bitte den Beamer, ... dort im Schrank steht?
3. Der Film, ... ich ausgeliehen habe, ist echt spannend!
4. Pierre, ... Jens viele Tipps gegeben hat, bewirbt sich bei einer deutschen Firma.
5. Iwona und Pierre, ... schon gut Deutsch sprechen, fahren nach München.

Kulturtipp
German punctuality

One of the characteristics often attributed to Germans is punctuality. However in private life it depends on an individual person. For ones it's very important, while others don't care very much. It may even be that the contact with other cultures in our globalized world made the Germans a bit more relaxed and tolerant regarding (un-) punctuality!?

But no matter how one's personal attitude is, punctuality really matters in business life. Here, even minutes can influence the mood of your colleagues and seniors. If you're going to be late (after all, it's not always your fault, isn't it?), then it's always good to give a brief call, especially if you've got an appointment.

In private life, it's usually OK to be late for 10–15 minutes (and not call).

If you're travelling by train or using buses and trams, you're probably soon going to realize that delays can occur (and those who value punctuality can get quite angry because of that and rant about the decay of values ...). But generally trains are quite punctual – so try not to be late (particularly when you bought a special offer train ticket for a particular train).

What can you already do?

	☺	😐	☹	
▪ make appointments	■	■	■	▸ Ü1, Ü2
▪ agree to appointments or decline	■	■	■	▸ Ü1, Ü2
▪ speak about date, time and days	■	■	■	▸ Ü1, Ü2

Day 26 Making contacts

In this lesson you will learn

- to talk about clothes and networks
- to prepare for a job interview

2/30 Gute Nachrichten

Jens sitzt in der Kantine beim Mittagessen. Da kommt Pierre dazu.

Pierre Hallo Jens! Eben hat einer von der Firma angerufen, bei der ich mich beworben habe.

Jens Hi Pierre, setz dich doch! Und? Was hat er gesagt?

Pierre Er hat mich zu einem Gespräch eingeladen! Ich bin schon richtig nervös.

Jens Ich gratuliere! Wann ist denn der Termin?

Pierre In zwei Wochen.

Jens Ach, das ist genug Zeit. Im Internet findet man viele Ratgeber zum Thema Bewerbungsgespräch – zum Beispiel auf fast jeder Webseite mit Stellenanzeigen.

Pierre Steht da auch, was ich anziehen soll?

Jens Sicher! Am besten ist wohl ein Anzug, aber lies das in den Ratgebern nach.

Pierre O. K., mache ich.

Jens Ach, ich wollte dir auch noch einen Tipp geben. Bist du schon Mitglied in einem Business-Netzwerk im Internet?

Pierre Nein.

Jens Ich finde das heute ziemlich wichtig. So kann man ganz einfach mit ehemaligen Kollegen in Kontakt bleiben und auch leicht neue Kontakte knüpfen. Und vielleicht ergibt sich ja auch der ein oder andere neue Job!

Pierre Verstehe! Und wo melde ich mich da an?

Jens Zum einen gibt es da LinkedIn, das ist das weltweit größte Netzwerk dieser Art. In Deutschland und Europa ist aber auch Xing sehr populär. Viele Kollegen hier sind dort Mitglied – ich auch! Wenn du willst, kann ich dir eine Einladung schicken.

Pierre Ja, mach das bitte.

Dialogue questions

Mark with a cross:

	right	wrong
1. Jens ist in seinem Büro als Pierre kommt.	☐	☐
2. Pierre soll im Internet nach Ratgebern suchen.	☐	☐
3. Pierre ist Mitglied bei LinkedIn.	☐	☐

Good news

Jens is sitting in the canteen at lunch. Then Pierre arrives.

Pierre Hello Jens! A moment ago I had a call from someone from the company I applied to.

Jens Hi Pierre, do sit down! And? What did they say?

Pierre They invited me to an interview! I'm really nervous already.

Jens Congratulations! When's the appointment?

Pierre In two weeks.

Jens Oh, there is enough time. You'll find many guides on the internet dealing with job interviews – for instance nearly on every website with job advertisements.

Pierre Is there also anything said about how I should dress?

Jens Sure! A suit will probably be the best, but you'd better read those guides.

Pierre O. K., I'll do.

Jens Oh, and I wanted to give you a tip, too. Are you already a member of a business network on the internet?

Pierre No.

Jens I think it's pretty important today. You can really easily keep in touch with former colleagues and make new contacts. So the one or other new job might come along!

Pierre I see! And where do I register?

Jens On one hand, there's LinkedIn, that's the world's biggest network of this kind. But in Germany and Europe Xing's very popular too. A lot of our colleagues are members of it – and me too! If you want I can send you an invitation.

Pierre Yes, please do that.

Day 26

Vocabulary

anmelden	register
anziehen	dress
Art, -en *f*	kind, type
auffällig	flashy
ausziehen	undress
bunt	colourful
eben	a moment ago
ehemalig	former
elegant	elegant
genug	enough
gepflegt	neat, groomed
Gespräch, -e *n*	conversation, talk
gratulieren	congratulate
in Kontakt bleiben	stay in touch
Kleidung *f* (*only Sg*)	clothes
Kleidungsstück, -e *n*	piece of clothing
Kontakt, -e *m*	contact
Kontakte knüpfen	to make new contacts
locker, sportlich	casual
Mitglied, -er *n*	member
nervös	nervous
Netzwerk, -e *n*	network
passend, geeignet	suitable
pflegen	maintain
populär	popular
Ratgeber, – *m*	guide
schick	chic, fashionable
Schmuck (*only Sg*) *m*	jewellery
Thema, Themen *n*	topic
Verstehe!	I see!, I get it!
verteilen	distribute
Visitenkarte, -n *f*	business card
Voraussetzung, -en *f*	requirement
wohl	probably
ziemlich	pretty, quite
zurückhaltend	conservative

Clothes	
Anzug, Anzüge *m*	suit
Bluse, -n *f*	blouse
Handschuh, -e *m*	glove
Hemd, -en *n*	shirt
Hose, -n *f*	trousers
Hosenanzug, -anzüge *m*	pantsuit
Hut, Hüte *m*	hat
Jacke, -n *f*	jacket, (shorter) coat
Jackett, -s *n*	jacket, suit jacket
Jeans, – *f*	jeans
Kleid, -er *n*	dress
Kostüm, -e *n*	female suit
Krawatte, -n *f*	tie
Mantel, Mäntel *m*	(longer) coat
Mütze, -n *f*	cap
Pullover, – *m*	jumper, sweater
Rock, Röcke *m*	skirt
Schal, -s *m*	scarf
Schuh, -e *m*	shoe
Socke, -n *f*	sock
T-Shirt, -s *n*	T-shirt
Unterwäsche (*only Sg*) *f*	underwear

Grammar and means of expression

The indefinite pronoun *man* ► *§ 3.5.1*

There's another indefinite pronoun in German: **man** *one/they/you*. It substitutes one or more unspecified persons. It's always the subject of the sentence and the referring verb is always in third person singular.
Im Internet findet **man** viele Ratgeber. *You'll find many guides on the internet.*
For accusative or dative objects you use the suitable forms of the indefinite pronoun **einer**.

Other articles ► *§ 2.2*

There are some words in German that are used like articles, i.e. before a noun. They are used to state more or less definite quantities or partial quantities. All of them can be used as pronouns as well, that is without the noun – but only if it's clear what you're referring to.
You saw some of them in the dialogue:
Im Internet findet man **viele** Ratgeber. *You'll find many guides on the internet.*
Auf fast **jeder** Webseite. *Nearly on every website.*
Or as a pronoun:

► Ich suche einen Ratgeber.
► *I'm looking for a guide.*

◄ Im Internet findest du **viele**.
◄ *You'll find many on the internet.*

The most important of these articles/pronouns are:
jeder, jede, jedes (no *Pl*, endings are similar to the indefinite pronoun **einer**) *each/every/any*
beide (*only Pl*) *both*
alle (*only Pl*) *all*
viele (*only Pl*) *many/a lot of*
mehrere (*only Pl*) *several*
einige, manche (*only Pl*) *some*

And also the following articles/pronouns which don't change with gender or case:
etwas, ein wenig (*only Sg* and only with mass nouns) *some, a little bit of*
viel (*only Sg* and only with mass nouns) *much*
ein paar (*only Pl*) *a few, a couple of*

Day 26 Exercises

1 Read the text from a job interview guide and answer the questions (multiple answers are possible).

Die richtige Kleidung ist eine wichtige Voraussetzung für ein gelungenes Bewerbungsgespräch. „Passend und authentisch" soll die Kleidung sein, liest man oft. Gemeint ist: passend zum zukünftigen Beruf und passend zu einem selbst! Wichtig ist, dass man sich selbst in seiner Kleidung wohlfühlt. Denn wenn nicht, merken das die anderen gleich. Auch sollte man darauf achten, dass die Kleidung nicht ablenkt. Ihr zukünftiger Arbeitgeber sollte sich während des Gesprächs nicht ständig Gedanken wegen Ihrer bunten Krawatte oder einer auffälligen Brosche* machen müssen. Treten Sie zurückhaltend, aber gepflegt auf – dann sind Sie auf der sicheren Seite!

1. Was ist wichtig für ein Bewerbungsgespräch?
   a) ☐ Richtige Kleidung. b) ☐ Passende Kleidung. c) ☐ Sportliche Kleidung.
2. Was ist an der Kleidung für ein Bewerbungsgespräch wichtig?
   a) ☐ Dass man sich darin wohlfühlt.
   b) ☐ Dass sie zum Beruf passt.
   c) ☐ Dass sie andere Menschen ablenkt.
3. Wie soll die Krawatte sein?
   a) ☐ Auffällig. b) ☐ Zurückhaltend. c) ☐ Bunt.
4. Welches Kleidungsstück ist gut geeignet für ein Bewerbungsgespräch?
   a) ☐ Jackett. b) ☐ T-Shirt. c) ☐ Hemd.

* die Brosche *brooch*

2/31 **2 Pierre and Iwona are talking about networks and contacts. Listen to their conversation on the CD and mark the right answer.**

	right	wrong
1. Iwona ist nur in einem Netzwerk Mitglied.	☐	☐
2. Iwona findet Netzwerke nicht wichtig.	☐	☐
3. Pierre hat keinen direkten Kontakt mit Kunden.	☐	☐
4. Iwona geht auf Veranstaltungen. Dort pflegt sie ihre Kontakte.	☐	☐
5. Pierre ist Mitglied in einem Business-Netzwerk.	☐	☐
6. Iwona ist schon seit vielen Jahren Mitglied bei Xing.	☐	☐

Kulturtipp My German job interview

Did you receive an invitation to a job interview? Congratulations! But now it's important to prepare accordingly.

First you need to collect as much information about the company as possible. Try to gather all information in German (even if the company has a website in your native language or English). Thus you won't have to translate it later and you will already have the right terminology.

One good method to prepare to the interview is to make a mind map. Write down the information you've gathered. Also write down any questions you might get asked and, of course, questions which you would like to ask. Then ask a German friend to look it over and correct if necessary. That's the base for your next step: Practise your job interview in a role play – preferably also with a German friend. And keep in mind that you're not supposed to just sit and answer, ask the questions you've prepared. It's a good sign to show some initiative – all the more since you're talking in a foreign language!

Now, fingers crossed and good luck!

What can you already do?

	☺	😐	☹	
▪ talk about clothes	▪	▪	▪	► *Ü1*
▪ prepare for a job interview	▪	▪	▪	► *Ü1*
▪ talk about networking	▪	▪	▪	► *Ü2*

Day 27

Meetings

In this lesson you will learn

- to welcome the members of a meeting
- to moderate a meeting
- about presentations and presentation media

2/32

Noch Fragen?

Die Besprechung, die Iwona organisiert hat, beginnt.

Iwona Guten Tag, mein Name ist Iwona Nowak und ich möchte Sie ganz herzlich zu dieser Besprechung begrüßen! Mein Kollege Herr Theus stellt Ihnen jetzt das Programm für heute vor.

Herr Theus Ja, als ersten Tagesordnungspunkt haben wir eine kurze Präsentation zum aktuellen Geschäftsbericht vorbereitet. Im Anschluss sagt Herr Steigmann ein paar Worte zur Situation in der Firma. Dann machen wir eine Pause. Danach ist Frau Nowaks Präsentation zu den zukünftigen Strategien an der Reihe und dann bespricht Frau Klein noch die Planung und das weitere Vorgehen mit Ihnen. Kommen wir also zum ersten Punkt ...

Herr Theus und Herr Steigmann halten ihre Vorträge. Nach der Pause fährt Iwona fort.

Iwona So, ich hoffe, Sie haben die Pause genossen. Ich will in meiner Präsentation die neuen Strategien ansprechen ...

Iwona hält ihre Präsentation.

Iwona Gibt es noch Fragen?

Teilnehmer Ja. Gibt es die Möglichkeit für uns, dass wir die Dinge, die Sie genannt haben, noch einmal nachlesen?

Iwona Ja, wir schicken Ihnen eine Zusammenfassung per E-Mail.

Teilnehmer Ah, gut. Vielen Dank.

Iwona Gern. Weitere Fragen?

Die Teilnehmer stellen noch einige weitere Fragen.

Iwona Gut, ich denke, dass wir alles Wichtige angesprochen und Ihre Fragen beantwortet haben. Ich möchte Ihnen für die Aufmerksamkeit danken und wünsche uns allen weiterhin gute Zusammenarbeit und eine erfolgreiche Zukunft. Vielen Dank und auf Wiedersehen!

Dialogue questions

Mark the right answer.

1. Wie heißt Iwonas Kollegin?	a) ☐ Frau Klein.	b) ☐ Frau Theus.
2. Wer spricht zuerst?	a) ☐ Herr Steigmann.	b) ☐ Frau Klein.
3. Worüber spricht Frau Klein?	a) ☐ Die Strategien.	b) ☐ Die Planung.
4. Wie gibt es die Zusammenfassung?	a) ☐ Als Handout.	b) ☐ Als E-Mail.

Any questions?

The meeting which Iwona organized begins.

Iwona Good morning, my name is Iwona Nowak and I would like to cordially welcome you to this meeting! My colleague Mr Theus is now going to present the programme for today.

Mr Theus Well, as the first topic we prepared a short presentation of the current report on the company. Next Mr Steigmann is going to say a few words about the situation in the company. Then we will have a break. After that there will be Ms Nowak's turn to present future strategies and finally Ms Klein is going to discuss with you the planning and further actions. Let's proceed thus to the first topic ...

Mr Theus and Mr Steigmann make their speeches. After the break Iwona continues.

Iwona Well, I hope you've enjoyed the break. I'd like to speak about the new strategies now ...

Iwona conducts her presentation.

Iwona Are there any questions?

Member Yes. Is there a possibility for us to read about those things you've mentioned once again?

Iwona Yes, we e-mail a summary to you.

Member Oh, well. Thank you very much.

Iwona You're welcome. Are there any other questions?

The members ask some more questions.

Iwona Well, I think that we have addressed all important topics and answered your questions. I'd like to thank you for your attention and also I wish us good cooperation and a successful future. Thank you very much and goodbye!

Day 27 **Vocabulary**

aktuell	current
alles Wichtige	all important topics
also	thus
an der Reihe sein	to be so.'s turn to …
ansprechen	address
Aufmerksamkeit *(only Sg) f*	attention
beantworten	answer
begrüßen	welcome
besprechen	talk, discuss
Dame, -n *f*	lady, madam
Ding, -e *n*	thing
einen Vortrag halten	make a speech
erfolgreich	successful
es geht um	it's about
fortfahren	continue
Frage, -n *f*	question
genießen	enjoy
Geschäftsbericht, -e *m*	company report
Herr, -en *m*	sir, mister
herzlich	dearly, cordially
heutig	today's
im Anschluss	subsequently
im Folgenden	in the following
Moderation, -en *f*	moderation
moderieren	moderate
Möglichkeit, -en *f*	possibility
nennen	mention
noch einmal	once again
Pause, -n *f*	break
Programm, -e *n*	programme
Punkt, -e *m*	here: topic, point
Situation, -en *f*	situation
Strategie, -n *f*	strategy
Tagesordnungs-punkt, -e *m*	topic
vorstellen	present
Vortrag, Vorträge *m*	speech
Wand, Wände *f*	wall
weiterhin	furthermore, also
zukünftig	future
Zukunft *(only Sg) f*	future
Zusammenarbeit *(only Sg) f*	cooperation
Zusammen-fassung, -en *f*	summary

Presentations

Einleitung, -en *f*	introduction
Hauptteil, -e *m*	main part/section
Schluss, Schlüsse *m*	conclusion
Diskussion, -en *f*	discussion
Handzettel, – *m*; **Handout, -s** *n*	handout
Tageslichtprojek-tor, Overhead-projektor, -en *m*	overhead projector
Medium, Medien *n*	medium

Grammar and means of expression

Adjectives I ▸ *§ 6*

There are two possible positions of adjectives. The one you have already used is after the verb **sein**. For example:
Das Museum ist interessant. *The museum is interesting.*
In this position the adjective does not change its form because of case, gender or number.
Now let us have a look at the adjectives positioned before nouns, where they have to be declined. That's what a lot of students consider really difficult to learn, but there really is nothing to fear. For now it's essential to understand what it's about – you can use in most cases the adjective after **sein**. But we'll do some exercises with adjectives here and there will be more than enough possibilities to practise once you start your B1 German class later! So let's just cut the preamble and jump right in at the deep end:
The declined form of the adjectives differs according to the article you used – let's start with the definite article:
Ich will **die** neue**n** Strategien ansprechen. – *I'd like to speak about the new strategies.*
Danach ist Frau Nowaks Präsentation zu **den** zukünftigen Strategien an der Reihe.
After that it's Ms Nowak's turn to present future strategies.
Now in this position (before the noun) after the definite article, the adjective gets -**e** or -**en** as an ending according to the noun's case, gender and number as you can see in the table.

	m (e.g. Plan)	f (e.g. Frage)	n (e.g. Buch)	Pl (e.g. Strategien)
Nom.	der neue	die neue	das neue	die neu**en**
Acc.	den neu**en**	die neue	das neue	die neu**en**
Dat.	dem neu**en**	der neu**en**	dem neu**en**	den neu**en**

Day 27 Exercises

2/33

1 Listen to the CD. You'll hear the phrases below. Fill in the gaps and repeat each sentence after the beep.

Guten Tag, ... (1.) Herren. – Ich .... (2.) zur heutigen Besprechung. – Ich möchte kurz .... (3.). – In der Präsentation .... (4.) neue Strategien. – Gibt es noch .... (5.)? – Dann sind alle Fragen .... (6.). – Vielen Dank .... (7.). – Auf .... (8.).

2 You have received an e-mail about the presentations for the next meeting. Read the e-mail and answer the questions.

Neue E-Mail

Guten Tag,
wie am Telefon besprochen, sende ich Ihnen die Planung für die Besprechung. Herr Maier präsentiert um 9.15 Uhr den Geschäftsbericht 2009. Um 10 Uhr ist Frau Leser an der Reihe. Sie spricht von der Firmenentwicklung* in den letzten Jahren. Von 10.45 Uhr bis 11 Uhr ist eine Pause. Danach hält Frau Berger ihren Vortrag zum Thema „Neue Strategien für die Zukunft". Herr Maier braucht um 9 Uhr einen Beamer und Frau Leser braucht für ihren Vortrag einen Tageslichtprojektor. Vielen Dank!
Mit freundlichen Grüßen
I. Schmitz

1. Das Thema von Herrn Maiers Präsentation? ....
2. Wann beginnt Frau Bergers Vortrag? ....
3. Wer spricht von der Firmenentwicklung? ....
4. Wer braucht einen Tageslichtprojektor? ....

* die Firmenentwicklung *the company's development*

3 Write the sentences again by placing the adjective before the noun.

1. Das Buch ist langweilig. ....
2. Der Anzug ist schick. ....
3. Die Hemden sind weiß. ....
4. Die Schuhe sind sportlich. ....

Kulturtipp
Body language

Germans are often perceived as cold and closed. One reason might be that the body language of German people – especially in a professional environment – is not so distinctive. But that depends on your point of view: analyses showed that there is more or less a decline where body language and contacts get more extensive from north to south.

In Germany you normally keep some distance (about an arm's length) to people you're not familiar with, like colleagues at work. The standard greeting is a handshake (pecks on the cheeks are possible only in familiar surroundings). It's uncommon to touch others during a conversation, except for the handshakes or maybe a motivating or praising back-slapping. But don't give your superiors a backslap – they may only come from someone higher in the hierarchy.

Of course all that can be very different among close friends!

What can you already do?

	☺ 😐 ☹	
▪ welcome the members of a meeting	▫ ▫ ▫	► *Ü1*
▪ present a topic	▫ ▫ ▫	► *Ü1*
▪ moderate a meeting	▫ ▫ ▫	► *Ü1*
▪ talk about presentations and presentation media	▫ ▫ ▫	► *Ü2*

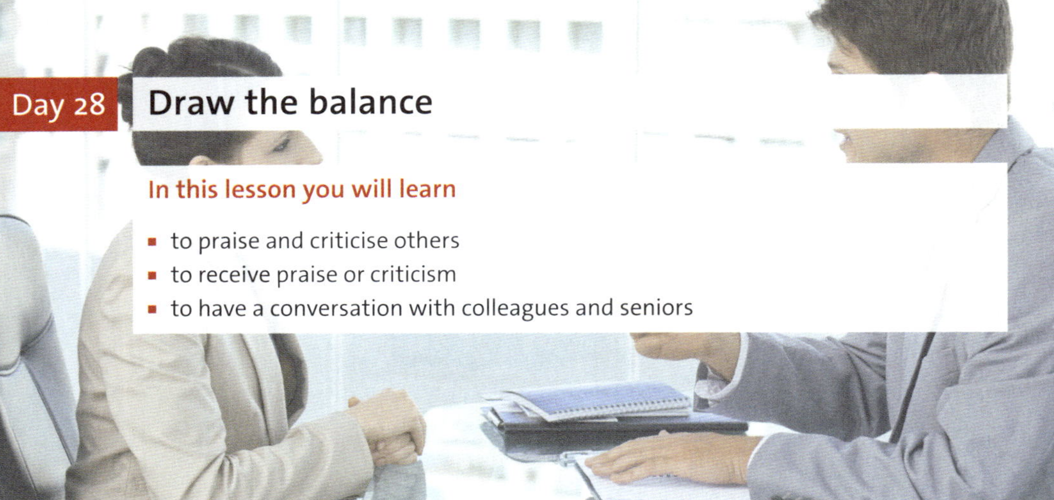

Day 28 Draw the balance

In this lesson you will learn

- to praise and criticise others
- to receive praise or criticism
- to have a conversation with colleagues and seniors

2/34 Gut gemacht!

Nach der Besprechung bittet Frau Klein Iwona zu sich in ihr Büro.

Frau Klein Frau Nowak, ich möchte Sie loben. Die Präsentation war wirklich hervorragend. Das haben Sie ganz toll gemacht!

Iwona Vielen Dank, Frau Klein. Ich habe mich auch lange darauf vorbereitet. Das war das erste größere Projekt auf Deutsch, deshalb war ich ganz schön nervös ...

Frau Klein Ja? Das hat man Ihnen aber nicht angemerkt. Und auch sprachlich war das einwandfrei. Sie haben in der kurzen Zeit hier wirklich gut Deutsch gelernt.

Iwona Stimmt, ich bin selbst zufrieden. Ich habe aber auch eine sehr gute Lehrerin!

Frau Klein Ich bin jedenfalls froh, dass Sie in meiner Abteilung sind.

Iwona Ich arbeite sehr gern in Ihrer Abteilung. Das angenehme Klima und die netten Kollegen erleichtern die Arbeit sehr!

Frau Klein Dann hoffe ich, dass Sie noch eine Weile bei uns bleiben. Wenn Sie im nächsten Quartal auch so gute Leistung bringen, dann können wir bald über eine Beförderung sprechen.

Iwona Vielen Dank. Die Arbeit macht mir einfach Spaß und das motiviert mich auch.

Frau Klein Das merkt man, Frau Nowak. Nun gut, ich freue mich schon auf das nächste Projekt, das Sie übernehmen.

Iwona Ja, ich auch!

Dialogue questions

Answer the questions briefly.

1. Wie findet Frau Klein Iwonas Präsentation? ....

2. Warum war Iwona nervös vor dem Projekt? ....

3. Wie findet Iwona ihre Kollegen? ....

4. Worauf freut sich Frau Klein? ....

Well done!

After the meeting Ms Klein asks Iwona to join her in her office.

Ms Klein Ms Nowak, I want to praise you. The presentation was really excellent. You've done great!

Iwona Thank you, Ms Klein. I had been preparing for it for a long time. That was the first bigger project in German, that's why I was pretty nervous ...

Ms Klein Oh, really? Nobody noticed. And also it was flawless as far as the language is concerned. You learnt German really well in such a short time.

Iwona That's true, I'm satisfied with myself. But I have a very good teacher, too!

Ms Klein Anyway, I'm glad that you're in my department.

Iwona I like working in your department. A pleasant atmosphere and nice colleagues make the work very easy!

Ms Klein Then I hope that you will stay with us for a while. If you perform so well in the next quarter too, we soon can talk about a promotion.

Iwona Thank you very much. I have pleasure doing the work and that motivates me too.

Ms Klein I have noticed it, Ms Nowak. Very well, I'm already looking forward to the next project you're going to take on.

Iwona So do I!

Day 28 Vocabulary

Abteilung, -en *f*	department
angenehm	kind
anmerken	notice
bald	soon
Beförderung, -en *f*	promotion
deshalb	therefore, that's why
Deutsch *(only Sg) n*	(the language) German
einwandfrei	flawless
erleichtern	to make ... easy
froh	glad
ganz schön	pretty
ganz	here: quite
Gern geschehen.	You're welcome.
Gut gemacht!	Well done!
hervorragend	excellent
hoffen	hope
Ich auch.	So do I.
jedenfalls	anyway
Leistung bringen	perform
Leistung, -en *f*	performance
merken	notice
nett	nice
Projekt, -e *n*	project
selbst	oneself
sich freuen	look forward to
Spaß, Späße *m*	fun
sprachlich	linguistic
übernehmen	take over
Verhalten *(only Sg) n*	behaviour
Weile *(only Sg) f*	while
zufrieden	satisfied

Praise and criticise	
auf etwas achten	mind, pay attention
beim nächsten Mal	next time
eine Bitte haben	have a favour to ask
Kritik, -en *f*	criticism
kritisieren	criticise
Lob *(only Sg) n*	praise
loben	praise
motivieren	motivate
üblich	common
unüblich	uncommon, not common
vermeiden	avoid

Learning tip

The plural ending of all feminine nouns ending with **-ung**, **-keit**, **-heit**, **-tion** is **-en**, e.g. **Leistung**, **Leistungen**.

Grammar and means of expression

Adjectives II ► §6

Now let's focus our attention on adjectives positioned before a noun with an indefinite article. Here there are more different endings.
Let's look at the table first:

	m (e.g. Plan)	f (e.g. Frage)	n (e.g. Buch)	Pl (e.g. Strategien)
Nom.	ein neu**er**	eine neu**e**	ein neu**es**	– neu**e**
Acc.	einen neu**en**	eine neu**e**	ein neu**es**	– neu**e**
Dat.	einem neu**en**	einer neu**en**	einem neu**en**	– neu**en**

Martina ist eine gut**e** Lehrerin. *Martina is a good teacher.*
Iwona hat eine gut**e** Lehrerin. *Iwona has a good teacher.*
Iwona ist mit einer gut**en** Lehrerin befreundet. *Iwona is friends with a good teacher.*
Iwona hat gut**e** Lehrerinnen. *Iwona has good teachers.*

Refer to the grammar in the appendix to see how adjectives are declined with other articles or possessive pronouns you learned (like **mein**, **jeder** or **viele**).

deshalb and *darum* ► §9

There are some words in German that look and are used like coordinating conjunctions (you remember: like **und**, **oder**, **aber**). Two such words probably most often used are **deshalb** *therefore/thus/hence* and **darum** *therefore/that is why* and they state a result:
Der Vortrag ist auf Deutsch, **deshalb/darum** bin ich nervös.
The speech is in German, therefore I am nervous.
Vice versa, to state the cause you can use **denn** or **weil** as you already know:
Ich bin nervös, denn der Vortrag ist auf Deutsch.
I am nervous, for the speech is in German.
The special thing about **deshalb** and **darum** is that they are full constituents and that's why in the examples above the verb follows directly **deshalb** – and not the subject like after **denn**.

Day 28 Exercises

1 Read the situations below. Then choose the appropriate phrase from the box and say it loud.

> Dieses Verhalten ist hier unüblich. Vermeiden Sie bitte die Anrede mit Du. Ich habe eine Bitte: Seien Sie bitte etwas pünktlicher. Das war hervorragend. Ihre Präsentation war etwas kurz. Achten Sie beim nächsten Mal bitte auf die Zeit. Das haben Sie gut gemacht.

Tell your colleague ...

1. that he should pay more attention to the timing.
2. that it was excellent.
3. that her presentation was a bit brief.
4. that he should avoid the informal language.
5. that this behaviour is not common here.
6. that she has done well.
7. that you'd ask him to be a bit more punctual.

2 Fill in the gaps with the adjectives in their correct form.

1. Pierre sieht einen .... Film. (interessant)
2. Iwona liest ein .... Buch. (langweilig)
3. Martina und Jens gehen mit .... Freunden essen. (gut)
4. Ich habe ein .... Auto. (schnell)
5. Das Oktoberfest ist ein .... Volksfest. (groß)
6. Du bist ein .... Lehrer. (toll)

2/35

3 Read the questions and listen to the conversation on the CD. Then answer the questions.

1. Wer hat den Vortrag gehalten?	a) ☐ Herr Kern.	b) ☐ Frau Roth.
2. Was kritisiert Herr Kern? Der Vortrag war	a) ☐ zu kurz.	b) ☐ zu lang.
3. Warum war der Vortrag nicht einwandfrei?	a) ☐ Das Handout war zu kurz.	b) ☐ Wenig Vorbereitung.
4. Wer hat die Materialien zu spät geschickt?	a) ☐ Herr Kern.	b) ☐ Frau Roth.
5. Wer ist der Chef?	a) ☐ Herr Kern.	b) ☐ Frau Roth.

Kulturtipp Intercultural misunderstandings

Do you feel bad because your boss criticised you openly? Germans are known for their directness which may be sometimes hurtful (in return a nice objective praise is a fine thing, isn't it?). But don't feel bad, it's not about you personally.

Punctuality, body contact, directness – these are only a few aspects of a whole multitude of possible intercultural misunderstandings and missteps. But – and that's true – there's nothing like "international cultural norms". And nobody can possibly expect you to fully adopt German norms and abandon your own cultural habits (but also you shouldn't ignore the habits of the culture in which you live). On the contrary: The more intercultural contacts there are in this globalized world, the more different cultures cultivate their peculiarities. And thus cultural tensions are unavoidable.

But what can you do when you happen to make someone cross because you were unpunctual, or touched the person you talked to? Talk about it: Explain your cultural habits and norms. When you know common stereotypes associated with your own culture and the culture you're now living in, it's easy to unmask them. It should then be possible to solve the problem and find an agreement.

What can you already do?

	☺ ☹︎ ☹	
▪ praise and criticise others	▪ ▪ ▪	► Ü1, Ü3
▪ receive praise or criticism	▪ ▪ ▪	► Ü3
▪ have a conversation with colleagues and seniors	▪ ▪ ▪	► Ü3

Day 29 Job-related plans

In this lesson you will learn

- to express and talk about wishes
- to express plans and intentions for the future

2/36 Was bringt uns die Zukunft?

Iwona, Martina, Pierre und Jens sitzen zusammen in einer Kneipe.

Martina Schön, dass wir wieder mal alle zusammensitzen. Es ist ja wirklich viel passiert in letzter Zeit ... Pierre, du willst also nach Hamburg, ja?

Pierre Ja! Aber zuerst findet noch das Bewerbungsgespräch statt und dann werde ich meinen Abschluss machen. Aber ich würde wirklich gern bei dieser Firma arbeiten!

Jens Ich glaube nicht, dass das Bewerbungsgespräch ein Problem ist. Ich würde Pierre gleich einstellen!

Pierre Danke. Hoffentlich sieht das die Firma auch so.

Martina Das wird schon klappen, Pierre! Und du, Iwona? Ich habe gehört, dass du auch sehr erfolgreich warst.

Iwona Oh ja. Die Präsentation war sehr gut. Und meine Chefin hat auch mein Deutsch gelobt.

Martina Schließlich hast du eine tolle Lehrerin!

Iwona Genau das Gleiche habe ich meiner Chefin auch gesagt. Und ich werde vielleicht auch bald eine Beförderung bekommen.

Martina Wow, das ging ja schnell! Ich drücke dir die Daumen für deine Karriere. Dann werdet ihr beide also in naher Zukunft in Deutschland bleiben?

Iwona u. Pierre Ja.

Martina Das ist toll. Ich hoffe, dass wir noch viele Dinge gemeinsam unternehmen werden. Hamburg ist ja nicht so weit weg!

Pierre Ich würde ja auch lieber in Berlin bleiben, aber hier habe ich einfach keine passende Arbeit gefunden. Aber ich liebe Berlin und werde euch oft besuchen!

Jens Hoffentlich! Aber jetzt lasst uns doch anstoßen: Auf das, was uns die Zukunft bringen wird!

Dialogue questions

Mark with a cross:

	right	wrong
1. Pierre will lieber in Hamburg leben.	☐	☐
2. Iwona und Pierre bleiben noch in Deutschland.	☐	☐
3. Pierre will seine Freunde oft besuchen.	☐	☐
4. Martina will noch viel mit Pierre und Iwona unternehmen.	☐	☐

What does the future hold for us?

Iwona, Martina, Pierre and Jens are sitting in a pub.

Martina It's nice that we are all sitting together once again. Quite a lot has happened lately ... Pierre, you want to go to Hamburg, do you?

Pierre Yes! But first there's the job interview and then I have to graduate. I'd really like to work for this company!

Jens I don't think that the job interview is going to be a problem. I'd employ Pierre at once!

Pierre Thanks. I hope that the company will see it the same.

Martina That'll go off all right, Pierre! And how about you, Iwona? I've heard that you've been very successful, too.

Iwona Oh, yes. The presentation was very good. And my boss praised my German.

Martina After all, you had a great teacher!

Iwona I said to my boss exactly the same. And maybe I'll get a promotion soon, too.

Martina Wow, that was fast! I'll keep my fingers crossed for your career. So both of you are going to stay in Germany for the near future?

Iwona u. Pierre Yes.

Martina That's great. I hope that we will yet undertake a lot of things together. Hamburg isn't that far away!

Pierre I'd rather stay in Berlin, but I couldn't find a satisfying job. But I love Berlin and I'm going to visit you often!

Jens I hope so! But now let's chink glasses: To what the future holds for us!

Day 29 Vocabulary

anstoßen	chink glasses
arbeitslos	unemployed
auch so, ebenso	the same, likewise
Ausbildung, -en *f*	education
beruflich	job-related
Das wird schon klappen!	That'll go off all right.
den/einen Abschluss machen	graduate
die Daumen drücken	keep one's fingers crossed
einstellen	hire, employ
genau	exactly
glauben	think, believe
gleich	here: at once
hoffentlich	hopefully, I hope so
hören	hear
in letzter Zeit	lately
in naher Zukunft	in the near future
Karriere, -n *f*	career
Kneipe, -n *f*	pub, bar
mal, einmal	once
Rente, -n *f*	pension
Ruhestand *(only Sg) m*	retirement
schließlich	after all
Schulung, -en *f*	training
Studium, Studien *n*	studies
weit weg	far away
Weiterbildung, -en *f*	further education
wieder	again
Wunsch, Wünsche *m*	wish
zuhören	listen
zusammen	together

Grammar and means of expression

The auxiliary verb *werden* ▸ *§ 8.4*

Apart from **haben** and **sein** there's a third auxiliary verb in German: **werden**. You already know it as a main verb where it means *become*. The auxiliary **werden** is used in the future tense.

werden	
ich werde	wir werden
du wirst	ihr werdet
er/sie/es wird	sie/Sie werden

Futur I ▸ *§ 8.4*

You have learnt to use the present tense and temporal adverbs to talk about the future. But sometimes the present tense can be ambiguous and/or the point in time is not specified by an adverb. In these cases you can use the **Futur I**. (It's called **Futur I**, because there's also the **Futur II** which is seldom used and is not mentioned in this book.)
The forms are quite easy. You use the auxiliary **werden** and the infinitive of the verb. The word order is the same as with **Perfekt**: the conjugated form of **werden** is in the second position and the infinitive is in the last position in the main clause, and in the subordinate clause the auxiliary comes after the infinitive in the last position.
Ich **werde** euch oft besuchen. *I'm going to visit you often.*
Ich denke, dass ich euch oft besuchen **werde**. *I think that I'm going to visit you often.*

Wishes

To express (unrealisable) wishes you use **ich würde (gerne/lieber/am liebsten)** *I would (like/rather/like ... best).* For a certain plan you use the already learnt
ich werde *I will*. The already familiar form **ich will** *I want* is between those two: it states a possible wish if not already a rather certain plan.
Ich würde Pierre gleich einstellen.
I'd employ Pierre at once. (But Jens isn't the personnel manager.)
Ich würde lieber in Berlin bleiben.
I'd rather stay in Berlin. (But Pierre didn't find a satisfying job there.)

Day 29 Exercises

1 Fill in the gaps with the correct form of *werden* to build the future tense.

1. Ich .... nächstes Jahr nach England fahren.
2. Er .... nach seinem Abschluss sicher Rechtsanwalt werden.
3. Wir .... euch im Sommer besuchen.
4. Im Winter .... sie *(Pl)* ihren Abschluss an der Universität machen.
5. .... ihr morgen einen Vortrag halten?
6. .... du die E-Mail an Frau Wagner noch schreiben?

2 Imagine you've won a big bunch of money. What would you do? The phrases in the box might help you, but feel free to write your own wishes.

nicht mehr arbeiten · eine Reise machen · noch ein Studium beginnen · ein schnelles Auto kaufen · meinen Eltern Geschenke kaufen · ein Haus bauen · anderen Menschen helfen

1. Ich würde ....
2. Ich würde gern ....
3. Ich würde am liebsten ....
4. ....
5. ....
6. ....

2/37

3 Read the different replies in the box. Then listen to the CD and say the appropriate reply after the beep. You'll hear the correct answer again after each sentence.

Ich würde am liebsten Russisch lernen! · Ich will Lehrerin werden. · Ich auch, aber ich habe leider keine Zeit. · Ich würde gern in Deutschland arbeiten. · Nein. Ich würde gern in Deutschland arbeiten, aber ich muss zurück nach Japan.

Kulturtipp
Further education

Well, this is the end (almost, at least). Now you're going to do the last repetition lesson and the final test ... and then? You've already learnt a lot, but there is still more to learn. And it's very important to keep practising. If you're in Germany there's a way to do that: book a German class at the **VHS**, the **Volkshochschule** *folk high school*. The **VHS** is usually a municipal non-profit organization. You can not only learn and improve your language skills there but it's a place for all kinds of advanced education, art and culture, sport and health. There are more than 2000 **Volkshochschulen** in Germany and Berlin alone has 14.

The courses there are not free but normally the fees aren't that high, like for example in private education centres, since the **VHS** doesn't have to make a profit.

What can you already do?

	☺	😐	☹	
▪ express and talk about wishes	▪	▪	▪	▸ *Ü2, Ü3*
▪ express plans and intentions for the future	▪	▪	▪	▸ *Ü1, Ü3*

You worked for a good base in the future. Of course it wasn't possible to address everything in the context of this book and some topics were dealt with only briefly. But now that you've acquired a taste for it, you won't stop, will you? We wish you all the best and lots of fun!

Day 30 Repeat and practise

Here you repeat

- making appointments
- leaving messages on the phone
- writing e-mails
- talking about clothes
- stating plans for the future

1 Which word does not belong here? Cross it out.

1. Beamer, Tageslichtprojektor, Flipchart, Dokument
2. Hemd, Schuhe, Jacke, Bluse
3. anrufen, verschicken, verwählen, telefonieren
4. Wunsch, Studium, Karriere, Ausbildung
5. Besprechung, Vortrag, Kantine, Präsentation
6. sportlich, nervös, gepflegt, elegant

2/38

2 Listen to the short dialogues on the CD and write the number of the matching situation.

1. Am Telefon: ....
2. Termin vereinbaren: ....
3. Bei einer Präsentation: ....
4. Bewerbungsgespräch: ....
5. Gespräch mit dem Chef: ....

3 *Welcher* or *was für ein*?

1. .... Vortrag war besser? – Der von Frau Krüger.
2. .... Film soll ich ausleihen? Einen Thriller oder einen Krimi?
3. Sieh mal, das rote Kleid dort. Und da, der braune Rock. .... soll ich nehmen?
4. ► Bei a) .... Firma hast du dich beworben? Bei der in Hamburg oder bei der in Berlin?
   ◄ Bei der in Hamburg!
   ► Und b) .... Firma ist das?
   ◄ Das ist eine kleine Consultingfirma.

4 Fill in the gaps with the adjectives. Pay attention to the gender.

voll/die volle   schön/das schöne   langweilig/die langweilige
jung/die jungen   zufrieden/der zufriedene
spannend/das spannende   rot/der rote   lang/die langen

1. Das Haus ist .... – .... Haus.
2. Der Pullover ist .... – .... Pullover.
3. Die Kinder sind .... – .... Kinder.
4. Die Präsentation ist .... – .... Präsentation.
5. Das Buch ist .... – .... Buch.
6. Die Vorträge sind .... – .... Vorträge.
7. Der Chef ist .... – .... Chef.
8. Die Kantine ist .... – .... Kantine.

5 Leave messages on the answering machines of your colleagues/friends.

1. Tell Mr Beck that he should call you back. Your number is 89771.
2. Tell Ms Sander that you need a video projector for your presentation on Monday 22.
3. Ask Brian from your German class if he has free time on Friday. You could go to the cinema.
4. Tell Mr Schumacher that you sent an e-mail on Tuesday and ask if he has read the summary you sent.
5. Tell Ms Engel that the presentation takes place at 11 am and not at 9 am.

6 Match the appropriate sentence parts.

1. Ich hatte keine Zeit zur Vorbereitung,
2. Wenn Sie keine Zeit haben,
3. Der Vortrag war schlecht,
4. Ich bewerbe mich bei einer deutschen Firma,
5. Ich habe keine Zeit,
6. Die Präsentation war gut,
7. Weil ich keine Zeit zur Vorbereitung hatte,

a) deshalb war mein Chef zufrieden.
b) weil ich in Deutschland arbeiten will.
c) war der Vortrag schlecht.
d) deshalb war der Vortrag schlecht.
e) rufen Sie mich bitte kurz an.
f) denn ich hatte keine Zeit zur Vorbereitung.
g) deshalb rufe ich kurz an.

2/39 **7 Pierre and Iwona are looking at photographs of their families. Listen to their conversation and answer the questions.**

1. Welche Farbe hat der Mantel von Iwonas Großvater?
   a) ☐ Schwarz. b) ☐ Grün. c) ☐ Braun.
2. Wer trägt das grüne Jackett?
   a) ☐ Iwonas Vater. b) ☐ Iwonas Bruder. c) ☐ Iwonas Onkel.
3. Welche Farbe hat der Hut von Iwonas Vater?
   a) ☐ Braun. b) ☐ Blau. c) ☐ Rot.
4. Wer trägt die blaue Mütze?
   a) ☐ Jean. b) ☐ Pierre. c) ☐ Julie.
5. Was trägt Camille?
   a) ☐ Ein blaues Kleid. b) ☐ Eine rote Mütze. c) ☐ Ein rotes Kleid.

8 Fill in the gaps with the pronouns/articles from the box.

alles dieser ein ein paar einen etwas jeden
jemand keiner man niemand viele

1. Wenn du den Weg nicht kennst, dann musst du ________ fragen.
2. In a) ________ Firma arbeiten b) ________ Menschen.
3. ► Ich suche a) ________ Tageslichtprojektor.
   ◄ Tut mir leid, aber hier ist b) ________.
4. ► Kennst du a) ________, der in dieser Firma arbeitet?
   ◄ Nein, ich kenne b) ________, der dort arbeitet.
5. Hier kann ________ Fahrräder ausleihen.
6. ► Möchtest du noch a) ________?
   ◄ Ja, kann ich bitte noch b) ________ Weintrauben bekommen?
7. ► Wie war der Vortrag? Hast du ________ verstanden?
   ◄ Ja, das war kein Problem.
8. ► Und hat dir a) ________ Kollege geholfen?
   ◄ Nein! Ich habe b) ________ gefragt, aber c) ________ wollte mir helfen!

9 Read about Pierre's plans. Then think about your own plans for the following dates and say them loud. Use *Futur I*.

1. Heute Abend schaue ich Fußball im Fernsehen.
2. Morgen gehe ich joggen.
3. Im Sommer fahre ich mit Iwona nach Polen.
4. Nächstes Jahr lerne ich Spanisch.
5. In naher Zukunft kaufe ich mir eine Wohnung.

10 What to wear? Choose 5 of the 10 clothes and combine each with one colour. Use the correct case!

ein Pullover ein Hemd eine Jacke eine Hose Schuhe
eine Mütze ein Schal Socken eine Jeans ein T-Shirt
rot grün blau gelb schwarz braun weiß

1. Heute ziehe ich .... an.
2. Morgen ziehe ich vielleicht .... an.
3. ....
4. ....
5. ....

11 Fill in the gaps with the words from the box.

die in weil oft deshalb viele dass

Frauen und Männer .... (1.) Deutschland sind gleichberechtigt. Das sagt das Gesetz. Aber in Wirklichkeit ist es .... (2.) anders. Zum Beispiel verdient eine Frau in ihrem Leben im Durchschnitt weniger Geld als ein Mann. Das bedeutet nicht, ... (3.) eine Frau für die gleiche Arbeit weniger Geld bekommt. Aber .... (4.) Frauen arbeiten weniger, ... (5.) sie mehr Zeit für Familie und Kinder brauchen. Es gibt in Deutschland auch nur wenige Frauen, ... (6.) in hoch bezahlten Führungspositionen* in deutschen Firmen arbeiten. Warum ist das so? Vielleicht sind diese Jobs als Manager für viele Frauen nicht interessant. Aber wir wissen das nicht genau.
Es gibt Statistiken, die sagen, dass heute viele Frauen bessere Abschlüsse haben als Männer. .... (7.) gibt es in naher Zukunft vielleicht doch mehr Frauen, die Manager in deutschen Firmen werden.

* eine hoch bezahlte Führungsposition *a highly paid leadership position*

 **12 Read the text from exercise 11 again and cross out the wrong answers.**

1. *Ein Mann | eine Frau* verdient im Durchschnitt mehr Geld.
2. Frauen arbeiten oft weniger, denn sie *brauchen Zeit für die Familie | sind keine Manager.*
3. *Viele | wenige* Frauen arbeiten in Deutschland in Führungspositionen.
4. *Männer | Frauen* haben bessere Abschlüsse.
5. Es gibt vielleicht bald *mehr | weniger* Frauen in Führungspositionen.

2/40  **13 Listen to the CD. You'll hear questions about appointments. Cross out the date you hear and answer after the beep, repeating the date. Decide for yourself if you have time or not. A possible answer is given before the next question. Not all dates in the box are used.**

8.12. 6.7. 3.10. 24.3. 8.9. 7.6. 13.10. 20.3.

 **14 Make relative clauses from the second sentence referring to the underlined noun.**

Er hat einen Bruder. Sein Bruder arbeitet als Kellner.

Er hat einen Bruder, der als Kellner arbeitet.

1. Ich lese das Buch. Das Buch habe ich vor einer Woche gekauft.

2. Deine Schwester geht noch in die Schule. Deine Schwester ist jünger.

3. Ich bringe den Kindern Geschenke mit. Ich besuche die Kinder.

4. Meine Freunde sind toll. Ich fahre mit den Freunden in Urlaub.

5. Pierres Mutter lebt in Frankreich. Er denkt oft an seine Mutter.

6. Ich denke an meinen Bruder. Ich muss meinem Bruder noch eine E-Mail schreiben.

15 Complete the crossword about clothes. The grey fields show the solution.

1. elegant
2. chic
3. hat
4. glove
5. neat
6. casual
7. flashy
8. underwear
9. jewellery
10. scarf
11. female dress
12. dress
13. clothes
14. tie
15. long coat
16. to dress
17. shoe
18. colourful

Solution (a–e): ....

Final test

1 Fill in the gaps with the verbs from the brackets in the right form of the present tense.

1. Er .... mit dem Auto nach München. (fahren)
2. Morgen .... du bei einem Freund. (schlafen)
3. Wir .... zusammen auf das Oktoberfest. (gehen)
4. Wann .... sie *(Sg)* ihren Vortrag? (halten)
5. Du .... sehr schnell! (laufen)
6. Sie .... gute Freunde. (sein)

__/6

2 Read the text and write down the infinitive of all main verbs (not the auxiliary verbs).

Ich mache gern Sport. Am liebsten klettere und schwimme ich. Und gestern habe ich mit einem Freund zwei Stunden lang Tennis gespielt. Das war toll! Ich fahre auch gern Rad. Nur leider habe ich kein Fahrrad. Aber morgen leihe ich eins aus und mache eine Radtour. Und wenn du willst, dann nehme ich dich mit. Wie findest du das?

1.	5.	9. ....
2.	6.	10. ....
3.	7.	11. ....
4.	8.	12. ....

__/12

3 Insert the missing adjectives. Pay attention to the endings and use comparative/superlative forms where necessary.

1. Pierre zieht für sein Bewerbungsgespräch eine a) .... (schwarz) Hose und ein b) .... (elegant) Jackett an.
2. Jens kann kochen, aber er ist kein a) .... (gut) Koch. Martina ist die b) .... (gut) Köchin.
3. Pierre fährt mit dem ICE nach Hamburg. Der ICE ist der .... (schnell) Zug in Deutschland.
4. Iwona isst mit ihren .... (nett) Kollegen zu Mittag.
5. Stell die a) .... (klein) Teller doch bitte in den b) .... (rot) Schrank neben dem c) .... (groß) Tisch.
6. Ich gratuliere! Du hast einen .... (toll) Vortrag gehalten!

__/10

4 Read the words and cross the odd ones out.

1. Hals, Wartezimmer, Krankenschwester, Röntgen
2. Feiertag, Freizeit, Film, Reise
3. Gast, Hobby, Party, Einladung
4. Bruder, Großvater, Onkel, Tante
5. Glas, Teller, Müll, Geschirr
6. Sprudel, Suppe, Saft, Cola

__/6

5 Listen to the short dialogues on the CD. Then write each dialogue's number next to the matching situation. Two situations remain unused. 2/41

1. Auf der Party: ....
2. Beim Einkaufen: ....
3. Im Café: ....
4. In der Kantine: ....
5. Im Kino: ....
6. Im Hotel: ....

__/4

6 Complete the sentences with the personal pronouns. Don't forget to use the correct case.

1. Iwona, wann hast .... die E-Mail geschrieben?
2. Hallo Martina, hallo Jens. Ich habe ein Geschenk für ....
3. Dort steht Iwona und neben .... steht Pierre.
4. Das ist mein Freund Klaus. Ich fahre mit .... nach Polen.
5. Ich richte das aus, Herr Lang. Herr Lehmann ruft .... morgen zurück.
6. Ich esse gern frisches Obst. Am liebsten kaufe ich .... auf dem Markt.

__/6

7 Read the word snake, separate the nouns and write them in the column with the right gender. (½ point for each correct word)

themavortragtelefonpunktgesprächbewerbungkleidungkontakt
bürobuchterminverabredungterminkalenderabschlussdokument
zeugnisnachrichtabteilungverhaltenprojektausbildung
karriererentearbeitgeber

m (der)	*f* (die)	*n* (das)
....	....	....
....	....	....
....	....	....
....	....	....
....	....	....

__/12

2/42 **8 Johanna tells you about her cleaning up routine. Listen to the CD and answer the questions.**

1. Wo ist das dreckige Geschirr? ....
2. Wo ist die Kleidung? ....
3. Wo stehen die sauberen Teller? ....
4. Und wo stehen die Gläser? ....
5. Wo sitzt Johanna nach dem Aufräumen? ....

__/5

9 Read the situations below. Choose the matching German phrase from the box and say it loud.

Darf ich dir Philipp vorstellen? Wir arbeiten zusammen.
Lass uns doch ins Kino gehen. Hallo, kommt bitte herein! Toll, dass ihr da seid.
Das haben Sie wirklich sehr gut gemacht.
Morgen koche ich für meine Freunde. Deshalb muss ich jetzt noch einkaufen.
Entschuldigung, wie komme ich zum nächsten Supermarkt?

1. Welcome your friends to your party and say how great it is, that they're here.
2. Ask your way to the next supermarket.
3. Make a proposal for your evening plans.
4. Introduce your friend from work.
5. Give a reason why you have to go shopping now.
6. Praise your colleague for his/her good work.

__/6

10 Iwona and Pierre are still looking at photographs of their families. Fill in the gaps with the missing possessive pronouns (used as articles).

dein deine deinen euren ihre ihrem mein seine unseren

Pierre Iwona, ist das .... (1.) Bruder?
Iwona Ja, das ist .... (2.) Bruder. Neben ihm steht .... (3.) Frau mit .... (4.) Kind.
Pierre Und das ist .... (5.) Großmutter?
Iwona Genau. Alle anderen Personen neben ihr sind .... (6.)Kinder.
Pierre Oh, sie hat aber viele Kinder.
Iwona Stimmt. Pierre, das hier bist du mit .... (7.) Schwestern, oder?
Pierre Ja.
Iwona Und das seid ihr mit .... (8.) Großeltern?
Pierre Richtig, das sind wir mit .... (9.) Großeltern!

__/9

11 Read the extract from a networking guide. Cross out the wrong answers.

Wenn Sie nach neuen Kontakten für Ihr persönliches Netzwerk suchen, dann ist es immer besser, nur einen oder zwei Kontakte zu knüpfen, die aber später auch von Nutzen sind*. Nur einfach viele Visitenkarten einsammeln, ist oft keine gute Idee. Gerade bei größeren Besprechungen hat man keine Zeit für mehr als ein oder zwei gute Gespräche. Deshalb ist es auch gut, wenn man vor einer Besprechung zum Beispiel im Internet schaut, welcher Teilnehmer ein interessanter Kontakt sein könnte. Und interessant ist ein beruflicher Kontakt, wenn man ähnliche Interessen hat.

* von Nutzen sein *be of use*

1. Man sollte *immer so viele Kontakte wie möglich | nur wenige gute Kontakte* knüpfen.
2. Man sollte *mit seinem Kontakt auch kurz sprechen | von seinem Kontakt nur eine Visitenkarte nehmen.*
3. Informationen über einen neuen Kontakt sollte man *schon vor | erst auf einer* Besprechung suchen.
4. Ein interessanter Kontakt hat ähnliche *Interessen | Hobbys.* __/4

12 Answer the question using a pronoun instead of the underlined noun.

1. Siehst du Pierre? – Ja, ...
2. Willst du ein Stück Kuchen? – Nein, ...
3. Gebt ihr den Kindern Geschenke? – Ja, ...
4. Hast du auch eine Schwester? – Ja, ...
5. Ist Martina da? – Nein, ...
6. Ist die E-Mail von deiner Schwester? Nein, ... __/6

2/43 **13 Listen to the conversation between Martina, Iwona and Pierre. They are talking about their plans once they've finished the German class. What are they going to do?**

1. Iwona: ....
2. Pierre: ....
3. Martina: ....

__/3

14 Read the semantic fields and find the fitting generic term in the box. Not all generic terms are used.

Monate Haus Gemüse Jahreszeiten Freizeit Wetter Sommer Sport Obst

1. ....: Treppe, Aufzug, Stockwerk, Schlüssel
2. ....: Sommer, Winter, Frühling, Herbst
3. ....: Regen, Schnee, Wind, Gewitter
4. ....: Juni, Januar, Juli, August
5. ....: Tennis, Radfahren, Joggen, Judo
6. ....: Banane, Apfel, Pfirsich, Weintraube

__/6

2/44 **15 Read the answers in the box below. Then listen to the questions on the CD and say the correct answer after the beep. You'll hear the correct answer again before the next question.**

Am liebsten am Donnerstag. Eine große Tasse Kaffee, bitte.
Ich will Lehrer werden.
Ich bin hingefallen und habe mich an der Hand verletzt.
Am besten mit dem Auto. Ich glaube, dass es morgen regnen wird.

__/6

16 Match the phrases with the corresponding situation. One situation remains.

1. Die Rechnung bitte.	a) Bahnhof
2. Herzlich Willkommen!	b) Arzt
3. Was unternehmen wir heute?	c) Fernsehen
4. Ich gehe noch joggen.	d) Sport
5. Herzlichen Glückwunsch!	e) Einladung
6. Wo ist der Fahrplan?	f) Geburtstag
7. Was kommt denn heute?	g) Markt
8. Ich hätte gerne ein Kilo Bananen.	h) Freizeit
	i) Restaurant

__/8

17 The articles in the text are missing. Can you fill in the gaps?

einen ein paar die seinen vielen der viel sein das viel ihrem den

Iwona und Pierre sind bald mit .... (1.) Deutschkurs fertig. Zum Schluss wird es .... (2.) großen Abschlusstest geben. Deshalb müssen Pierre und Iwona noch lernen. Aber sie haben nicht .... (3.) Zeit. Iwona muss sich mit .... (4.) Kunden treffen. Darum kann sie nur .... (5.) Stunden in .... (6.) Woche lernen. Auch Pierre hat .... (7.) Arbeit: Er muss .... (8.) Bewerbungsgespräch vorbereiten. Pierre will .... (9.) Test gut machen, aber .... (10.) Bewerbungsgespräch ist wichtiger! Wir drücken ihnen .... (11.) Daumen für .... (12.) Test! __/12

18 Read the text and answer the questions in full sentences.

Claudias Wohnung
Wir haben eine kleine Wohnung mit vier Zimmern. Im Wohnzimmer steht ein brauner Tisch mit vier schwarzen Stühlen. Es gibt auch einen weißen Schrank mit Geschirr und zwei grüne Regale mit Büchern. Unser Fernseher steht auch dort. In der Küche haben wir einen Tisch mit zwei Stühlen. Der Tisch hier ist gelb. Dort essen wir oft unser Frühstück. Das große Bett steht im Schlafzimmer. Dort steht auch unser roter Schrank, in dem wir unsere Kleidung haben. Rechts neben dem Bett steht eine rote Kommode. Dort haben wir unsere Unterwäsche. Im Bad haben wir eine Dusche, ein WC und einen kleinen weißen Schrank.

1. Wie viele Stühle hat Claudia? ....
2. Wo steht der gelbe Tisch? ....
3. Wo steht ein weißer Schrank? ....
4. Welche Farbe haben die Regale? ....
5. Welche Möbel stehen im Wohnzimmer? .... __/5

19 **The verbs in brackets are missing in these sentences. Which is the correct position for each verb? Don't forget about the appropriate form and – where necessary – tense.**

1. Wenn ihr wollt, dann .... wir euch .... (helfen)
2. Ich .... gern auf dem Markt .... (einkaufen)
3. Du .... heute die Rechnung im Restaurant .... (bezahlen)
4. .... Sie mir bitte .... , wo der Bahnhof ist? (sagen, können)
5. Wir fahren am Wochenende nach Hamburg, denn .... ich .... noch nicht in Hamburg .... (sein *Präteritum*)
6. Ich denke, dass .... du .... den Vortrag gestern gut .... (machen *Perfekt*)

__/6

20 **The following sentences got mixed up. Additionally, the verbs are still in infinitive forms. Can you put the sentences back in the correct order and the verbs in the right form and tense (and don't forget the auxiliary verbs where necessary)?**

1. am Donnerstag / um 9 Uhr / ich / einen wichtigen Termin / haben (*Präsens*) / .

   ....

2. wir / einen interessanten Vortrag / halten (*Futur I*) / zusammen / .

   ....

3. du / wann / E-Mail / verschicken (*Perfekt*) / die / ?

   ....

4. jetzt / in / ein / ihr / Café / gehen (*Futur I*) / ?

   ....

5. er / einen / müssen (*Präteritum*) / erst / vereinbaren / Termin / .

   ....

6. anrufen (*Perfekt*) / wen / gestern / Sie / ?

   ....

__/6

21 Read the questions below and then listen to the phone conversation on the CD. Answer the questions. 2/45

1. Mit wem will Herr Meyer sprechen?
   a) ☐ Mit Herrn Maurer. b) ☐ Mit Herrn Schneider. c) ☐ Mit Herrn Thomas.
2. Wann ist der alte Termin von Herrn Meyer?
   a) ☐ Am 7.4., um 9.30 Uhr. b) ☐ Am 17.4., um 9.30 Uhr. c) ☐ Am 17.4., um 11 Uhr.
3. Wann ist der neue Termin?
   a) ☐ Um 4 Uhr. b) ☐ Um 11 Uhr. c) ☐ Um 14 Uhr.
4. Wie ist die Telefonnummer von Herrn Meyer?
   a) ☐ 0431 98223. b) ☐ 0341 92832. c) ☐ 0431 92833. __/4

22 Complete the text to make sensible sentences.

Iwona ist in ihrem Büro. Heute muss sie viel .... (1.). Zuerst schreibt sie eine .... (2.) an Frau Engel von der Firma Bärmann. Danach muss sie mit Herrn Meier von der Firma Meier & Co. .... (3.), denn sie muss ihn einige Dinge fragen. Um 13 Uhr isst sie in der Kantine zu Mittag. Am .... (4.) hat sie einen Termin mit einem Kollegen. Sie müssen zusammen eine .... (5.) mit einem Kunden vorbereiten. Am Abend trifft sie sich mit Freunden und sie gehen in eine .... (6.), wo sie etwas trinken. Dann .... (7.) sie mit dem Bus nach Hause und geht bald ins .... (8.) . __/8

__/150

Grammatical terminology

German Term	English Term	Example
Adjektiv	adjective	der nette Kollege
Adverb (*Pl* Adverbien)	adverb	morgen, dort
Akkusativ	accusative	Ich rufe den Mann an.
Akkusativobjekt	direct object	Ich sehe den Mann.
Artikel	article	einem Mann, meine Mutter, die Schwester
bestimmter Artikel	definite article	der Apfel, das Buch
Dativ	dative	Ich gebe den Kindern Obst.
Dativobjekt	indirect object	Ich gebe dem Mann einen Kuchen.
Deklination	declension	der Mann, den Mann, dem Mann
Demonstrativartikel	demonstrative determiner	diese Frau
Diphthong	diphthong	au, ei, eu
Fragepronomen	interrogative pronoun	Wer ist das?
Futur I	a German future tense	Ich werde nach Berlin fahren.
Hauptsatz	main clause	Ich denke, dass du gut bist.
Hilfsverb	auxiliary verb	Er hat eine E-Mail geschrieben.
Imperativ	imperative	Ruf mich an!
Infinitiv	infinitive	gehen, essen
Kardinalzahl	cardinal numeral	eins, zwei drei
Komparativ	comparative	schneller, schöner
Konjugation	conjugation	ich gehe, du gehst, er geht
Konjunktion	conjunction	und, oder, dass, weil
Konsonant	consonant	b, c, d, f, g
Modalverb	modal verb	wollen, müssen, dürfen
Nebensatz	subordinated clause	Ich denke, dass du gut bist.
Nominativ	nominative	der Mann
Ordinalzahl	ordinal numeral	Der erste April.
Partizip Perfekt	past participle	gegessen, gewartet
Perfekt	a German past tense	Ich habe dich angerufen.
Person	person	erste Person Singular: ich
Personalpronomen	personal pronoun	ich, sie, wir
Plural	plural	(zwei) Bücher
Possessivpronomen	possessive pronoun	mein Vater, seine Schwester

German Term	English Term	Example
Präposition	preposition	Er ist in einem Museum.
Präsens	the German present tense	Ich bin in Deutschland.
Präteritum	simple past	Ich war in Berlin.
Pronomen	pronoun	sie, man, alle, jemand
Relativpronomen	relative pronoun	Meine Schwester, die Kathrin heißt, ...
Singular	singular	(ein) Buch
Steigerung	comparison	schön, schöner, am schönsten
Subjekt	subject	Martina geht einkaufen.
Substantiv/Nomen	noun	das Haus, die Frage
Superlativ	superlative	am schnellsten, am schönsten
Umlaut	umlaut	ä, ö, ü
unbestimmter Artikel	indefinite article	ein Auto, eine Frau
Verb	verb	fahren, er fährt
Vokal	vowel	a, e, i, o, u

Short Grammar

§1 Nouns

Nouns in German are always written with a capital letter. All nouns have a gender and are either masculine (m), feminine (f) or neuter (n). They have a plural and there are different cases to differentiate the role of the noun in the sentence.

§1.1 Gender • *Day 2*

The gender is not always logical and can differ from the natural gender of a noun – e.g. **das Mädchen** *girl* is neuter (in most cases, luckily, the gender of a person is like the natural gender, though). There are a few endings that give the gender away:

m: -ling, -ismus, -er	**f:** -heit, -keit, -ung, -ion	**n:** -chen, -lein, -(t)um

But since the exception proves the rule (e.g. **die** Mutt**er**), it's best to learn a noun right away with its definite article (▸ *§ 2.1*), because the definite article shows the gender! The gender of compound nouns is always that of the last part of the compound: ***die* Stadt** + ***das* Zentrum** → ***das* Stadtzentrum**.

§1.2 Plural

There are no general rules as to how to build the plural. Here too, the best advice is to learn the correct plural form together with the noun itself.

§1.3 Cases ▸ *Day 4, Day 5, Day 6*

German has four cases: **Nominativ**, **Genitiv**, **Dativ**, **Akkusativ**. Most nouns look the same in the different cases – it's mostly the article (▸ *§ 2.1*) that is declined (mostly, because nouns in the dative plural get an **-n** ending if they do not already end with **-n**).

The nominative is the case of a sentence's subject. Then there's the accusative for things or people you see, have or in general do something with and the dative is usually an object that receives something. The case of a noun depends on its role in the sentence and that role is given by the verb (or a preposition ▸ *§ 5*). For example the verb **sehen** *see* needs a subject (that is always needed!) that sees and an object in the accusative that is seen. Or the verb **geben** *give* needs a subject, an accusative object (what is given) and a dative object (whom is it given).

Pierre sieht den Mann. *Pierre sees the man.*

Pierre gibt dem Mann den Apfel. *Pierre gives the man the apple.*

The dative object usually stands before the accusative object.

§ 2 Articles

Articles are the companions of nouns. And where the noun does not so easily reveal its case or gender, the article does (especially the definite article). There are different kinds of articles in German, but all share one characteristic: they stand in front of a noun and have the same gender, case and number as the noun.

§ 2.1 The definite and indefinite article ► *Day 2, Day 5*

The definite article **der/die/das** *the* usually is used when the noun is known or it's a singular distinct person/thing. Use the indefinite article **ein/eine/ein** *a* (but also *one*) when referring to something in general or yet unknown. The use of German articles is often similar to English. The indefinite article has no plural!

	m	f	n	Pl
Nom.	der/ein	die/eine	das/ein	die/–
Acc.	den/einen	die/eine	das/ein	die/–
Dat.	dem/einem	der/einer	dem/einem	den/–

§ 2.2 Other articles ► *Day 7, Day 26*

There are some other articles in German. As said above, they all stand in front of a noun and have the same gender, case and number as that noun. Most can be used as pronouns (i.e. instead of the noun) too, so they will be explained in the next paragraph.

§ 2.2.1 Demonstrative determiner

The demonstrative determiner **dieser/diese/dieses** *this, that* has the same function as in English. The forms are similar to the forms of **der/die/das**.
Dieser Mann ruft **diese** Frau an. *That man calls that woman.*

§ 2.2.2 kein ► *Day 4*

kein (► *§ 4*) is the negative indefinite article and the forms are the same as those of the indefinite article. It has, however, a plural form that is **keine** in nominative and accusative and **keinen** in dative.
Kein Mensch ruft mich an. *Nobody calls me.*
Jens kauft heute **kein** Obst. *Jens buys no fruit today.*

§ 2.2.2 Nullartikel ▸ *Day 7*

Nullartikel means that there is no article. It is used for example with mass nouns of undefined quantity or professions (note that in English professions have the indefinite article!).
Ich brauche noch Milch. *I still need milk.*
Ich bin Lehrer. *I'm a teacher.*

§ 2.2.4 Interrogative article ▸ *Day 25*

There are two interrogative articles: **welcher/welche/welches?** *which?* and **was für ein/eine/ein?** *what (kind of)?* The forms of **welcher** are similar to the definite article and those of **was für ein** to the indefinite article.
Was für einen Film willst du sehen? – Einen Actionfilm.
What (kind of) film would you like to see? – An action movie.
Welches Buch willst du lesen? – Harry Potter 4.
Which book would you like to read? – Harry Potter 4.

§ 3 Pronouns

§ 3.1 Personal pronouns ▸ *Day 2, Day 8*

Personal pronouns can replace known persons or things, i.e. all nouns.

Declination of the personal pronouns						
Nom.	ich	du	er/sie/es	wir	ihr	sie/Sie
Acc.	mich	dich	ihn/sie/es	uns	euch	sie/Sie
Dat.	mir	dir	ihm/ihr/ihm	uns	euch	ihnen/Ihnen

Let's have a look at the verb **geben** *give*. It needs a subject (**Pierre**), a dative object (**Iwona**) and an accusative object (**einen Apfel**):
Pierre gibt Iwona einen Apfel. *Pierre gives Iwona an apple.*
Pierre gibt **ihr** den Apfel. *Pierre gives her the apple.*
If, however, the accusative object is represented by a pronoun, that pronoun stands even before the dative object (▸ *§ 1.3*):
Pierre gibt **ihn** Iwona. *Pierre gives it Iwona.*
Pierre gibt **ihn ihr**. *He gives it to her.*

The formal address **Sie** *you* always has the same form as the third person plural (**sie**). The formal address pronouns are always written with a capital **S** and are the same in singular and plural.

§ 3.1.1 The impersonal *es* ▸ *Day 19*

Since every sentence has to have a subject and sometimes there is no real subject, you use **es** *it*. It's mostly used with time and weather, like in English:
Es ist Viertel nach drei. *It's a quarter past three.*
Es ist sonnig. *It's sunny.*

§ 3.2 Possessive pronouns (used as articles)

The possessive articles are:

Personal pronouns	Possessive articles (in the nominative)	
ich	mein	my
du	dein	your
er/sie/es	sein/ihr/sein	his/her/its
wir	unser	our
ihr	euer	your
sie/Sie	ihr/Ihr	their/your

Note that the third person singular has different pronouns depending on the gender of the possessing person (or thing). Additionally, all possessive articles have to have the same gender, case and number as their related noun, i.e. the possessed person or thing. It sounds complicated but a few examples will help:
Das ist **mein** Vater. *This is my father.*
Ich gebe **meiner** Schwester ein Buch. *I give my sister a book.*
Ich fahre mit **meinen** Freunden nach München. *I go to Munich with my friends.*
Which pronoun you choose depends therefore on the possessing person or thing. The ending, though, depends on the following, related noun. Those endings are similar to the endings of the indefinite article:

	Nom.	Acc.	Dat.
Sg	mein/mein**e**/mein	mein**en**/mein**e**/mein	mein**em**/mein**er**/ mein**em**
Pl	mein**e**	mein**e**	mein**en**

The other possessive articles have the same endings. Note, that if **euer** gets an ending, the **e** before the **r** is omitted:
Wo sind **eure** Freunde? *Where are your friends?*
Wir sitzen auf **eurem** Sofa. *We're sitting on your sofa.*

§ 3.3 Interrogative pronouns

Wer? Wen? Wem?	Wie?	Was?	Wann?	Warum?	Wo?	Wohin?	Womit?
Who? Who(m)? Who(m)?	How?	What?	When?	Why?	Where?	Where to?	With what?

§ 3.4 Relative pronouns ▸ *Day 25*

The relative pronouns **der/die/das** *who, which, that* are used in relative clauses. The number and gender of the relative pronoun is always the same as that of the related noun. The case of the relative pronoun depends on the role of the pronoun in the subordinate clause. It can be any kind of object!
The forms of the relative pronouns are identical to the definite article (▸ *§ 2.1*), with one exception: the dative of plural relative pronouns is **denen**.
Der Kunde, **dem** ich schreibe, ist wichtig. *The client, to whom I'm writing, is important.*

§ 3.5 Indefinite pronouns ▸ *Day 26*

§ 3.5.1 einer/keiner

You can use the indefinite article **ein** and the negative indefinite article **kein** as pronouns. For example in short answers.
Willst du einen Apfel? – Nein, ich will **keinen**.
Do you want an apple? – No, I don't want any.
The forms are similar to the indefinite article with following exceptions:
Nominative masculine: **ein*er*/kein*er*** and nominative/accusative neuter: **ein*s*/kein*s***.

§ 3.5.2 man

The indefinite pronoun **man** can replace any unknown or unspecified person.
It's always the subject of the sentence and the verb always has the ending for the third person singular. It's often used to paraphrase passive constructions.
Man kann in Berlin viele Sachen sehen. *One can see a lot of things in Berlin.*
Hier darf **man** nicht rauchen. *Smoking is not allowed here.*

§ 3.5.3 jemand/niemand ▸ *Day 23*

jemand *someone/somebody* and **niemand** *no one/nobody* have accusative and dative endings:

Nom.	Acc.	Dat.
jemand/niemand	jeman**den**/nieman**den**	jemand**em**/niemand**em**

Ich habe dort **niemanden** gesehen. *I have seen nobody there.*
Luckily in spoken language they are often not declined:
Ich habe dort **jemand** gesehen. *I have seen somebody there.*

§ 3.5.4 Other indefinite pronouns

German knows a lot of other pronouns that are indefinite regarding gender or number. In most cases they can be used as pronouns as well as articles. You can find an overview in (▸ *Day 23*) and (▸ *Day 26*).

§ 4 Negation ▸ *Day 4*

To negate single nouns you use the negative indefinite article **kein** (▸ *§ 2.2*). It always stands right in front of the noun.
To negate other words or a whole sentence you use **nicht** *not*.
Das Haus ist **nicht** schön. *The house is not nice.*
Ich schreibe dir **nicht**. *I am not writing to you.*
When negating a whole sentence **nicht** tends to stand as near to the end as possible (at the end of the middle field, ▸ *§ 10*) like in the second example.
With modal verbs **nicht** stands usually near the modal verb:
Ich will **nicht** ins Museum gehen. *I don't want to go to the museum.*

§ 5 Prepositions

Some verbs need an object that is neither an accusative object nor a dative object, but begins with a preposition. For example the verb **gehen** *go* needs an object that specifies the destination.
Ich gehe **in** ein Museum. *I go to a museum.*
Commonly prepositions are used for local or temporal information. Most prepositions need the following noun in a specific case. Thus it's good to learn the preposition together with a noun in the correct case. The prepositions themselves do not change!

§ 5.1 Prepositions with the dative or the accusative ► *Day 11, Day 12*

in	an	auf	über	unter	neben	zwischen	vor	hinter
in	at	on	over	beneath	by, next to	between	in front of	behind

After these prepositions the noun can be in the accusative or the dative. One of these prepositions plus a dative noun says where something is. A preposition plus an accusative noun gives a direction to somewhere.
The rule is as follows: If you ask *where?* it's the dative, and if you ask *where to?* the accusative.
Some prepositions can merge with a following definite article:

in + dem → **im**	an + dem → **am**	in + das → **ins**	an + das → **ans**

§ 5.2 Prepositions with the dative ► *Day 17*

aus	von	nach	zu	bei	mit	seit
from	from, of	to, toward, after, past	to, toward	at, by, next to	with	since, for

These prepositions are always followed by a noun in the dative. Here also the prepositions can merge:

von + dem → **vom**	zu + dem → **zum** zu + der → **zur**	bei + dem → **beim**

§ 5.3 Prepositions with the accusative

bis	durch	für	gegen	ohne	um
until, to	through, by	for	against, around	without	around, at

These prepositions are always followed by a noun in the accusative. They don't merge with articles!

§ 5.4 Temporal prepositions ▸ *Day 15*

For certain temporal statements you always use the same prepositions:

um	time	Wir treffen uns **um** 17.30 Uhr.
am	times of the day	Ich komme **am** Morgen zu dir. Wir gehen **am** Abend ins Kino.
	for days and dates	Er fährt **am** Mittwoch nach Potsdam. Sie besuchen die Eltern **am** 4. März.
im	months and seasons	**Im** Sommer ist es sehr heiß. **Im** November beginnt der Winter.

§ 6 Adjectives ▸ *Day 27, Day 28*

Adjectives have the function to specify nouns. To fulfil this role they stand either in front of nouns or with the verbs **sein** *be* (or **werden** *get*).

§ 6.1 Adjectives with *sein* or *werden*

Adjectives in this position are not declined – which is great, isn't it? You use the adjective's basic form – the one you can find in the dictionary.
Der Apfel ist **rot**. *The apple is red.* Es wird **heiß**. *It's getting hot.*

§ 6.2 Adjectives in front of the noun

An adjective in front of the noun has to be declined. That means that the case, gender and number of the adjective is the same as that of the noun (and article).
The endings of the adjectives differ whether you use the definite or indefinite article.

	m (e.g. **Plan**)	**f** (e.g. **Frage**)	**n** (e.g. **Buch**)	**Pl** (e.g. **Strategien**)
Adjectives in front of nouns with a definite article				
Nom.	der gut**e**	die gut**e**	das gut**e**	die gut**en**
Acc.	den gut**en**	die gut**e**	das gut**e**	die gut**en**
Dat.	dem gut**en**	der gut**en**	dem gut**en**	den gut**en**
Adjectives in front of nouns with an indefinite article				
Nom.	ein gut**er**	eine gut**e**	ein gut**es**	– gut**e**
Acc.	einen gut**en**	eine gut**e**	ein gut**es**	– gut**e**
Dat.	einem gut**en**	einer gut**en**	einem gut**en**	– gut**en**

The declination of adjectives with other articles always follows one of these two paradigms.
Like with definite articles: the interrogative article **welcher**, **welche**, **welches** *which*, the articles **jeder**, **jede**, **jedes** *each* and **alle** *all* and the demonstrative article **dieser**, **dieser**, **dieses** *this/that*.
Dieses neu**e** Haus ist schön. *This new house is nice.*
Er sieht **jeden** neu**en** Film. *He watches each new film.*
Like with indefinite articles: possessive articles (**mein** *my*, **dein** *your* ... – but: adjectives with possessive articles have an **-en** ending in the plural!), the interrogative article **was für ein** *what* and the remaining articles from Day 26 (► *Day 26*).
Mein neu**er** Kollege ist Franzose. *My new colleague is a Frenchman.*
Sie haben **viele** alt**e** Weine. *They have many old wines.*

§ 6.3 Adjective (and adverb) comparison ► *Day 9*

For the comparison of adjectives with **sein** you need two suffixes: **-er** for the comparative and **-sten** (or **-esten** after d, t, s, sch, z and vowels) for the superlative. Just add them to the basic form: neu – neu**er** – am neu**esten**.
Comparative adjectives in front of a noun are built with the basic form *plus* **-er-** for comparative or **-(e)st-** for superlative *plus* the ending according to the table in (► *§ 6.2*): das neu**ere** Haus – der neu**este** Parkplatz.
Contrary to English the superlative of an adjective with **sein** has **am** in front of the adjective. In front of the noun the superlative is only used with the definite article.
Most monosyllabic adjectives with **a**, **o**, **u** get the respective umlaut **ä**, **ö**, **ü** in the comparative and superlative: lang – l**ä**nger – der l**ä**ngste.
And finally there are some adjectives that are compared irregularly. The few adverbs that can be compared, are also in this list.

	Basic form	Comparative	Superlative
good	gut	besser	am besten
high	hoch	höher	am höchsten
near	nah	näher	am nächsten
much	viel	mehr	am meisten
gladly	gern	lieber	am liebsten
often	oft	öfter/häufig	am häufigsten/(*rare:* am öftesten)
soon	bald	eher	am ehesten

§ 7 Adverbs

Adverbs specify other words or the whole sentence. They are not declined and usually have no comparison (► *§ 6.3*). There are three big groups of adverbs:
With temporal adverbs you can say when something happens or in what order.
Ich gehe **morgen** ins Museum. *I go to the museum tomorrow.*
Danach mache ich einen Spaziergang. *Afterwards I go for a walk.*
The local adverbs determine the position or (often with prepositions) the direction.
Ich bin **hier**. *I am here.*
Gehen Sie **dort vorne** nach **rechts**. *Turn right there up ahead.*
Often you use more than one local adverb in a sentence (e.g. **dort vorne** *there up ahead*, **hinten links** *in the back left*).
Finally you can use adverbs of grade and frequency if you want to specify how much or how often you do something.
Sie mag ihren Freund **sehr**. *She likes her friend much.*
Ich telefoniere **oft** mit meiner Freundin. *I call my friend often.*

§ 7.1 Position in the sentence ► *Day 11*

An adverb can take the first position in a sentence:
Morgen gehe ich ins Museum. *Tomorrow I go to the museum.*
If you have more than one adverb, the temporal adverbs usually come first and the local last.
Ich bin **morgen sicher dort**. *I am there tomorrow for sure.*

§ 8 Verbs

Verbs express actions, events or states. The basic form (which you can find in the vocabulary) is infinitive. Most verbs in the infinitive end with **-en**: geh**en**, wart**en**, hab**en**, einkauf**en** ... In sentences they show the tense and they are conjugated. That means that the verb's ending shows the person of the subject.

§ 8.1 Präsens ► *Day 2, Day 3*

Präsens is the German simple present. Be aware that German has no progressive forms like English! So there is no grammatical way in German to differ between habitual and actual ongoing actions and events. You can use the **Präsens** to express both (differences can be made with adverbs like **immer** *always*).
Verbs have different endings according to the subject of the sentence.

	gehen go	**reisen** travel	**warten** wait	**ending**
ich	geh**e**	reis**e**	wart**e**	**-e**
du	geh**st**	reis**t**	wart**est**	**-st**
er/sie/es	geh**t**	reis**t**	wart**et**	**-t**
wir	geh**en**	reis**en**	wart**en**	**-en**
ihr	geh**t**	reis**t**	wart**et**	**-t**
sie/Sie	geh**en**	reis**en**	wart**en**	**-en**

If the stem of the verb ends with an **s**, **ss**, **ß** or **z** the second person singular (**du**) gets only a **-t** as ending. If it ends with **t** or **d** there's an additional **-e-** between the stem and the ending in the second and third person singular (**du**, **er/sie/es**) and second person plural (**ihr**).

There are also some verbs which have irregular forms in the present tense:

	laufen walk, run	**geben** give	**sehen** see
ich	laufe	gebe	sehe
du	**läufst**	**gibst**	**siehst**
er/sie/es	**läuft**	**gibt**	**sieht**
wir	laufen	geben	sehen
ihr	lauft	gebt	seht
sie/Sie	laufen	geben	sehen

You can see, the endings are the same as those of the regular forms. But the vowels in the second and third person singular change! **a/au** become **ä/äu**, **e** becomes **i** or **ie**. Be careful, because there are only a handful of those verbs:

essen → du **i**sst, er **i**sst	fahren → du f**ä**hrst, er f**ä**hrt	lesen → du l**ie**st, er l**ie**st

As you saw above, not all verbs with **e** have this change (e.g. **gehen**).

§ 8.2 Perfekt ▸ *Day 20, Day 21*

Perfekt is the past tense that is most commonly used in spoken German. The modal verbs (▸ *§ 8.6*) and **haben** and **sein** (▸ *§ 8.5*) are mostly used in their **Präteritum** forms, though.

The structure of the German **Perfekt** (the auxiliary verb **haben** or **sein** in the Präsens plus past participle) is similar to the English present perfect – the use, however, differs. Just use the **Perfekt** for all statements about the past.

When to use **haben** and when **sein**? Most verbs of movement (like **gehen** *go*, **fahren** *drive*) or change of state (like **einschlafen** *fall asleep*) build the **Perfekt** with **sein**. The rest (which is by far the bigger part) use **haben**.
And how to build the past participle? Like in English there are regular and irregular verbs. A lot of verbs used in every day language fall into the irregular category – you will find a list of those verbs to learn and consult at the end of this grammar. The regular verbs use the infinitive as a base for the past participle. In most cases the infinitive gets the prefix **ge-** and the **-en** ending is chopped of and replaced with a **-t** (or **-et** if there's a t or d before the **-en**):

hören → **gehört**	kosten → **gekostet**

If the infinitive already has a non-separable prefix (like **ver-**, **ent-**, **be-**) this prefix stays instead and just the **-en** ending is replaced with **-(e)t**:

verletzen → verletz**t**	sich beeilen → sich beeil**t**

A separable prefix (like **mit-**, **ab-**, **aus-**) also stays but the past participle additionally gets the prefix **-ge-** right after the separable prefix. And don't forget the **-(e)t** ending.

aufhängen → auf**ge**häng**t**	vorstellen → vor**ge**stell**t**

Together, the conjugated form of **haben** or **sein** and the past participle build the **Perfekt**:
Die Äpfel **haben** 1,90 Euro **gekostet**. *The apples cost 1,90 Euro.*
Er **ist** nach Paris **gereist**. *He traveled to Paris.*
Ich **bin** zu spät zur Arbeit **gekommen**. *I've come too late to work.*

Most verbs that build the **Perfekt** with **sein** are irregular. There are only a few regular verbs with **sein**, among them **passieren** *happen* and **reisen** *travel*. However, not all irregular verbs build the **Perfekt** with **sein**!

§ 8.3 Präteritum

The **Präteritum** is rarely used in spoken German (which is our main goal in this book). However, there are a few verbs (**haben**, **sein** and the modal verbs) that are more often used in **Präteritum** than **Perfekt** (▸ *§ 8.5, § 8.6*).
The list with irregular verbs after this grammar contains the **Präteritum** forms, because it's sensible to learn all forms at once. The **Präteritum** endings for regular verbs are the same as for modal verbs (▸ *Day 13*).

§ 8.4 Futur ▸ *Day 9, Day 29*

There are two different ways to talk about the future. You can either use the verb in the present tense and a temporal adverb (like **später** *later*, **morgen** *tomorrow* ...) or use the forms of the **Futur I**.

The **Futur I** is built with the appropriate form of **werden** and the infinitive:
Jens **geht** morgen mit Martina ins Kino. = Jens **wird** morgen mit Martina ins Kino **gehen**.

In spoken language the present tense with a temporal adverb is more common. The **Futur I**, however, is often used to underline the certainty of a future plan – like the English future with *going to*.

§ 8.5 haben and sein ▸ *Day 4, Day 12*

haben and **sein** are often used but conjugated irregularly:

	ich	du	er/sie/es	wir	ihr	sie/Sie
Präsens present tense						
haben	habe	hast	hat	haben	habt	haben
sein	bin	bist	ist	sind	seid	sind
Präteritum simple past						
haben	hatte	hattest	hatte	hatten	hattet	hatten
sein	war	warst	war	waren	wart	waren

Even if a text is written in **Perfekt** (▸ *§ 8.2*) **haben** and **sein** are usually used in their simple past forms. However, they have **Perfekt** forms too: **ich habe gehabt**, **du hast gehabt**, .../**ich bin gewesen**, **du bist gewesen**, ...

§ 8.6 Modal verbs ▸ *Day 5, Day 8, Day 10, Day 13*

Modal verbs are used to express wishes, necessities or prohibitions. They have a few grammatical peculiarities. Refer to Day 13 (▸ *Day 13*) for a comprehensive overview of their forms of **Präsens** and **Präteritum**. When you look at the tables you'll see that the first and third person singular (**ich**, **er**/**sie**/**es**) have no endings and (with the exception of **sollen**) the singular forms have a different vowel than the infinitive and plural. Modal verbs are usually combined with a verb in the infinitive. The modal verb is always the conjugated verb and therefore stands in the second position in a declarative sentence or the last in a subordinated clause (▸ *§ 10*).

Du **sollst** deinen Chef anrufen! *You should call your boss.*

Ich denke, dass wir uns morgen treffen **wollen**. *I think, that we want to meet tomorrow.*

Müssen *must/have to* expresses duty and necessity, often used when giving commands. Be careful with the negation: **nicht müssen** means *there's no need to.*
Sollen *shall/should* is often used for the same purposes as **müssen**. Commonly used for advice too.
Wollen *want* is used for wishes.
Können *can* expresses the possibility or ability to do something.
Dürfen *may/might* expresses permission to do something. The negation **nicht dürfen** expresses a prohibition and means *must not.*
Apart from these basic modal verbs there are some others (which are actually subjunctive forms of those above – so they have no own infinitive):

können → du könntest	sollen → Sie sollten	mögen → ich möchte

These are often considered more polite forms than the above and are used generally for the same purposes as the normal forms.
Mögen *like* itself is not a modal verb (although it conjugates like one: **ich mag, du magst, er mag, wir mögen, ihr mögt, sie mögen**), because it does not join with a verb in the infinitive but a noun. The forms **möcht-**, however, are modal verbs.
Another verb that conjugates like a modal verb is **wissen** *know*:

	ich	du	er/sie/es	wir	ihr	sie
present	weiß	weißt	weiß	wissen	wisst	wissen
past	wusste	wusstest	wusste	wussten	wusstet	wussten

The **Perfekt** forms (▸ *§ 8.2*) are **ich habe gewusst**, **er hat gewusst** ...

§ 8.7 Verbs with prefixes ▸ *Day 10*

The German has a lot of verbs with prefixes. Often there is a basic verb, like **nehmen** *take*, and a lot of additional different forms with different prefixes, like **aufnehmen** *record*, **mitnehmen** *take along*, **annehmen** *accept/assume*. These verbs always conjugate in the same way as the basic form!
Most prefixes that are prepositions (like the above examples) are so called separable prefixes and the verbs are called **trennbare Verben** *verbs with separable prefixes.* That means in the present tense, the prefix is separated from the conjugated form and put at the end of the sentence:
Iwona **nimmt** Pierre ins Kino **mit**. *Iwona takes Pierre along to the cinema.*
Ich **komme** um 19.15 Uhr in Berlin **an**. *I will arrive at 19.15 in Berlin.*

Other prefixes are, for example, **ver-**, **ent-**, **be-**, **ge-**. These prefixes are never separable:
Er **ver**letzt sich. *He hurts himself.*
Wir **be**eilen uns. *We have to hurry.*
This differentiation is important for the past participle (► *§ 18.2*).
Note that for pronunciation these separable prefixes are always stressed (non separable prefixes are not)!

§ 8.8 Reflexive verbs ► *Day 18*

Some verbs in the vocabulary have the word **sich** added (like the two verbs from the examples above with non-separable prefixes). **Sich** is the reflexive pronoun. That means that the verb's object is identical to the subject.
The forms of the reflexive pronoun are the same as those of the personal pronouns in the accusative with the exception of the third persons in singular and plural and the formal **Sie**:

Personal pronoun (Nom.)	ich	du	er/sie/es	wir	ihr	sie/Sie
Reflexive pronoun	mich	dich	**sich**	uns	euch	**sich**

Real reflexive verbs (i.e. the object can not be different from the subject) are rare in German. Examples are **sich beeilen** *to hurry*, **sich freuen** *look forward to* or **sich treffen** *meet*. Note that these examples are not reflexive in English!
A lot of verbs can be used like reflexive verbs: e.g. **waschen** *wash*.
Ich wasche mich. *I wash myself.*
Ich wasche dich. *I wash you.*
Ich wasche meine Wäsche. *I wash my clothes.*
Wir waschen uns. *We wash ourselves./We wash each other.*
Note the ambiguity in the last example. The plural pronouns (**uns**, **euch**, **sich**) can be reflexive or mean *each other*!

§ 8.9 Imperative ► *Day 7*

The imperative is used for commands and requests, just like in English. There are three different forms:

	Declarative sentence	Imperative sentence
informal **du** *(Sg)*	Du nimmst Platz. You take a seat.	**Nimm** Platz. Take a seat.
informal **ihr** *(Pl)*	Ihr nehmt Platz. You take a seat.	**Nehmt** Platz. Take a seat.
formal **Sie** *(Sg+Pl)*	Sie nehmen Platz. You take a seat.	**Nehmen Sie** Platz. Take a seat.

You can see the English translation is always the same, but the German makes a difference depending on who you're talking to. In the imperative sentence the verb always takes the first place. For the formal address you keep the pronoun (but put it behind the verb). For the informal address the pronoun is omitted. For the informal plural the verb does not change, for the singular you leave the **-st** ending out.

§ 9 Conjunctions ▸ *Day 15, Day 16, Day 17, Day 21, Day 24, Day 28*

There are two different kinds of conjunctions in German (just like in English): coordinating conjunctions and subordinating conjunctions.
A **coordinating conjunction** connects two main clauses. A coordinating conjunction is not a full sentence element and therefore the word order (▸ *§ 10*) of the two main clauses is not changed.
The most important coordinating conjunctions are:

und and	**oder** or	**aber** but	**denn** for/because

They are used like in English, with the exception of **denn** which can't stand at the beginning of a sentence.
Subordinating conjunctions connect a main clause with a subordinated clause. The word order in the subordinated clause is different (▸ *§ 10*).

dass that	**weil** because	**wenn** when	**als** when	**wenn** if

Dass stands after certain verbs (**glauben**, **denken**, **meinen**, **sagen**, **wissen** ...) in the main clause similar to the English.
Ich denke, **dass** du sehr gut Deutsch sprichst.
I think, that you speak German very well.
Wenn and **als** are temporal conjunctions. **Wenn** is used for events that keep repeating (in the past, the present or the future) – **als** is only used for singular events (or periods) in the past.

Als ich ein Kind war, bin ich oft ins Museum gegangen.
When I was a kid, I often went to the museum.
Ich gehe immer in ein Museum, **wenn** ich in Berlin bin.
I always visit a museum when I'm in Berlin.
Wenn has yet another meaning: if. It's used in conditional clauses, i.e. the subordinate clause with **wenn** states a condition and the main clause states the outcome if the condition comes true.
Wenn ich dieses Jahr nach Berlin fahre, besuche ich das Ägyptische Museum.
If I'm going to Berlin this year, I'll visit the Egyptian Museum.
Additionally you can begin subordinate clauses with interrogative pronouns.
It's a different way to express questions and stands often after verbs like **wissen**, **sagen**, **schreiben** ...
Weißt du, **wann** wir uns treffen? *Do you know, when we meet?*
Schreib ihm, **wo** er uns treffen kann! *Write him, where he can meet us.*
Deshalb *therefore/thus/hence* and **darum** *therefore/that's why* look like coordinating conjunctions and are used similarly to connect main clauses. However, they are full sentence elements and push the subject from the first position to the position after the verb.
Ich will nach Deutschland fahren, **darum** lerne ich Deutsch.
I want to go to Germany, that's why I learn German.
Subordinated clauses and coordinated main clauses with **aber** or **denn** are always separated from the main clause by a comma. The same applies for relative clauses.

§10 Word order ▸ *Day 2, Day 5, Day 16*

The previous paragraph already described a lot of main and subordinate clauses.
Let's have a look at a normal main clause:
Ich sehe das Haus. *I see the house.*
The word order is similar to the English: subject – verb – object.
According to these constituents you separate the sentence in different positions:
The **first position**: that's where, in our example, the subject (**ich**) stands. The **second position**: that's where, in every declarative sentence, the conjugated verb stands.
The **middle field**: that's where the object (**das Haus**) stands.
You might ask, why is it called "middle field" – it's at the end of the sentence.
But look at a declarative sentence in the **Perfekt** for example:
Ich habe das Haus gesehen. *I have seen the house.*

Now there is a last position which is connected to the second position and has a place for parts of complex verbs. Together the second and last position build a brace around the sentence, the so called **Satzklammer**.
The following table shows the different word orders for different main clauses:

		1st position	2nd position	middle field	last position
Declarative sentence		Ich	gehe	in die Stadt.	
		Er	muss	das Geschirr	abspülen.
		Gestern	wollte	er in ein Museum	gehen.
		Wir	sind	gestern ins Kino	gegangen.
		In einem Jahr	wird	er nach Russland	fliegen.
Imperative sentence			Spül	das Geschirr	ab!
Wh question		Wann	fährt	der Zug?	
Coordinated main clauses		Pierre	macht	eine Stadt-rundfahrt	
	und	Iwona	geht	in eine Ausstellung.	

You can see, the second and last position are for the verb and its parts.
The conjugated part (e.g. a modal verb or the conjugated part of a verb with separable prefix) is in the second position in a main clause, the other, not conjugated part (e.g. an infinitive or a past participle) in the last.

In subordinated clauses the word order is different: all parts of the verb are always in the last position and the conjugated part comes last of all:

		1st position	2nd position	middle field	last position
Main		Wir	fahren	mit dem Zug,	
and subordinate clause	weil	wir		dann nicht im Stau	stehen.
Main		Ich	denke,		
and subordinate clause	dass	er		gestern noch lange	gearbeitet hat.
Main		Er	fragt	eine Passantin,	
and subordinate clause	wie	er		den Weg zum Hotel	finden kann.

The second position in the subordinated clauses is empty!
One word about the first position: In most cases the subject stands there. Temporal adverbs like to go there as well – in this case the subject comes first after the verb in the middle field.
But it's also possible that a whole subordinated clause stands there. Let's take a conditional clause for example:
Ich fahre nach München, wenn ich Zeit habe. *I go to Munich if I have time.*
If the main clause comes first, all is as shown above. However, like in English you can put the if-clause in front:

		1st position	2nd position	middle field	last position
Subordinate	Wenn	ich		Zeit	habe,
and main clause	(dann)		fahre	ich nach München.	
Subordinate	Weil	wir		dann nicht im Stau	stehen,
and main clause			fahren	wir mit dem Zug.	

Now the main clause starts with the verb, because the first position is occupied by the subordinate clause! And that's why the subject stands in the middle field here. That's possible for most subordinate sentences.

Irregular verbs

The forms of **Präsens**, **Präteritum**, **Perfekt** are all in the third person singular (**er/sie/es**).

	Infinitiv	Präsens	Präteritum	Perfekt
begin	**beginnen**	beginnt	begann	hat begonnen
ask, beg	**bitten**	bittet	bat	hat gebeten
stay	**bleiben**	bleibt	blieb	ist geblieben
break	**brechen**	bricht	brach	ist gebrochen
bring	**bringen**	bringt	brachte	hat gebracht
think	**denken**	denkt	dachte	hat gedacht
may	**dürfen**	darf	durfte	hat gedurft
advise	**empfehlen**	empfiehlt	empfahl	hat empfohlen
eat	**essen**	isst (ihr esst)	aß	hat gegessen
drive	**fahren**	fährt	fuhr	ist/hat gefahren
fall	**fallen**	fällt	fiel	ist gefallen
find	**finden**	findet	fand	hat gefunden
fly	**fliegen**	fliegt	flog	ist geflogen
be cold, freeze	**frieren**	friert	fror	hat gefroren
give	**geben**	gibt	gab	hat gegeben
go	**gehen**	geht	ging	ist gegangen
succeed	**gelingen**	gelingt	gelang	ist gelungen
happen	**geschehen**	geschieht	geschah	ist geschehen
win	**gewinnen**	gewinnt	gewann	hat gewonnen
have	**haben**	hat	hatte	hat gehabt
hold	**halten**	hält	hielt	hat gehalten
hang	**hängen**	hängt	hing	hat gehangen
be called	**heißen**	heißt	hieß	hat geheißen
help	**helfen**	hilft	half	hat geholfen
know	**kennen**	kennt	kannte	hat gekannt
come	**kommen**	kommt	kam	ist gekommen
can	**können**	kann	konnte	hat gekonnt
invite	**einladen**	lädt ein	lud ein	hat eingeladen
let	**lassen**	lässt	ließ	hat gelassen
run, walk	**laufen**	läuft	lief	ist gelaufen
borrow, lend	**leihen**	leiht	lieh	hat geliehen
read	**lesen**	liest	las	hat gelesen
lie	**liegen**	liegt	lag	hat gelegen
lie	**lügen**	lügt	log	hat gelogen
like	**mögen**	mag	mochte	hat gemocht

	Infinitiv	Präsens	Präteritum	Perfekt
must	**müssen**	muss	musste	hat gemusst
take	**nehmen**	nimmt	nahm	hat genommen
mention	**nennen**	nennt	nannte	hat genannt
run	**rennen**	rennt	rannte	ist gerannt
smell	**riechen**	riecht	roch	hat gerochen
shout	**rufen**	ruft	rief	hat gerufen
shine	**scheinen**	scheint	schien	hat geschienen
sleep	**schlafen**	schläft	schlief	hat geschlafen
close	**schließen**	schließt	schloss	hat geschlossen
write	**schreiben**	schreibt	schrieb	hat geschrieben
cry	**schreien**	schreit	schrie	hat geschrien
swim	**schwimmen**	schwimmt	schwamm	ist/hat geschwommen
see	**sehen**	sieht	sah	hat gesehen
be	**sein**	ist	war	ist gewesen
send	**senden**	sendet	sandte	hat gesandt
sit	**sitzen**	sitzt	saß	hat gesessen
shall	**sollen**	soll	sollte	hat gesollt
speak	**sprechen**	spricht	sprach	hat gesprochen
jump	**springen**	springt	sprang	ist gesprungen
stand	**stehen**	steht	stand	hat gestanden
die	**sterben**	stirbt	starb	ist gestorben
argue	**streiten**	streitet	stritt	hat gestritten
carry	**tragen**	trägt	trug	hat getragen
meet	**treffen**	trifft	traf	hat getroffen
drink	**trinken**	trinkt	trank	hat getrunken
do	**tun**	tut	tat	hat getan
forget	**vergessen**	vergisst	vergaß	hat vergessen
grow	**wachsen**	wächst	wuchs	ist gewachsen
wash	**waschen**	wäscht	wusch	hat gewaschen
become	**werden**	wird (du wirst)	wurde	ist geworden
throw	**werfen**	wirft	warf	hat geworfen
know	**wissen**	weiß (du weißt)	wusste	hat gewusst
want	**wollen**	will	wollte	hat gewollt

Solutions and listening texts

Day 2

Dialogue questions

1. Martina | ~~Iwona~~ – **2.** German | ~~English~~. – **3.** ~~19~~ | 29 – **4.** ~~Brian~~ | Susan – **5.** ~~Australia~~ | France.

1 **1.** Mein Name ist Pierre. – **2.** Ich komme aus Australien. – **3.** Yoko ist 21 Jahre alt. – **4.** Susan kommt aus England und ist 23. – **5.** Ich komme aus Polen und bin 30 Jahre alt. / Ich bin 30 Jahre alt und komme aus Polen.

2 **Listening text** 14, 7, 20, 3, 12, 8, 17, 5, 16, 9; *Remaining:* 2

3 **1.** Du – **2.** heißt, Sie – **3.** Ich – **4.** kommt, Er – **5.** komme

4 **Listening text**
1. Guten Tag. Ich bin **Paul**. Ich bin 27 Jahre alt. Ich komme aus **Schottland**. – **2.** Hallo. Mein Name ist **Mary**. Ich bin aus **Australien**. Ich bin 24. – **3.** Guten Morgen. Mein Name ist **Lucy** und ich komme aus **den USA**. – **4.** Hi! Mein Name ist **George**. Ich bin 21 und aus **England**.

Day 3

Dialogue questions

1. wrong – **2.** right – **3.** wrong – **4.** right – **5.** wrong

1 **1.** a) Woher kommst du? b) e.g. Ich komme aus England. – **2.** a) Wie geht es dir? b) e.g. Mir geht es gut. – **3.** a) Wo ist das? b) e.g. Das ist in der Nähe von Barcelo-na. – **4.** a) Was machst du? b) e.g. Ich studiere. / Ich arbeite in einer Firma. – **5.** a) Kommst du aus Deutschland? b) e.g. Nein, ich komme aus Polen. **6.** a) Bist du schon lange in Deutschland? b) e.g. Nein, erst seit zwei Wochen. – **7.** a) Arbeitest du hier? b) e.g. Ja, ich arbeite in einer Firma. / Nein, ich studiere hier.

2 **1.** kommt – **2.** arbeiten – **3.** kommen – **4.** arbeiten – **5.** arbeitet – **6.** kommen

3 **Listening text**
1. Hallo Jens, wie geht's? – Danke gut. – **2. Woher kommst du?** – Aus Jena. – **3. Wo ist das?** – Jena ist in Thüringen. – **4. Und was machst du?** – Ich arbeite in einer Firma für Druckmaschinen.

Day 4

Dialogue questions

1. right – **2.** wrong – **3.** right – **4.** wrong

1 **1.** ist – **2.** Seid – **3.** bin – **4.** haben – **5.** Hast

2 **Possible answers**
1. Mein Name ist Iwona. – **2.** Ich komme aus Polen. – **3.** Ich bin 30 (Jahre alt). – **4.** Ja, ich habe einen Bruder. – **5.** Mein Vater ist Rechtsanwalt.
Listening text
1. Wie heißt du? – **2.** Woher kommst du? – **3.** Wie alt bist du? – **4.** Hast du Geschwister? – **5.** Was ist dein Vater von Beruf?

3 **1.** e) – **2.** d) – **3.** b) – **4.** a) – **5.** f) – **6.** c)

4 **1.** zwei – **2.** keinen – **3.** keine – **4.** einen – **5.** eine – **6.** drei

Day 5

Dialogue questions

1. ~~laptop~~ | video projector – **2.** some | ~~no~~ – **3.** similar | ~~other~~ **4.** ~~the same as~~ | something completely different than

1 **1.** e) – **2.** d) – **3.** c) – **4.** b) – **5.** f) – **6.** a)

2 **Listening text**

1. Entschuldigung, ich verstehe das nicht. – **2.** Kannst du das wiederholen? – **3.** Heißt es der Laptop oder das Laptop? – **4.** Garten und *garden* sind sehr ähnlich. – **5.** Dieses Wort kenne ich nicht. – **6.** Leider gibt es einige falsche Freunde.

Remaining: Das ist etwas ganz anderes.

3 **1.** a) Er muss den Satz wiederholen. b) He has to repeat the sentence. – **2.** a) Kannst du (bitte) den Beamer (bitte) holen (, bitte)? b) Can you get the video projector please? – **3.** a) Musst du viel arbeiten? – b) Do you have to work a lot? – **4.** a) Iwona muss diese Wörter nachschauen. – b) Iwona has to look up these words. – **5.** a) Wir können unseren Sohn oft besuchen. – b) We can visit our son often. – **6.** a) Ich verstehe das nicht. – b) I don't understand that. – **7.** a) Können Sie das bitte wiederholen? – b) Can (Could) you repeat please?

Day 6

1 **1.** Du arbeitest ... – **2.** Er studiert ... – **3.** Wir sind ... – **4.** Sie ist ...

2 **1.** Unsere – **2.** Mein – **3.** Ihre – **4.** Ihr –**5.** Eure – **6.** Ihr

3 Correct order: **3.** – **6.** – **5.** – **7.** – **1.** – **8.** – **2.** – **4.**

4 **a)** vier – **b)** zwei – **c)** elf – **d)** drei – **e)** zehn – **f)** sieben – **g)** acht – **h)** neun

5 **1.** a) – **2.** a) – **3.** b) – **4.** b)

Listening text

Hallo, mein Name ist Martin. Ich bin 31 Jahre alt und Deutschlehrer. Ich arbeite hier in Berlin. Ich bin seit einem Jahr in Berlin. Ich habe seit drei Jahren eine Freundin. Sie heißt Lynn. Sie ist 29 Jahre alt und kommt aus England. Sie ist schon seit fünf Jahren in Berlin.
Sie ist Architektin.

6 **1.** Onkel – **2.** Geschäftsmann – **3.** Monat – **4.** Deutschland – **5.** Guten Abend – **6.** Eltern

Remaining: Auf Wiedersehen *(You use it to say goodbye, the others are to say hello.)*

7 **1.** Sie – **2.** du – **3.** du – **4.** Sie – **5.** Sie (*maybe also* du) – **6.** Sie

8 **1.** Das ist nicht schwer. – **2.** Martina hat keine Schwester. – **3.** Ich verstehe das nicht. – **4.** Das ist kein englisches Wort. – **5.** Du weißt es nicht. – **6.** Ich habe keinen Laptop.

9 **1.** wrong – **2.** wrong – **3.** right – **4.** wrong – **5.** right – **6.** wrong

10 **1.** Es geht. – **2.** Freut mich! – **3.** Viel Spaß! – **4.** Bis später! – **5.** Hallo!

11 **1.** Sie sehen zwei Männer. – **2.** Wir haben keine Schwester / Schwestern. – **3.** Du hast einen Sohn. – **4.** Sie hat vier Geschwister.

12 **1.** e) – **2.** c) – **3.** d) – **4.** b) – **5.** a)

13 **Possible solution**

Hallo, mein Name ist ... Ich komme aus ... Das liegt in ... Ich bin ... Jahre alt.
Ich studiere / arbeite in ... Ich habe ... Schwester / Bruder. Sie heißt / heißen ... Mein Vater ist ... von Beruf. Meine Mutter arbeitet in ...

14 **1.** Kannst du den Mann sehen? – **2.** Ich muss Deutsch lernen. – **3.** Wo arbeitest du? – **4.** Arbeitest du in einer Consultingfirma? – **5.** Wir müssen sehr viel lernen. – **6.** Sie können diese Wörter nicht verstehen.

15 **Possible solution**
Hallo, es geht mir gut. Ich bin schon 6 Monate in Deutschland. Ja, ich mache einen Deutschkurs. Deutsch ist schwer! Ja, ich arbeite in einer Firma. Aber ich kenne noch nicht viele Deutsche. Tschüs!

16 **1.** einen – **2.** a) Der b) einen – **3.** ein – **4.** — – **5.** a) einen b) Der c) eine d) Die

17 **Listening text**
1. Hallo, wie geht es dir? – **Mir geht es prima.** – **2.** Wie lange bist du schon in Deutschland? – **Ich bin seit 6 Monaten hier.** – **3.** Hast du Geschwister? – **Ja, ich habe einen Bruder.** – **4.** Was arbeiten deine Eltern? – **Mein Vater ist Rechtsanwalt. Meine Mutter ist Architektin.** – **5.** Bist du verheiratet? – **Nein, ich bin Single.** – **6.** Verstehst du alles? – **Ja, kein Problem.**

18 **1.** geht – **2.** bin (arbeite) – **3.** mache – **4.** ist – **5.** habe – **6.** heißt – **7.** kommt – **8.** ist – **9.** kenne – **10.** machst – **11.** Arbeitest (Bist)

19 **Listening text**
1. Guten Abend, Herr Schneider. – Ah, Herr Maier, guten Abend! *(10 pm)* – **2.** Hi, wie heißt du? – Hallo, ich bin Martin. *(possible at all times)* – **3.** Ich muss gehen! Gute Nacht. – Auf Wiedersehen und gute Nacht! *(10 pm)* – **4.** Guten Morgen und herzlich willkommen! – Vielen Dank. *(8 am)* – **5.** Guten Tag! Kann ich helfen? – Ja. Wo ist der Deutschkurs? *(2 pm, also possible at 8 am)*

20 **1.** Sie fragen Ihren Nachbarn. – **2.** Woher kommen Sie? – **3.** Arbeiten Sie viel? – **4.** Können Sie das bitte wiederholen? – **5.** Sie sind aus Deutschland.

Intermediate test 1

1 **1.** die Architektin – **2.** die Präsentation – **3.** der Garten – **4.** die Zeit – **5.** der Monat – **6.** das Restaurant – **7.** die Woche – **8.** der Dialog

2 **1.** Sie muss den Laptop holen. – **2.** Ich kann über meine Familie sprechen. – **3.** Ihr müsst den Satz wiederholen. – **4.** Müssen Sie sehr viel arbeiten?

3 **1.** right – **2.** right – **3.** wrong – **4.** wrong – **5.** wrong
Listening text

1. Mann	Verstehen Sie das, Frau Schneider?
Frau Schneider	Ja, ich verstehe alles.
2. Pierre	Kannst du das bitte wiederholen, Martina?
Martina	Ja, Gift ist „poison" auf Englisch.
3. Martina	Ihr macht das sehr gut. Ich bin sehr zufrieden!
4. Iwona	Yoko, hast du einen Bruder?
Yoko	Nein. Ich habe eine Schwester.
5. Jens	Ich muss sehr viel arbeiten. Aber ich bin glücklich.

4 **1.** Länder – **2.** Stunde – **3.** Firma – **4.** Familien – **5.** Lehrer – **6.** Sohn – **7.** Schwestern – **8.** Mütter – **9.** Haus **10.** – Restaurants

5 **1.** Woher kommen Sie? – **2.** Kannst du das (bitte) wiederholen? – **3.** Holst du (bitte) den Beamer? – **4.** Wo arbeiten Sie?

6 **1.** b) – **2.** c) – **3.** a) – **4.** c) – **5.** a)

7 **1.** Woher – **2.** Wo – **3.** Wie – **4.** Wie – **5.** Wo – **6.** Wie

8 **Listening text**
1. Monika Maier, guten Tag. Ich bin Rechtsanwältin. Meine Telefonnummer ist 07623 – **862274**. – **2.** Mein Name ist **Martin Schneider**. Ich arbeite in Hamburg. Ich bin **Architekt**. **3.** Hallo. Ich bin **Claudia**. Ich bin Deutschlehrerin und arbeite in **Berlin**.

9 **1.** Kannst du / Können Sie mir helfen? – **2.** Ich muss den Laptop holen. – **3.** Er muss viel arbeiten. – **4.** Jens kann seine Mutter oft besuchen. – **5.** Kannst du / Können Sie diese Wörter (bitte) wiederholen (bitte)?

Evaluation

You reached .... of 50 points.

45–50	**Sehr gut!** *Very good!* Keep it up!
35–44	**Gut!** *Good!* You're on the right way.
25–34	**In Ordnung.** *OK.* You've already accomplished a lot. Repeat the exercises where you still had problems and full points won't be problem.
0–24	**Das können Sie noch besser.** *You can still do better.* But hey, it's not the end of the world! Review the lessons where you had problems and use the solutions actively: don't just correct your exercises but try to understand why the solution is correct.

Day 7

Dialogue questions

1. wrong – **2.** wrong – **3.** wrong – **4.** right – **5.** wrong – **6.** wrong

1 **Obst:** Apfel, Banane, Birne, Orange, Pfirsich, Weintraube – **Gemüse**: Gurke, Kartoffel, Möhre (Karotte), Paprika, Tomate, Zucchini, Zwiebel – **Milchprodukte**: Butter, Joghurt, Käse, Milch, Sahne – **Anderes**: Brot, Brötchen, Ei, Fisch, Hähnchen, Fleisch, Honig, Marmelade, Müsli, Schinken, Wein, Wurst

2 **1.** b) – **2.** c) – **3.** d) – **4.** a)

3 **1.** 80 Cent pro Kilo – **2.** 1,50 Euro pro Kilo – **3.** 1,99 Euro pro Packung – **4.** 3 Euro pro Flasche

Listening text

Verehrte Kunden, heute für Sie im Sonderangebot: Kartoffeln – ein Kilo nur 80 Cent. Außerdem für Sie: frisches Obst – Birnen nur 1,50 Euro das Kilo. Im Kühlfach finden Sie Schinken: Die Packung für nur 1,99 Euro. Und als besonderes Angebot: Wein aus Frankreich – eine Flasche nur 3 Euro.

Day 8

Dialogue questions

1. Apfelkuchen | ~~Schokoladentorte~~. – **2.** etwas | ~~keine~~ – **3.** nicht | sehr – **4.** heute | ~~morgen~~

2 **Martina**: Wasser, Fisch mit Kartoffeln – **Jens**: Bier, Schnitzel mit Pommes, die Rechnung

Listening text

Kellner	Guten Tag, was darf ich Ihnen bringen?
Martina	Guten Tag. Ich hätte gerne den Fisch und dazu Kartoffeln.
Jens	Für mich bitte das Schnitzel mit Pommes.
Kellner	Ja, natürlich. Was möchten Sie trinken?
Jens	Ich hätte gerne ein Bier.
Martina	Und ich möchte bitte ein Wasser.
Kellner	Sehr gerne. [...] Möchten Sie noch etwas?
Jens	Nein, danke. Aber bringen Sie uns bitte die Rechnung?

3 *Begin your sentences with* **„Ich hätte gerne ..."** *or* **„Ich möchte ..."**. *Just be careful to use the accusative* **„einen Salat"**.

Day 9

Dialogue questions

1. b) – **2.** b) – **3.** a) – **4.** a)

1 **1.** ist größer – **2.** geht lieber in ein Museum – **3.** ist besser – **4.** geht lieber ins Theater – **5.** ist interessanter – **6.** ist toller

2 **1.** Ich hätte gerne eine normale Eintrittskarte und zwei für Studenten. **2.** Ich gehe lieber einkaufen als ins Theater. **3.** Um wie viel Uhr macht das Museum zu? **4.** Gibt es eine Studentenermäßigung? **5.** Ich möchte lieber eine Stadtrundfahrt machen. **6.** Ich faulenze lieber. **7.** Was kostet eine normale Eintrittskarte?

3 **1.** 3) – **2.** 4) – **3.** 6) – **4.** 5) – **5.** 7) – **6.** 1) – **7.** 2) – **8.** –

Listening text

1. Wir treffen uns um **halb 4**. – **2.** Das Museum schließt um **18.30 Uhr**. – **3.** Es ist **Viertel nach 11**. – **4.** Mein Deutschkurs beginnt um **2**. – **5.** Martina wartet seit **Viertel vor 9**. – **6.** Es ist **9.45 Uhr**. – **7.** Um **19.15 Uhr** gehe ich auf den Fernsehturm.

Day 10

Dialogue questions

1. right – **2.** right – **3.** wrong – **4.** wrong – **5.** wrong

1 **1.** b) – **2.** e) – **3.** d) – **4.** c) – **5.** f) – **6.** a)

2 **1.** right – **2.** wrong – **3.** wrong – **4.** wrong – **5.** wrong – **6.** right

Listening text

Pierre Am Morgen frühstücke ich nicht – ich trinke nur einen Kaffee. Dann gehe ich in die Arbeit. Zu Mittag esse ich in der Firma. Nach der Arbeit besuche ich einen Deutschkurs oder treffe mich mit Freunden.

Martina Ich muss früh aufstehen. Aber ich mag das nicht! Dann frühstücke ich – meistens Obst oder Müsli. Ich mache Deutschkurse und komme oft erst am Abend nach Hause. Oft sehe ich dann noch fern.

Iwona Ich stehe gern früh auf und gehe dann joggen. Ich komme oft schon am Nachmittag nach Hause. Dann gehe ich in die Stadt und kaufe ein oder treffe mich mit Freunden. Am Abend lese ich gern und gehe früh ins Bett.

3 *Orient yourself using the text in the exercise and the dialogue.*

Day 11

Dialogue questions

1. Jens hat Geburtstag. – **2.** Andreas ist der Freund von Martinas Schwester / von Kathrin. – **3.** Die Getränke stehen auf einem / dem Tisch (im Wohnzimmer). – **4.** Sie wohnt in Potsdam.

1 **1.** 3) – **2.** 5) – **3.** 4) – **4.** 1) – **5.** 2)

Listening text

1.

Frau Hallo Jens. Ich wünsche dir alles Gute zum Geburtstag.

Jens Danke sehr!

Frau Hier, ich habe ein Geschenk für dich!

2.
Jens Hi Kathrin. Hallo Andreas. Herzlich willkommen.
Kathrin Hi Jens, danke für die Einladung.
Jens Gern! Kommt doch herein!
3.
Jens Martina, das ist Paul, ein Kollege von mir. Paul, das ist Martina, meine Freundin.
Paul Hallo Martina. Freut mich dich kennenzulernen.
Martina Freut mich auch, Paul.
4.
Frau Wo sind denn die Getränke?
Pierre Da, auf dem Tisch. Essen kannst du in der Küche holen.
Frau Danke.
5.
Kathrin Hi, wie geht's dir?
Iwona Gut, danke.
Kathrin Du bist aus Martinas Deutschkurs, ja?

2 **Andreas**: Toilette – **Jens**: Flur – **Kathrin**: Flur – **Martina**: Wohnzimmer – **Pierre**: Bad

3 **1.** Freut mich sehr Sie kennenzulernen. – **2.** Ich wünsche dir alles Gute zum Geburtstag. – **3.** Ich möchte euch kurz vorstellen. – **4.** Herzlich willkommen in unserer Wohnung.– **5.** Das ist mein Kollege Paul.

Day 12

Dialogue questions

1. im Wohnzimmer | ~~in der Küche~~ – **2.** ~~kehrt gerne~~ | spült gerne ab – **3.** ~~Iwona~~ | Pierre – **4.** ~~sehr~~ | nicht.

1 **Iwona:** ☺ staubsaugen, Wäsche waschen – ☹ abspülen, bügeln – **Pierre**: ☺ Müll wegbringen – ☹ aufräumen, abspülen, staubsaugen, Wäsche waschen, bügeln

Listening text

Iwona Pierre, räumst du gerne auf?
Pierre Nein.
Iwona Na, das ist in Ordnung. Ich spüle dafür nicht gern ab.
Pierre Ja, ich spüle auch nicht gern ab. In Frankreich habe ich einen Geschirrspüler.
Iwona Das ist gut. Ich mag Staubsaugen und Wäsche waschen. Aber ich bügle nicht gern.
Pierre Das mag ich auch alles nicht.
Iwona Aber Pierre, du magst ja keine Hausarbeit!
Pierre Stimmt! Oh, doch ... ich bringe gern den Müll weg!

2 **1.** Abspülen ist in Ordnung. – **2.** Was ist los? – **3.** Stell das dreckige Geschirr in den Geschirrspüler. – **4.** Das macht nichts. – **5.** Was soll ich machen? – **6.** Das tut mir leid! – **7.** Kehren mag ich nicht.

3 **1.** Regal *(article is already in "im"!)* – **2.** das Sofa – **3.** dem Stuhl – **4.** dem Tisch – **5.** den Schrank – **6.** der Kommode – **7.** der Lampe – **8.** dem Teller

Day 13

Dialogue questions

1. right – **2.** wrong – **3.** right – **4.** right

1 **1.** a) – **2.** a) – **3.** a) – **4.** b) – **5.** a) – **6.** a)

Listening text

Martina Gehen wir ins Kino?
Jens Ich will lieber zu Hause bleiben und einen Film im Fernsehen oder auf DVD sehen.
Martina Was kommt denn heute Abend?
Jens Also im Fernsehen kommt „Insomnia" – ein Thriller mit Al Pacino.
Martina Nein, ich habe keine Lust auf einen Thriller. Kommt vielleicht eine Komödie?
Jens Das weiß ich nicht. Ich muss erst die Fernsehzeitschrift holen. Nein, heute kommt keine Komödie.
Martina Wollen wir vielleicht eine DVD ausleihen?
Jens Ja, das können wir machen.
Martina Dann suche ich einen Film im Internet aus. Okay? „Rush Hour 3" – was meinst du?
Jens Das ist gut. Dann hole ich den Film.

2 **1.** Tagesschau – **2.** 20.15 Uhr – **3.** 21.45 Uhr – **4.** Nachrichten – **5.** 24 hours daily in Europe

3 **Listening text**

1. Hast du Lust auf einen Film? – **Nein, ich will lieber lesen.** – **2.** Wo spielt der Tatort? – **Heute spielt er in Hamburg.** – **3.** Um wie viel Uhr kommen die Nachrichten? – **Um 19 Uhr.** – **4.** Was kommt heute Abend im Fernsehen? – **Heute Abend gibt es einen Actionfilm.**

Day 14

1 **fahren**: ich fahre, du fährst, er / sie / es fährt, wir fahren, ihr fahrt, sie / Sie fahren – **essen**: ich esse, du isst, er / sie / es isst, wir essen, ihr esst, sie / Sie essen – **schlafen**: ich schlafe, du schläfst, er / sie / es schläft, wir schlafen, ihr schlaft, sie / Sie schlafen – **fernsehen**: ich sehe fern, du siehst fern, er / sie / es sieht fern, wir sehen fern, ihr seht fern, sie / Sie sehen fern – **geben**: ich gebe, du gibst, er / sie / es gibt, wir geben, ihr gebt, sie / Sie geben

2 **1.** Um halb acht steht Jens auf. – **2.** Um acht (acht Uhr) fährt er in die Arbeit. – **3.** Um 12.45 isst er zu Mittag. – **4.** Um Viertel nach sechs kommt er nach Hause.

3 **1.** 5 Tomaten – **2.** 1 Zucchini – **3.** 1 Kilo Kartoffeln – **4.** 4 Bananen – **5.** 0,5 kg Äpfel – **6.** 400 g Schinken – **7.** 2 Flaschen Wein – **8.** 1 Karton Milch

Listening text

So, auf dem Markt kaufe ich Gemüse und Obst. Ich möchte 5 Tomaten und 1 Zucchini kaufen – ach ja, und 1 Kilo Kartoffeln. Außerdem möchte ich noch 4 Bananen und ein halbes Kilo Äpfel kaufen. Dann gehe ich in den Supermarkt. Ich brauche 400 Gramm Schinken, 2 Flaschen Wein und 1 Karton Milch.

4 **1.** Zucchini – **2.** joggen – **3.** Fleisch – **4.** Tüte – **5.** unten – **6.** Zeitschrift – **7.** rot – **8.** Wasser

5 **1.** Räum dein Zimmer auf! – **2.** Macht mehr Sport! – **3.** Reden Sie mit dem Kunden! – **4.** Gehen Sie einen Kaffee trinken! – **5.** Besuch deinen Freund! – **6.** Macht eine Stadtrundfahrt!

6 **1.** ihr – **2.** Sie – **3.** ihn – **4.** ihm – **5.** Er – **6.** sie

7 **1.** Fernsehen – **2.** aufstehen – **3.** Gurke – **4.** Zimmer – **5.** Saft – **6.** Müll wegbringen

8 **1.** dem – **2.** — – **3.** — – **4.** ein – **5.** ein – **6.** einen – **7.** einen – **8.** eine – **9.** — – **10.** — – **11.** den – **12.** das

9 **1.** ein Freund von Martina / Martinas Freund – **2.** im Kindergarten – **3.** neben Martinas Eltern – **4.** in Hamburg – **5.** gern ins Kino – **6.** eine Radtour (oder gehen schwimmen) – **7.** gern Fußball. / am liebsten Fußball. / einmal in der Woche Fußball – **8.** sieht Klaus fern und (er) geht früh ins Bett

Listening text

Hallo, ich bin Klaus. Ich bin ein Freund von Martina. Wir waren zusammen im Kindergarten. Ich kenne sie also schon sehr lange. Meine Eltern wohnen neben Martinas Eltern – sie sind Nachbarn. Martina lebt jetzt in Berlin. Ich lebe in Hamburg. Hamburg ist eine tolle Stadt. Ich besuche Martina und ihren Freund Jens gern. Martina kommt auch oft nach Hamburg. Wir gehen gern ins Kino oder reden lang. Das macht viel Spaß. Wir machen aber lieber eine Radtour oder gehen schwimmen. Ich mache gern Sport. Am liebsten spiele ich Fußball. Aber ich bin nicht in einem Sportverein. Einmal in der Woche treffe ich mich mit Freunden und wir spielen. Am Abend sehe ich gern fern und gehe früh ins Bett.

10 **1.** dreihundertsiebenundfünfzig – **2.** achthundertzwölf – **3.** tausendeins / eintausendeins – **4.** zweitausendzehn – **5.** neuntausendneunhundertneunundneunzig

11 **1.** ausleihen – **2.** mitnehmen – **3.** einkaufen – **4.** aufräumen – **5.** abspülen – **6.** fernsehen

12 **1.** kann sie ein Fahrrad ausleihen – **2.** wollen sie auf eine Radtour mitnehmen – **3.** wollen an den Wannsee außerhalb von Berlin fahren – **4.** können sie auch schwimmen – **5.** muss Iwona im Supermarkt einkaufen – **6.** will sie auf eine Party gehen – **7.** muss sie aufräumen und abspülen – **8.** will noch fernsehen – **9.** möchte sie ins Bett gehen und schlafen

13 *Begin your sentences with* **„Ich hätte gerne …“** or **„Ich möchte …“**. *Just be careful to use the accusative* **„einen Becher Sahne“**. **„0,5 kg”** *can be* **„fünfhundert Gramm“** *or* **„ein halbes Kilo(-gramm)“**.

14 **1.** Iwona wollte nicht an der Straße joggen. – **2.** Ich sollte etwas im Internet suchen. – **3.** Wir hatten viel Freizeit. – **4.** Ihr konntet alles auf dem Markt kaufen. – **5.** Du musstest den Müll wegbringen. – **6.** Das Museum war interessant.

15 0.40 Uhr: 6 – 15.30 Uhr: 2 – 4.30 Uhr: — – 15.45 Uhr: 1 – 5.15 Uhr: — – 16.30 Uhr: 5 – 9.15 Uhr: 4 – 16.45 Uhr: 7 – 13.00 Uhr: 8 – 21.20 Uhr: 3 – 13.15 Uhr: 10 – 23.30 Uhr: 9

Listening text

1. Es ist 15.45 Uhr. – **2.** Um halb 4. – **3.** Um 21.20 Uhr. – **4.** Es ist Viertel nach 9. – **5.** Um 16.30 Uhr. – **6.** Um 0.40 Uhr. – **7.** Es ist Viertel vor 5. – **8.** Es ist eins. – **9.** Um halb 12. – **10.** Um 13.15 Uhr.

16 **1.** vor das Haus – **2.** auf dem Tisch – **3.** hinter den Pfirsichen – **4.** zwischen dem Messer und der Gabel – **5.** an den Tisch – **6.** im (!) Schrank – **7.** neben seinen Schwestern – **8.** sich auf das Sofa – **9.** ins (!) Regal

17 **1.** a) euch b) Uns – **2.** a) dir b) mir – **3.** a) Ihnen b) mir

18 **1.** b) – **2.** a) – **3.** b) – **4.** b) – **5.** c) – **6.** c)

Listening text

Iwona	Hi Pierre! Wo warst du denn gestern? Du warst nicht im Deutschkurs …
Pierre	Hi Iwona. Ja, ich konnte nicht kommen. Wir mussten so viel arbeiten.
Iwona	Das macht nichts. Aber es war sehr interessant! Martina hatte eine Präsentation über Freizeit in Deutschland.
Pierre	Na ja … ich hatte keine Freizeit. Ich musste arbeiten.
Iwona	Ja. Und morgen? Hast du morgen Abend Zeit? Es gibt eine Party in der Goethestraße.
Pierre	Um wie viel Uhr beginnt die Party denn?
Iwona	Um acht.
Pierre	Ja, da habe ich Zeit. Cool.
Iwona	Und was machst du heute noch? Triffst du noch Freunde?

Pierre	Nein ... Ich gehe nur ins Bett.
Iwona	Na, dann wünsche ich dir eine gute Nacht!

19 **1.** Löffel – **2.** Teller – **3.** essen – **4.** Hauptgericht – **5.** Tasse – **6.** Glas – **7.** trinken – **8.** Gabel – **9.** Beilage – **10.** Messer – **11.** Serviette – **12.** Nachtisch
Solution: Restaurant

Intermediate test 2

1 **1.** einem – **2.** ihnen – **3.** möchten – **4.** Apfelschorle – **5.** Kartoffeln – **6.** Glas – **7.** lecker – **8.** Spaziergang – **9.** kauft – **10.** Ermäßigung – **11.** interessanter – **12.** muss – **13.** Wurst – **14.** nach Hause – **15.** aufräumen – **16.** Tschüs

2 **1.** b) – **2.** d) – **3.** h) Die Rechnung bitte. – **4.** f) – **5.** g) – **6.** c) – **7.** a) – **8.** e)

3 **Iwona**: Eintrittskarten kaufen, Viertel nach sechs / 18.15 Uhr – **Kathrin**: auf ein Konzert gehen, morgen – **Pierre**: in die Arbeit fahren, halb neun / 8.30 Uhr

Listening text

Iwona	Hier ist Iwona. Es ist Viertel nach sechs und ich will die Eintrittskarten kaufen. Hast du einen Studentenausweis? Ruf mich an!
Kathrin	Hey, ich bin's, Kathrin. Ich gehe morgen auf ein Konzert. Kommst du mit? Hast du Lust? Tschüs!
Pierre	Hi, Pierre hier. Ich fahre um halb neun in die Arbeit. Soll ich dich mitnehmen?

4 **1.** zwischen der – dem – **2.** neben dem – **3.** hinter (über) dem – **4.** auf dem – **5.** an der

5 **1.** ihm – **2.** es – **3.** ihr – **4.** er – **5.** ihn

6 **1.** c) – **2.** b) – **3.** — – **4.** d) – **5.** a)

7 **1.** will – **2.** waren – **3.** hat – **4.** mussten – **5.** hast – **6.** darfst

Evaluation

maximal:	50 points
sehr gut:	45–50
gut:	35–44
in Ordnung:	25–34

Day 15

Dialogue questions

1. wrong – **2.** right – **3.** right – **4.** wrong

1 **Listening text**
1. 1. Januar – **2.** 14. Februar – **3.** 4. März – **4.** 28. April – **5.** 12. Mai – **6.** 8. Juni – **7.** 17. Juli – **8.** 21. August – **9.** 11. September – **10.** 3. Oktober – **11.** 9. November – **12.** 24. Dezember

2 **1.** Mir gefällt dein Vorschlag. – **2.** Ich finde Ihre Idee gut. – **3.** Nein, ich muss an dem Tag arbeiten.

3 **1.** 110 Euro – **2.** Ja – **3.** Ja – **4.** 24 Zimmer

4 Anreise: 28. Juli / 28.7. – Abreise: 4. August / 4.8. – Erwachsene: 2 – Kinder: 0 – Einzelzimmer [ ] Doppelzimmer [X] – Inkl. Frühstück? Nein [ ] Ja [X]

Listening text

Jens	Martina, ich möchte das Hotel buchen. Wann fahren wir weg?
Martina	Das weißt du doch! Wir fahren am 28. Juli hier weg und bleiben bis 4. August.

Jens Stimmt, also sieben Nächte. Wir nehmen ein Doppelzimmer, oder?
Martina Ja, natürlich! Dachtest du, wir nehmen zwei Einzelzimmer?
Jens Nein. Wollen wir auch im Hotel frühstücken?
Martina Ja, ich denke das ist eine gute Idee. Dann müssen wir nicht jeden Morgen erst ein Café suchen.
Jens Okay!

Day 16

Dialogue questions

1. fahren | ~~fliegen~~ – **2.** ~~ersten~~ | zweiten – **3.** sechs | ~~vierzehn~~ – **4.** ~~am Schalter~~ | online.

1 **1.** Gleis 14 – **2.** 16.29 Uhr – **3.** Basel – **4.** 18.52 Uhr

2 Hin- und Rückfahrt – Von: Berlin – Nach: München – Hinfahrt am: 2.10. – Uhrzeit: 14.00, Abfahrt *or* 20:00, Ankunft – Rückfahrt am: 5.10.

3 **1.** Ich fahre lieber mit dem ICE, weil er schneller ist. – **2.** Ich denke, dass die Regionalbahn zu langsam ist. – **3.** Iwona und Pierre wollen nach München fahren. – **4.** Pierre sagt, dass ein Flug zu teuer ist.

Day 17

Dialogue questions

1. b) – **2.** a) – **3.** b) – **4.** b)

1 **1.** Entschuldigen Sie bitte. – **2.** Können Sie mir vielleicht helfen? – **3.** Entschuldigung, wo ist der Bahnhof? – **4.** Wissen Sie, wo die Schillerstraße ist? – **5.** Entschuldigen Sie, ich suche das Theater.

2 **Possible solution**

1. Gehen Sie an der Kreuzung / Baustelle nach rechts. / Biegen Sie ... rechts ab. – **2.** Gehen Sie hier vorne rechts und dann die nächste Straße links. – **3.** An der Kreuzung gehen Sie geradeaus. Dann müssen Sie rechts gehen. Nehmen Sie dann die zweite Straße links. / Fahren Sie an der Kreuzung nach rechts. Dann nehmen Sie die zweite Straße links und dann rechts. – **4.** Gehen Sie hier vorne (an der Kreuzung) rechts. Dann gehen Sie die erste / zweite Straße links und gleich wieder rechts. Dann geradeaus bis ans Ende der Straße.

Day 18

Dialogue questions

1. right – **2.** right – **3.** right – **4.** wrong

2 *Correct order:* 4 – 6 – 2 – 9 – 1 – 7 – 3 – 8 – 5

3 **1.** (Die Sauna kostet) 5 Euro. – **2.** In der Bar. – **3.** Fahrräder und DVDs. – **4.** Schwimmbad und Filmverleih.

Listening text

Jens Schau mal, Martina. Hier ist ein Faltblatt mit zusätzlichen Services im Hotel.
Martina Und was bieten sie an?

Jens Es gibt zum Beispiel ein Schwimmbad und eine Sauna. Das Schwimmbad ist kostenlos, aber die Sauna kostet 5 Euro.
Martina Aha. Kann man hier auch etwas essen oder trinken? Oder gibt es einen Zimmerservice?
Jens Nein, es gibt keinen Zimmerservice und auch kein Essen, nur das Frühstück. Aber es gibt eine Bar mit Getränken.
Martina O. K., eine Bar ist gut.
Jens Wir können auch Fahrräder ausleihen.
Martina Das kostet sicher auch etwas, oder?
Jens Ja, aber nicht viel: 10 Euro für einen ganzen Tag. Oh, und wir können auch kostenlos Filme auf DVD ausleihen.
Martina Jens, Filme schauen wir uns zu Hause an, nicht im Urlaub!
Jens Ja, du hast recht.

Day 19

Dialogue questions

1. gut | ~~schlecht~~ – **2.** dem Riesenrad | ~~der Achterbahn~~ – **3.** ~~sehr gern~~ | lieber nicht – **4.** Iwona | ~~Pierre,~~ Martina | ~~Jens~~.

1 **1.** 3) – **2.** 4) – **3.** 2) – **4.** 5) – **5.** 1) – **6.** *remaining*

Listening text

1. Am Abend sinken die Temperaturen. In der ganzen Nacht ist mit Gewittern zu rechnen. – **2.** Vor allem im Süden heute den ganzen Tag Schneefall. Die Temperaturen liegen um -5 Grad. – **3.** Heute wird es richtig warm! Die Sonne scheint den ganzen Tag und die Temperaturen steigen bis auf 28 Grad. – **4.** Im Norden scheint zwar immer wieder die Sonne, aber es bleibt den ganzen Tag bewölkt. Die Temperaturen liegen zwischen 5 und 10 Grad. – **5.** Vergessen Sie heute Ihren Regenschirm nicht! Am Nachmittag ziehen dicke Regenwolken auf und es regnet bis in die Nacht.

2 **Possible solution**

1. Hi! Ich bin auf dem Oktoberfest. Es ist toll, die Sonne scheint und es gibt viele Leute. LG – **2.** Wie geht's dir? Wie ist das Wetter (bei euch)? bb – **3.** Ich bin jetzt auf dem Oktoberfest und warte an / bei der Achterbahn. cu! – **4.** Hier ist es bewölkt und kühl. Aber ich mag das!

3 **1.** c) – **2.** d)– **3.** a) – **4.** e) – **5.** b)

Day 20

Dialogue questions

1. a) – **2.** a) – **3.** b) – **4.** b)

1 **1.** Mein Bauch tut weh. – **2.** Mein Zahn schmerzt. / Meine Zähne schmerzen. – **3.** Mein Hals tut weh. – **4.** Mein Ohr schmerzt. / Meine Ohren tun weh. – **5.** Mein Kopf schmerzt.

2 **1.** eine Allergie – **2.** eine Erkältung – **3.** gebrochen – **4.** eine Grippe – **5.** Rückenschmerzen – **6.** eine Verletzung – **7.** gesund

Listening text

1. Martina In der Nähe einer Katze muss ich immer niesen.
2. Jens Ich fühle mich schlecht und muss viel husten.

3. Johannes — Ich kann gar nicht mehr gehen.
4. Pierre — Ich habe starkes Kopfweh und hohes Fieber.
5. Iwona — Oh, mein Rücken tut so weh.
6. Peter — Mein Arm ist stark geschwollen und schmerzt.
7. Claudia — Also ich fühle mich so richtig gut!

3 **Es war** Freitag, der 13. März. **Ich bin** im Park spazieren **gegangen**. **Ich habe** ein Fahrrad kommen **gehört** und **mich umgedreht**. Ein Mann auf einem Fahrrad **ist** sehr schnell in **meine** Richtung **gefahren**. Er **hat mich** nicht **gesehen**. Im letzten Moment **konnte** der Mann ausweichen. Aber **ich bin ausgerutscht** und **hingefallen**. **Meine** rechte Hand **hat wehgetan** und **ich konnte** sie nicht mehr bewegen.

Day 21

Dialogue questions

1. Am Samstag. – **2.** Sie sind ins/zum Hotel gegangen. – **3.** Die Stadtrundfahrt. – **4.** Am Nachmittag.

1 *Grade:* **1.** gar nicht – **2.** wenig – **3.** nicht so – **4.** ein bisschen – **5.** etwas – **6.** sehr – **7.** total – *Frequency:* **1.** nie **2.** selten **3.** manchmal **4.** oft **5.** immer

2 **1.** Prag: ☺ Martina, Jens – **2.** die Fahrt: ☹ Jens – **3.** die Innenstadt: ☺ Martina – **4.** die Kirchen: ☺ Martina, ☹ Jens – **5.** die Burg: ☺ Jens, ☹ Martina – **6.** die Läden: ☺ Martina, Jens – **7.** der Urlaub: ☺ Martina, Jens

Listening text

Martina Wir waren ein paar Tage in Prag. Prag ist eine tolle Stadt. Der Urlaub hat mir total gefallen.

Jens Ja, mir hat Prag auch gefallen. Aber die Fahrt war nicht so toll, denn wir sind lange im Stau gestanden.

Martina Besonders schön finde ich die alte Innenstadt von Prag – die Häuser und Kirchen ...

Jens Naja, die Kirchen waren etwas langweilig – das mag ich nicht so sehr. Mir hat aber die Burg gefallen. Die war total spannend!

Martina Ach, du und deine Burgen. Ich finde, dass die Burg etwas langweilig war. Aber wir waren auch shoppen. Prag hat viele Läden. Das finde ich toll!

Jens Ja, stimmt. Das ist interessant, fast wie im Museum. Da kann man alles finden. Ach, es war einfach ein schöner Urlaub!

3 **Possible solution**

1. Ich war in einer Ausstellung. Das hat mir gefallen. Das war interessant. – **2.** Ich war in einer Kirche. Das hat mir wenig gefallen. Das war eintönig. – **3.** Ich habe einen Spaziergang gemacht. Das hat mir sehr gefallen. Das war toll. – **4.** Ich bin mit dem Zug gefahren. Das hat mir gar nicht gefallen. Das war langweilig. – **5.** Ich war auf dem Markt. Das hat mir nicht so gefallen. Das war nicht interessant. – **6.** Ich war in einem Restaurant. Das hat mir total gefallen. (Das Essen war gut.)

Day 22

1 **haben**: geregnet, angesehen, ausgefüllt, eingecheckt, gefunden, gefallen, gehustet, gemacht, geniest, geplant, geschmerzt, übernachtet, übersehen, verletzt, wehgetan, geschneit – **sein**: ausgerutscht, gefahren, gegangen, hingefallen, weggefahren

2 **1.** Halsweh – **2.** Baustelle – **3.** Gesundheit – **4.** Sitzplatz – **5.** Bratwurst – **6.** wenig

3 **1.** bin – **2.** habe – **3.** habe – **4.** sind – **5.** habe – **6.** hat – **7.** haben – **8.** haben – **9.** sind – **10.** war – **11.** hat – **12.** haben – **13.** habe – **14.** bin

4 **1.** die Kirche – **2.** der Bahnhof – **3.** die Post – **4.** das Restaurant – **5.** der Supermarkt

Listening text

1. Fahren Sie hier vorne rechts. Am Kino biegen Sie links ab und fahren dann immer geradeaus bis ans Ende der Straße. – **2.** Ah, das ist einfach. Gehen Sie einfach geradeaus. Dann die zweite Straße links. Dann ist es nicht mehr weit. – **3.** Hmm, am besten gehen Sie hier vorne links und dann die nächste Straße rechts. Dann geradeaus und die zweite Straße links. – **4.** Gehen Sie geradeaus. An der zweiten Kreuzung gehen Sie rechts und dann einfach geradeaus bis ans Ende der Straße. – **5.** Hier vorne biegen Sie links ab. Dann die zweite Straße rechts und Sie sind fast da.

5 **1.** Im – **2.** um – **3.** Am – **4.** im – **5.** a) Am b) um – **6.** a) Am b) am

6 **1.** Iwona und Pierre sind gestern einkaufen gegangen. / Gestern sind Iwona und Pierre ... – **2.** Du hast die Aufgabe richtig gemacht! – **3.** Wann hat Martina im Hotel eingecheckt? – **4.** Was hast du in München gesehen? – **5.** Ich bin gestern nach Hamburg gefahren. / Gestern bin ich nach H. gefahren. / Nach H. bin ich gestern gefahren.

7 **Listening text**

1. Und wann gehen wir dann ins Theater? – **Am Mittwoch, den 3. Juli**. – **2.** Oh, ich dachte wir gehen am 6. Juli. – **Nein, am Samstag wollen wir eine Radtour machen**. – **3.** Ach so, stimmt. Und um wie viel Uhr beginnt das Theater? – **Um 19.30 Uhr**. – **4.** Gut. Wie kommen wir zum Theater? – **Am besten nehmen wir den Bus**. – **5.** Gibt es dort denn eine Bushaltestelle? – **Nicht direkt. Wir müssen noch 5 Minuten laufen**.

Not used: Im Sommer fahren wir Fahrrad.

8 **1.** uns – **2.** a) sich b) mich – **3.** dich – **4.** sich – **5.** euch

9 **1.** wrong – **2.** right – **3.** wrong – **4.** right – **5.** right

Listening text

In Berlin scheint heute die Sonne. Die Temperaturen liegen dabei um 20 Grad. Am Abend ziehen Wolken auf und es ist mit Gewittern zu rechnen. – München. Vormittags bewölkt und windig, nachmittags starker Regen und kühl. Die Höchsttemperaturen liegen bei 11 Grad. – Guten Morgen in Köln. Achtung auf den Straßen: Dichter Nebel und Temperaturen um -2 Grad. Fahren Sie vorsichtig! – Hallo Hamburg! Heute haben wir wieder richtiges Sommerwetter. Der Regen ist vorbei, die Sonne scheint und es wird bis zu 30 Grad heiß! – Stuttgart. Heute den ganzen Tag Temperaturen unter null Grad und Schnee.

10 **1.** denn – **2.** aber – **3.** und – **4.** oder – **5.** und – **6.** aber – **7.** denn

11 **1.** 15 Minuten. – **2.** Aus Hamburg. – **3.** Nach Potsdam. – **4.** Der Eurocity (146). – **5.** Auf Gleis 7. – **6.** Nach München.

Listening text

Bitte Vorsicht an Gleis 3. Der Intercity aus Hamburg fährt soeben ein. – Verehrte Fahrgäste, der ICE 935 nach München, planmäßige Abfahrt 9.15 Uhr, hat voraussichtlich 15 Minuten Verspätung. Ich wiederhole: Der ICE 935 nach München hat voraussichtlich 15 Minuten Verspätung. – Verehrte Reisende, aufgrund von Gleisarbeiten fährt der Regionalexpress nach Potsdam heute von Gleis 7 ab. Ich wiederhole: Der Regionalexpress nach Potsdam fährt heute von Gleis 7 ab. – Herzlich Willkommen in Berlin Hauptbahnhof. Sie haben Anschluss an den Eurocity 146 nach Hamburg, Abfahrt 14.27 Uhr auf Gleis 2.

12 Im Frühling gibt es selten Schnee. Aber es regnet oft und es ist kühl. Es ist auch häufig windig. – Im Sommer ist es oft heiß. Manchmal gibt es Gewitter und ab und zu regnet es. – Im Herbst ist es oft bewölkt und neblig. Manchmal scheint die Sonne. Es schneit selten, aber es ist oft kalt. – Im Winter ist es oft kalt. Manchmal schneit es und ab und zu regnet es auch. Es gibt auch oft Eis.

13 *Think about a city you'd like to visit and say, what you would do there. Use* **"ich will"** and **"ich möchte"** *or* **"ich plane"**. *You'll find additional vocabulary in lesson 9.*

14 **1.** Körperteile – **2.** Fahrgeschäfte – **3.** Züge / Bahn – **4.** Wetter – **5.** Bahnhof – **6.** Krankenhaus – **7.** Krankheiten

15 **1.** Als – **2.** wenn – **3.** a) Als b) wenn – **4.** Wenn – **5.** wenn

16 **Grippe**: Ich habe Fieber und Kopfweh. – **Allergie**: Ich muss oft niesen. – **Erkältung**: Ich muss husten und fühle mich schlecht. – **Halsweh**: Mein Hals tut weh (und ich muss husten). – **Verletzung am Knöchel**: Mein Knöchel ist geschwollen und schmerzt.

17 **1.** Grippe – **2.** niesen – **3.** Halsweh – **4.** Bauch – **5.** Erkältung – **6.** Hand – **7.** Knochen – **8.** Krankheit – **9.** Fieber – **10.** husten – **Solution**: Gesundheit

Intermediate test 3

1 **1.** Jugendherberge – **2.** sind – **3.** haben – **4.** Doppelzimmer – **5.** Betten – **6.** Stockwerk – **7.** Morgens – **8.** für – **9.** Wir – **10.** einen Fahrradverleih – **11.** Wollen – **12.** immer – **13.** Fragen – **14.** Sehenswürdigkeiten – **15.** denn – **16.** Englisch – **17.** sprechen – **18.** uns

2 **1.** wrong – **2.** right – **3.** right – **4.** wrong – **5.** wrong – **6.** wrong – **7.** right – **8.** right

3 **1.** 4) – **2.** 5) – **3.** 2) – **4.** 1) – **5.** 3)

Listening text

1.

▸ Du, wollen wir damit auch fahren?

◂ Na klar, mit der Achterbahn wollte ich immer schon mal fahren!

2.

▸ Guten Tag, was kann ich für Sie tun?

◂ Ich möchte heute abreisen.

▸ Kein Problem. Ich brauche dann den Zimmerschlüssel und mache die Rechnung fertig.

3.

▸ Entschuldigen Sie bitte. Können Sie mir sagen, wie ich zum Bahnhof komme?

◂ Ja, natürlich. Gehen Sie die nächste Straße rechts und an der Baustelle links. Dann einfach geradeaus.

▸ Vielen Dank. Auf Wiedersehen.

4.

▸ Guten Tag, Herr Schirmer. Haben Sie Ihre Versicherungskarte dabei?

◂ Ja ... bitte schön.

▸ Danke. Sie können dann im Wartezimmer Platz nehmen.

5.

▸ Der Zug nach Hamburg fährt von Gleis 12. Das ist dort hinten.

◂ Ja, ich weiß. Ich brauche aber noch eine Fahrkarte ...

4 **1.** aus – **2.** nach – **3.** zur – **4.** a) nach b) mit dem c) mit der – **5.** Seit – **6.** beim

5 **1.** c) – **2.** b) – **3.** c) – **4.** b) – **5.** c)

Listening text
Hallo, ich bin David. Das sind meine Pläne für den Sommer: Am 14. Juli gehe ich nach England. Dort bleibe ich 8 Tage. Zuerst besichtige ich London. Dort bin ich 4 Tage. Dann fahre ich nach Oxford und zuletzt nach Brighton. In London will ich den Tower sehen und zu Madame Tussauds. Ich möchte auch in den Hyde Park, aber nicht ins British Museum. Weil ich Geschichte* sehr spannend finde und Städte mag, fahre ich danach nach Oxford. Das wollte ich schon immer sehen. In Brighton möchte ich dann schwimmen und faulenzen, aber nichts mehr besichtigen und nichts einkaufen.
* die Geschichte = *history*

6 **1.** was du in Prag besichtigt hast. – **2.** wo das Hotel „Seeblick" ist? – **3.** wie Sie sich verletzt haben. – **4.** wer dir geschrieben hat? – **5.** wann du im Urlaub warst. – **6.** warum du das gemacht hast?

Evaluation

maximal:	50 points
sehr gut:	45–50
gut:	35–44
in Ordnung:	25–34

Day 23

Dialogue questions

1. wrong – **2.** wrong – **3.** right – **4.** right

1 Listening text

1.
► Wollen Sie eine Nachricht hinterlassen?
◄ Ja. Richten Sie Frau Meier bitte aus, dass sie mich zurückrufen soll.
► Wie ist Ihre Telefonnummer?
◄ **0165 238723219**.

2. Sabine Keller. Rufen Sie mich bitte zurück. Meine Nummer ist **0049 89 874650**.

3.
► Silke Hinrichs.
◄ Pfeiffer, guten Tag. Kann ich bitte mit Herrn Rösner sprechen?
► Tut mir leid, Herr Rösner ist nicht hier. Aber Sie können ihn am Handy erreichen. Seine Nummer ist **0187 90274823**.
◄ Gut, vielen Dank. Auf Wiederhören!

4. Guten Tag. Sie sprechen mit dem Anschluss der Rufnummer **0221 2347854**. Bitte hinterlassen Sie eine Nachricht nach dem Piepston.

5.
► Gibst du mir deine Telefonnummer?
◄ Ja, gern. **069 134963**.
► Klasse! Ich melde mich bei dir!

6.
► Hallo?
◄ Becker hier, kann ich bitte Frau Greis sprechen?
► Nein, hier gibt es keine Frau Greis.
◄ Ist das nicht der Anschluss **0511 129873**?

▸ Nein, Sie haben sich verwählt.
◂ Entschuldigung, auf Wiederhören.
▸ Wiederhören.

2 **1.** Rufen Sie mich bitte zurück. – **2.** Meine Telefonnummer ist 030 998766. – **3.** Kann ich bitte mit Frau Meisner sprechen? – **4.** Am Apparat. – **5.** Bleiben Sie bitte am Apparat. – **6.** Entschuldigung, ich habe mich verwählt. – **7.** Kann ich etwas ausrichten? – **8.** Sagen Sie ihm bitte, dass ich angerufen habe. – **9.** Auf Wiederhören.

3 **1.** keinen – **2.** a) einen b) keinen – **3.** niemand / keiner – **4.** nichts / niemand / keinen – **5.** a) jemand / einer b) alle – **6.** keiner

Day 24

Dialogue questions

1. Ein paar Tipps für seine Bewerbung. – **2.** Er will in Deutschland arbeiten / weiterarbeiten / bleiben. – **3.** Per E-Mail. – **4.** Er scannt seine Zeugnisse ein. / Er verschickt seine Zeugnisse per E-Mail. / Er macht eine PDF-Datei aus seinen Zeugnissen.

1 **1.** Besprechung – **2.** Sehr geehrte – **3.** telefoniert – **4.** schicken – **5.** zwei – **6.** geplant – **7.** Fragen – **8.** Sie – **9.** mich – **10.** Mit freundlichen Grüßen

2 **1.** Iwona soll (Frau List) Details zur Besprechung schicken. – **2.** Drei Personen. – **3.** Wenn Frau List Fragen hat, soll sie Iwona anrufen oder eine E-Mail schreiben. / Sie soll (Iwona) anrufen oder eine E-Mail schicken.

3 **1.** Ich esse etwas, wenn ich Hunger habe. – **2.** Wenn wir nach München fahren, (dann) gehen wir auf das Oktoberfest. – **3.** Ich rufe dich an, wenn du mir deine Telefonnummer gibst.

Day 25

Dialogue questions

1. ~~Maler~~ | Gleisser – **2.** ~~Kaffee und Kuchen~~ | einem Bewerbungsgespräch – **3.** ~~ein Bewerbungsgespräch~~ | einen Zahnarzttermin – **4.** ~~an der Rezeption warten~~ | direkt ins Büro gehen

1 **1.** Am 4.5. – **2.** a) Im September. b) Um 14 Uhr. – **3.** a) Um 16 Uhr. b) Nein, er hat keine Zeit. – **4.** Der Termin ist am Donnerstag, im Juni 2011, um 9.30 Uhr (halb zehn). – **5.** Um 13.42 Uhr.

Listening text

1. ▸ Wann haben Sie denn Zeit?
◂ Ich habe am Dienstag, den 4. Mai, Zeit. Geht das?
▸ Ja, das geht! Danke.

2. ▸ Ich kann Ihnen einen Termin am 13.9. um 14 Uhr anbieten.
◂ Am 13.9.? Ja, das passt mir.

3. ▸ Können Sie am Freitagnachmittag um 4 Uhr zu mir kommen?
◂ Nein, tut mir leid. Am Freitagnachmittag habe ich keine Zeit.

4. ▸ Und wie ist es am Donnerstag, den 29.6.2011, um 9.30 Uhr morgens?
◂ Moment bitte ... Ja, der Termin passt – da habe ich Zeit!

5. ▸ Wann fahren Sie wieder nach Hause?
◂ Mein Zug fährt ab am Dienstag, um 13.42 Uhr.

2 **1.** Am Montag. / Im Juli. / Am Mittwoch um 16 Uhr. – **2.** An diesem Tag habe ich keine Zeit. / Tut mir leid. Leider nicht. / Ich habe meinen Terminkalender leider nicht hier. – **3.** An diesem Tag habe ich keine Zeit. / Ja, das passt mir gut. / Tut mir leid. Leider nicht. – **4.** An diesem Tag habe ich keine Zeit. / Ja, das passt mir gut. / Tut mir leid. Leider nicht. / Ich habe meinen Terminkalender leider nicht hier. – **5.** Am Montag. / Im Juli. / Am Mittwoch um 16 Uhr. – **6.** Am Mittwoch um 16 Uhr. / Am Montag.

3 **1.** die – **2.** der – **3.** den – **4.** dem – **5.** die

Day 26

Dialogue questions

1. wrong – **2.** right – **3.** wrong

1 **1.** a), b) – **2.** a), b) – **3.** b) – **4.** a), c)

2 **1.** wrong – **2.** wrong – **3.** right – **4.** right – **5.** right – **6.** wrong

Listening text

Pierre Iwona, bist du Mitglied bei einem Business-Netzwerk im Internet?

Iwona Ja, ich bin bei einigen Netzwerken Mitglied. Ich habe so schon einige interessante Kontakte geknüpft.

Pierre Denkst du auch, dass das wichtig ist?

Iwona Ja, das ist wichtig. Aber es ist auch sehr wichtig, dass man persönlich Kontakte knüpft und vor allem pflegt – nicht nur im Internet.

Pierre Aha. Und wie?

Iwona In deinem Beruf ist das vielleicht nicht wichtig, Pierre. Aber wenn man direkt mit Kunden arbeitet, dann ist das wichtig. Du gehst auf Veranstaltungen, redest mit den Leuten, verteilst deine Visitenkarten und so weiter.

Pierre Ah, ich verstehe. Vielleicht reicht ein Netzwerk im Internet für mich! Jens ist Mitglied bei Xing und ich seit zwei Tagen auch. Bist du dort auch?

Iwona Ja, aber noch nicht lange. Erst seit ich in Deutschland bin.

Pierre Cool, dann werde ich dich zu meinen Kontakten hinzufügen!

Iwona Mach das!

Day 27

Dialogue questions

1. a) – **2.** a) – **3.** b) – **4.** b)

1 **Listening text**

1. Guten Tag, **meine Damen und** Herren. – **2.** Ich **begrüße Sie sehr herzlich** zur heutigen Besprechung. – **3.** Ich möchte kurz **die Tagesordnungspunkte vorstellen**. – **4.** In der Präsentation **geht es um** neue Strategien. – **5.** Gibt es noch **Fragen**? – **6.** Dann sind alle Fragen **beantwortet**. – **7.** Vielen Dank **für Ihre Aufmerksamkeit**. – **8.** Auf **Wiedersehen**.

2 **1.** Geschäftsbericht 2009 – **2.** 11 Uhr – **3.** Frau Leser – **4.** Frau Leser

3 **1.** Das langweilige Buch. – **2.** Der schicke Anzug. – **3.** Die weißen Hemden. – **4.** Die sportlichen Schuhe.

Day 28

Dialogue questions

1. Sie findet sie wirklich hervorragend. – **2.** Das war das erste größere Projekt auf Deutsch. – **3.** Sie findet die Kollegen nett. – **4.** Auf das nächste Projekt, das Iwona übernimmt.

1 **1.** Achten Sie beim nächsten Mal bitte auf die Zeit. – **2.** Das war hervorragend. – **3.** Ihre Präsentation war etwas kurz. – **4.** Vermeiden Sie bitte die Anrede mit Du. – **5.** Dieses Verhalten ist hier unüblich. – **6.** Das haben Sie gut gemacht. – **7.** Ich habe eine Bitte: Seien Sie bitte etwas pünktlicher.

2 **1.** interessanten – **2.** langweiliges – **3.** guten – **4.** schnelles – **5.** großes – **6.** toller

3 **1.** b) – **2.** b) – **3.** b) – **4.** a) – **5.** a)

Listening text

Herr Kern	Frau Roth, vielen Dank, dass Sie den Vortrag gehalten haben.
Frau Roth	Gern geschehen, Herr Kern.
Herr Kern	Sie haben das gut gemacht. Aber achten Sie bitte etwas mehr auf die Zeit. Es war ein wenig lang.
Frau Roth	Ja, entschuldigen Sie. Ich hatte wenig Zeit für die Vorbereitung.
Herr Kern	Ich weiß. Das ist auch kein großes Problem. Aber Ihr Handout war sehr gut! Beim nächsten Mal bereiten Sie sich länger vor, dann ist die Präsentation sicher einwandfrei!
Frau Roth	In Ordnung. Ich hätte auch eine Bitte: Können Sie mir bitte beim nächsten Mal die Materialien früher schicken?
Herr Kern	Ja, natürlich.
Frau Roth	Vielen Dank.

Day 29

Dialogue questions

1. wrong – **2.** right – **3.** right – **4.** right

1 **1.** werde – **2.** wird – **3.** werden – **4.** werden – **5.** Werdet – **6.** Wirst

2 Ich würde (gern / am liebsten) eine Reise machen / anderen Menschen helfen / ...

3 **Listening text**

1. Was willst du später von Beruf werden? – **Ich will Lehrerin werden.** – **2.** Wo willst du in der Zukunft arbeiten? – **Ich würde gern in Deutschland arbeiten.** – **3.** Bleibst du nach deinem Praktikum in Deutschland? – **Nein. Ich würde gern in Deutschland arbeiten, aber ich muss zurück nach Japan.** – **4.** Ich würde mich gerne mit dir treffen. – **Ich auch, aber ich habe leider keine Zeit.** – **5.** Welche Sprache möchtest du am liebsten lernen? – **Ich würde am liebsten Russisch lernen!**

Day 30

1 **1.** Dokument – **2.** Schuhe – **3.** verschicken – **4.** Wunsch – **5.** Kantine – **6.** nervös

2 **1.** 3) – **2.** 2) – **3.** 1) – **4.** 4) – **5.** –

Listening text

1.

▸ Herzlich Willkommen. Als erstes spricht heute Herr Hahn von der Situation in der Firma.

◂ Ja, danke Frau Winkler. Kommen wir gleich zum ersten Punkt: dem aktuellen Geschäftsbericht ...

2.

▸ Haben Sie denn am Dienstag Zeit?

◂ Nein, tut mir leid. Da muss ich zum Arzt. Geht es auch am Mittwochnachmittag?

▸ Ja, das geht auch.

3.

▸ Kann ich bitte mit Frau Lorenz sprechen?

◂ Am Apparat!

▸ Ah, guten Tag, Frau Lorenz!

4.

▸ Wo haben Sie denn vorher gearbeitet?

◂ Ich habe nach meinem Studium ein Praktikum in einer deutschen Maschinenbaufirma gemacht.

3 **1.** Welcher – **2.** Was für einen – **3.** Welchen – **4.** a) welcher b) was für eine

4 **1.** schön, Das schöne – **2.** rot, Der rote – **3.** jung, Die jungen – **4.** langweilig, Die langweilige – **5.** spannend, Das spannende – **6.** lang, Die langen – **7.** zufrieden, Der zufriedene – **8.** voll, Die volle

5 **Possible solution**

(You normally say your name first. It's not necessary but polite to use a hello and a goodbye.)
1. Herr Beck, rufen Sie mich bitte zurück. Meine (Telefon-) Nummer ist 89771. (Auf Wiederhören.) – **2.** Frau Sander, ich brauche einen Beamer für meine Präsentation am Montag, den 22. (Auf Wiederhören.) – **3.** Hallo Brian. Hast du am Freitag Zeit? Wir können ins Kino gehen. (Tschüs!) – **4.** Guten Tag, Herr Schumacher. Ich habe am Dienstag eine E-Mail geschrieben. Haben Sie die Zusammenfassung gelesen, die ich Ihnen geschickt habe? – **5.** Frau Engel, die Präsentation findet um 11 Uhr statt und nicht um 9 Uhr.

6 **1.** d) – **2.** e) – **3.** f) – **4.** b) – **5.** g) – **6.** a) – **7.** c)

7 **1.** a) – **2.** c) – **3.** a) – **4.** b) – **5.** c)

Listening text

Pierre	Iwona, wer ist das dort auf dem Foto?
Iwona	Wen meinst du?
Pierre	Den Mann im langen, schwarzen Mantel.
Iwona	Das ist mein Großvater.
Pierre	Aha ... und der Mann daneben mit dem grünen Jackett – ist das dein Vater?
Iwona	Nein, sein Bruder, also mein Onkel.
Pierre	Dann ist der Mann mit dem braunen Hut dein Vater, ja?
Iwona	Genau! Auf dem Foto hier: Pierre, bist du der kleine Junge mit der roten Mütze?
Pierre	Nein, das ist mein Freund Jean. Ich bin der mit der blauen Mütze.
Iwona	Oh, ihr seid euch aber sehr ähnlich.
Pierre	Stimmt. Und das Mädchen im roten Kleid ist meine Schwester Camille.
Iwona	Und deine andere Schwester?
Pierre	Julie? Sie ist nicht auf dem Bild. Sie ist da erst ein paar Monate alt.

8 **1.** jemand – **2.** a) dieser b) viele – **3.** a) einen b) keiner – **4.** a) jemand b) niemand – **5.** man – **6.** a) etwas b) ein paar – **7.** alles – **8.** a) ein b) jeden c) keiner

9 *Start your sentences with the same temporal adverbs as already there and then use* **"werde ich"** *and whatever your plans are. For example:* **"Heute Abend werde ich in eine Kneipe gehen."**

10 *Build your sentences with* **"Ich ziehe ... an."** *or like the two examples already there. Use the accusative. Possible combinations are:* einen roten Pullover, ein weißes Hemd, eine schwarze Jacke, eine blaue Hose, braune Schuhe, eine gelbe Mütze, einen grünen Schal, rote Socken, eine schwarze Jeans, ein grünes T-Shirt

11 **1.** in – **2.** oft – **3.** dass – **4.** viele – **5.** weil – **6.** die – **7.** Deshalb

12 **1.** Ein Mann | ~~eine Frau~~ – **2.** brauchen Zeit für die Familie | ~~sind keine Manager~~ – **3.** ~~Viele~~ | wenige – **4.** ~~Männer~~ | Frauen – **5.** mehr | ~~weniger~~

13 **Listening text**

1.

▸ Können wir uns am **24. März** treffen?

◂ Ja, wir können uns am 24. März treffen.

2.

▸ Hast du am **8. September** Zeit?

◂ Nein, ich habe am 8. September keine Zeit.

3.

▸ Und geht es vielleicht am **13.10.**?

◂ Ja, am 13.10. geht es.

4.

▸ Haben Sie am **6. Juli** Zeit?

◂ Nein, am 6. Juli habe ich keine Zeit.

14 **1.** Ich lese das Buch, das ich vor einer Woche gekauft habe. – **2.** Deine Schwester, die jünger ist, geht noch in die Schule. – **3.** Ich bringe den Kindern, die ich besuche, Geschenke mit. – **4.** Meine Freunde, mit denen ich in Urlaub fahre, sind toll. – **5.** Pierres Mutter, an die er / Pierre oft denkt, lebt in Frankreich. – **6.** Ich denke an meinen Bruder, dem ich noch eine E-Mail schreiben muss.

15 **1.** elegant – **2.** schick – **3.** Hut – **4.** Handschuh – **5.** gepflegt – **6.** locker – **7.** auffällig – **8.** Unterwäsche – **9.** Schmuck – **10.** Schal – **11.** Kostüm – **12.** Kleid – **13.** Kleidung – **14.** Krawatte – **15.** Mantel – **16.** anziehen – **17.** Schuh – **18.** bunt

Solution: Bluse

Final test

1 **1.** fährt – **2.** schläfst – **3.** gehen – **4.** hält – **5.** läufst – **6.** sind

2 **1.** machen – **2.** klettern – **3.** schwimmen – **4.** spielen – **5.** sein – **6.** (Rad) fahren – **7.** haben – **8.** ausleihen – **9.** machen – **10.** wollen – **11.** mitnehmen – **12.** finden

3 **1.** a) schwarze b) elegantes – **2.** a) guter b) beste (bessere) – **3.** schnellste – **4.** netten – **5.** a) kleinen b) roten c) großen – **6.** tollen

4 **1.** Hals – **2.** Film – **3.** Hobby – **4.** Tante – **5.** Müll – **6.** Suppe

5 **1.** 4) – **2.** 1) – **3.** – – **4.** 2) – **5.** 3) – **6.** –

Listening text

1.

▸ Möchten Sie mit Kreditkarte zahlen?

◂ Ja. Hier, bitte.

▸ Möchten Sie auch eine Tüte?

◂ Oh ja, bitte.

2.
‣ Ich hätte gerne das Schnitzel mit Reis und einen Salat.
◂ Gut. Wollen Sie auch eine Suppe?
‣ Nein, danke.
3.
‣ Mensch, ist das langweilig.
◂ Ja, das nächste Mal sehen wir uns einen Thriller an.
4.
‣ Wo stehen denn die Getränke?
◂ Dort, im Wohnzimmer. Da gibt es auch etwas zu essen.
‣ Danke!

6 **1.** du – **2.** euch – **3.** ihr – **4.** ihm – **5.** Sie – **6.** es

7 ***m* (der):** Vortrag, Punkt, Kontakt, Termin, Terminkalender, Abschluss, Arbeitgeber – ***f* (die)**: Bewerbung, Kleidung, Verabredung, Nachricht, Abteilung, Ausbildung, Karriere, Rente – ***n* (das)**: Thema, Telefon, Gespräch, Büro, Buch, Dokument, Zeugnis, Verhalten, Projekt

8 **1.** In der Küche. / Das dreckige Geschirr ist in der Küche. – **2.** Im Schrank (im Schlafzimmer). / Die Kleidung ist im Schrank. – **3.** Auf dem Tisch. / Die sauberen Teller stehen auf dem Tisch. – **4.** Im Regal. / Die Gläser stehen im Regal. – **5.** Am Tisch. / Johanna sitzt (nach dem Aufräumen) am Tisch.

Listening text

Hallo, ich bin Johanna. Wenn ich aufräume, dann trage ich zuerst das dreckige Geschirr in die Küche. Dann lege ich meine Kleidung in den Schrank im Schlafzimmer. Dann staubsauge ich und spüle ab. Wenn das Geschirr sauber ist, dann stelle ich zwei Teller auf den Tisch. Die Gläser kommen ins Regal. Wenn ich dann fertig bin, setze ich mich an den Tisch und lese ein Buch.

9 **1.** Hallo, kommt bitte herein! Toll, dass ihr da seid. – **2.** Entschuldigung, wie komme ich zum nächsten Supermarkt? – **3.** Lass uns doch ins Kino gehen. –
4. Darf ich dir Philipp vorstellen? Wir arbeiten zusammen. – **5.** Morgen koche ich für meine Freunde. Deshalb muss ich jetzt noch einkaufen. – **6.** Das haben Sie wirklich sehr gut gemacht.

10 **1.** dein – **2.** mein – **3.** seine – **4.** ihrem – **5.** deine – **6.** ihre – **7.** deinen – **8.** euren – **9.** unseren

11 **1.**~~immer so viele Kontakte wie möglich~~ | nur wenige gute Kontakte – **2.** mit seinem Kontakt auch kurz sprechen | ~~von seinem Kontakt nur eine Visitenkarte nehmen~~ – **3.** schon vor | ~~erst auf~~ – **4.** Interessen | ~~Hobbys~~.

12 **1.** Ja, ich sehe ihn. – **2.** Nein, ich will keins. – **3.** Ja, wir geben ihnen Geschenke. – **4.** Ja, ich habe eine. – **5.** Nein, sie ist nicht da. – **6.** Nein, die E-Mail / sie ist nicht von ihr.

13 **1.** Iwona will viele deutsche Bücher lesen. – **2.** Pierre muss für seinen Abschluss lernen. – **3.** Martina fliegt (mit Jens) ein paar Tage nach London.

Listening text

Martina Und was werdet ihr machen, wenn unser Deutschkurs zu Ende ist?

Iwona Ich habe wirklich viel gelernt. Ich glaube nicht, dass ich wieder einen Kurs mache. Aber ich will viele deutsche Bücher lesen.

Martina Das ist eine gute Idee! Und du, Pierre?

Pierre Zuerst werde ich jetzt für meinen Abschluss lernen. Vielleicht mache ich danach wieder einen Kurs, aber das weiß ich noch nicht. Was wirst du denn machen, Martina?

Martina Nach dem Kurs habe ich zwei Wochen frei und muss nicht arbeiten. Ich werde ein paar Tage mit Jens nach London fliegen.

Pierre Das ist toll. Viel Spaß dabei.
Martina Danke.

14 **1.** Haus – **2.** Jahreszeiten – **3.** Wetter – **4.** Monate – **5.** Sport – **6.** Obst

15 Listening text

1. Wie wird das Wetter morgen? – **Ich glaube, dass es morgen regnen wird.** – **2.** Was ist passiert? – **Ich bin hingefallen und habe mich an der Hand verletzt.** – **3.** Wann wollen wir uns treffen? – **Am liebsten am Donnerstag.** – **4.** Was hätten Sie denn gerne? – **Eine große Tasse Kaffee, bitte.** – **5.** Wie fahren wir denn nach Köln? – **Am besten mit dem Auto.** – **6.** Was machst du nach deinem Studium? – **Ich will Lehrer werden.**

16 **1.** i) – **2.** e) – **3.** h) – **4.** d)– **5.** f) – **6.** a) – **7.** c) – **8.** g)

17 **1.** ihrem – **2.** einen – **3.** viel – **4.** vielen – **5.** ein paar – **6.** der – **7.** viel – **8.** sein – **9.** seinen – **10.** das – **11.** die – **12.** den

18 **1.** Claudia hat 6 / sechs Stühle. – **2.** Der gelbe Tisch steht in der Küche. – **3.** Ein weißer Schrank steht im Wohnzimmer und im Bad. – **4.** Die Regale sind grün. – **5.** Im Wohnzimmer stehen ein brauner Tisch, (vier) schwarze Stühle, ein weißer Schrank, (zwei) Regale (und der Fernseher).

19 **1.** Wenn ihr wollt, dann **helfen** wir euch. – **2.** Ich **kaufe** gern auf dem Markt **ein**. – **3.** Du **bezahlst** heute die Rechnung im Restaurant. – **4. Können** Sie mir bitte **sagen**, wo der Bahnhof ist? – **5.** Wir fahren am Wochenende nach Hamburg, denn ich **war** noch nicht in Hamburg. – **6.** Ich denke, dass du den Vortrag gestern gut **gemacht hast**.

20 **1.** Ich habe einen wichtigen Termin am Donnerstag um 9 Uhr. / Am Donnerstag um 9 Uhr habe ich einen wichtigen Termin. / Ich habe am Donnerstag um 9 Uhr einen wichtigen Termin. – **2.** Wir werden zusammen einen interessanten Vortrag halten. / Wir werden einen interessanten Vortrag zusammen halten. – **3.** Wann hast du die E-Mail verschickt? – **4.** Werdet ihr jetzt in ein Café gehen? – **5.** Er musste erst einen Termin vereinbaren. / Erst musste er einen Termin vereinbaren. – **6.** Wen haben Sie gestern angerufen?

21 **1.** c) – **2.** b) – **3.** c) – **4.** c)

Listening text

- ▸ Firma Maurer. Gabriele Schneider am Apparat.
- ◂ Paul Meyer. Guten Tag, Frau Schneider.
- ▸ Guten Tag, wie kann ich Ihnen helfen?
- ◂ Ich würde gerne mit Herrn Thomas sprechen. Ist er da?
- ▸ Nein, tut mir leid. Herr Thomas ist heute nicht im Büro. Kann ich Ihnen helfen?
- ◂ Ja, vielleicht. Es geht um einen Termin nächste Woche. Ich bin am Donnerstag, den 17.4., um 9.30 Uhr mit Herrn Thomas verabredet.
- ▸ Einen Moment bitte. Ich sehe eben im Terminkalender nach. Ah ja, hier steht ihr Termin.
- ◂ Gut. Leider habe ich vor 11 Uhr nun doch keine Zeit. Mein Chef braucht mich zu dieser Zeit. Kann ich um 11 Uhr kommen?
- ▸ Nein, tut mir leid. Herr Thomas hat schon einen Termin um 11 Uhr. Haben Sie am Nachmittag Zeit? Vielleicht um 14 Uhr?
- ◂ Ja, 14 Uhr geht bei mir auch.
- ▸ Gut. Kann ich Ihnen sonst noch helfen?
- ◂ Ja, können Sie Herrn Thomas bitte ausrichten, dass er mich zurückrufen soll. Ich muss ihm persönlich noch einige Fragen stellen, bevor wir uns treffen.
- ▸ Ich werde das ausrichten. Hat er Ihre Telefonnummer?
- ◂ Nein. Meine Nummer ist 0431 92833.

► 0431 92833. Gut, er wird sie anrufen.
◄ Vielen Dank. Auf Wiederhören.
► Auf Wiederhören.

22 **1.** arbeiten – **2.** E-Mail – **3.** telefonieren (sprechen) – **4.** Nachmittag – **5.** Besprechung – **6.** Kneipe / Bar – **7.** fährt – **8.** Bett

Evaluation

maximal:	150 points
sehr gut:	125–150
gut:	100–124
in Ordnung:	75–99

Alphabetical word list

A

abbiegen ['apbi:gn] turn
Abend, -e *m* [a:bənt] evening
Abendessen, – *n* ['a:bənt,ɛsn] dinner
abends ['abənts] in the evening
aber ['a:bɐ] but
abfahren ['apfa:rən] depart
Abfahrt, -en *f* ['apfa:rt] departure
abgeben ['apge:bn] deliver
ablenken ['aplɛŋkn] distract
Abreise, -n *f* ['apraɪzə] departure
Abschluss, -schlüsse *m* ['apʃlʊs] degree
Abschlusstest, -s *m* ['apʃlʊstɛst] final test
Absender, – *m* ['apzɛndɐ] sender
abspülen ['apʃpy:lən] wash up
Abteilung, -en *f* [ap'taɪlʊŋ] department
Ach! [ax] Oh!, Alas!
achten auf ['axtn auf] mind, pay attention
Achterbahn, -en *f* ['axtɐba:n] roller coaster
Actionfilm, -e *m* ['ɛkʃnfɪlm] action movie
ägyptisch [ɛ'gʏptɪʃ] Egyptian
Aha! [a'ha(:)] I see!
ähnlich ['ɛ:nlɪç] similar, alike
Aikido *(only Sg) n* [ai'ki:do] aikido
aktuell [aktu'ɛl] current
alle ['alə] all
Allergie, -n *f* [alɛr'gi:] allergy
alles ['aləs] all, everything
Alles Gute! ['aləs 'gu:tə] All the best!
als [als] than
also ['alzo] thus
alt [alt] old
am [am] on
am Apparat [am apa'ra:t] speaking
Amerika *(only Sg) n* [a'me:rika] America
Ampel, -n *f* ['ampəl] traffic light
an [an] to, at, by
anbieten ['anbi:tn] offer
anderer, andere, anderes ['andərɐ, 'andərə, 'andərəs] other
anders ['andɐs] different
Angebot, -e *n* ['angəbo:t] offer
angenehm ['angəne:m] kind, pleasant
Anhang, -hänge *m* ['anhaŋ] attachment
ankommen ['ankomən] arrive
Ankunft, -künfte *f* ['ankunft] arrival
anmelden ['anmɛldn] register
anmerken ['anmɛrkn] notice
Anrede, -n *f* ['anre:də] title
Anreise, -n *f* ['anraɪzə] arrival
anreisen ['anraɪzn] arrive
Anruf, -e *m* ['anru:f] call
Anrufbeantworter, – *m* ['anru:fbə,-antvɔrtɐ] answering machine
anrufen ['anru:fn] call, phone
Anschluss, -schlüsse *m* ['anʃlʊs] line, telephone connection
ansehen ['anze:ən] see, view
ansprechen ['anʃpreçn] address
anstoßen ['anʃto:sn] chink glasses
Antwort, -en *f* ['antvɔrt] reply, answer
antworten ['antvɔrtn] reply, answer
anziehen ['antsi:ən] dress
Anzug, Anzüge *m* ['antsu:k] suit
Apfel, Äpfel *m* ['apfəl] apple
Apotheke, -n *f* [apo'te:kə] pharmacy
April *(only Sg) m* [a'pril] April
Arbeit *(only Sg) f* ['arbaɪt] job, work
arbeiten ['arbaɪtn] work
Arbeitgeber, – *m* [,arbaɪt'ge:bɐ] employer

Arbeitnehmer, – *m* [ˌarbaɪtˈneːmɐ] employee
arbeitslos [ˈarbaɪtsloːs] unemployed
Arbeitsplatz, -plätze *m* [ˈarbaɪtsplats] job, position
Architekt, -en *m* [arçiˈtɛkt] architect (male)
Architektin, -nen *f* [arçiˈtɛktɪn] architect (female)
Arm, Arme *m* [arm] arm
Art, -en *f* [aːrt] kind, type
Arzt, Ärzte *m* [artst] doctor (male)
Ärztin, -nen *f* [ˈɛrtstɪn] doctor (female)
Asien *(only Sg) n* [ˈaːzjən] Asia
auch [aux] too
auf [auf] on, to
Auf Wiederhören! [auf ˈviːdɐˌhøːrən] Good-bye! (on the phone)
Auf Wiedersehen! [auf ˈviːdɐˌzeːən] Good-bye!
Aufenthalt, -e *m* [ˈaufɛnthalt] stay
auffällig [ˈauffɛlɪç] flashy
Aufgabe, -n *f* [ˈaufgaːbə] exercise
aufgehen [ˈaufgeːən] rise
aufhängen [ˈaufhɛŋən] put, hang up
Aufmerksamkeit *(only Sg) f* [ˈaufmɛrksamkaɪt] attention
aufräumen [ˈaufrɔʏmən] clean up
aufrufen [ˈaufruːfn] call
aufstehen [ˈaufʃteːən] get up
auftreten [ˈauftreːtən] tread; appear
Aufzug, -züge *m* [ˈauftsuːk] elevator
August *(only Sg) m* [auˈgʊst] August
aus [aus] from
Ausbildung, -en *f* [ˈausbɪldʊŋ] education
auschecken [ˈaustʃɛkn] check out
ausdrucken [ˈausdrʊkn] print
Ausflug, -flüge *m* [ˈausfluːk] trip, tour
ausfüllen [ˈausfʏlən] fill
Ausgang, -gänge *m* [ˈausgaŋ] exit
ausgerechnet [ˈausgərɛçnət] just
ausleihen [ˈauslaɪən] borrow
ausrichten [ˈausrɪçtn] leave/deliver a message
ausrutschen [ˈausrʊtʃn] slip
außerhalb [ˈausɐhalp] out of
aussteigen [ˈausʃtaɪgn] alight, get off
Ausstellung, -en *f* [ˈausʃtɛlʊŋ] exhibition
aussuchen [ˈaussuːxən] choose
Australien *(only Sg) n* [ausˈtraːljən] Australia
ausweichen [ˈausvaɪçn] dodge
ausziehen [ˈaustsiːən] undress
authentisch [auˈtɛntɪʃ] authentic
Auto, -s *n* [ˈauto] car
Autobahn, -en *f* [ˈautobaːn] motorway

B

Bäckerei, -en *f* [ˈbɛkəraɪ] baker's shop
Bad, Bäder *n* [baːt] bathroom
Badezimmer, – *n* [ˈbaːdəˌtsɪmɐ] bathroom
Bahn, -en *f* [baːn] train, railway
Bahnhof, -höfe *m* [ˈbaːnhoːf] station
Bahnsteig, -e *m* [ˈbaːnʃtaɪk] platform
bald [balt] soon
Banane, -n *f* [baˈnaːnə] banana
Bar, -s *f* [baːɐ] bar
Bauch, Bäuche *m* [baux] stomach, belly
Bauchweh *(only Sg) n* [ˈbauxveː] stomachache
bauen [ˈbauən] build
Baustelle, -n *f* [ˈbauʃtɛlə] construction site
beachten [bəˈaxtn] mind
Beamer, – *m* [ˈbiːmɐ] video projector
beantworten [bəˈantvɔrtn] answer
Becher, – *m* [ˈbɛçɐ] pot, cup

bedeuten [bə'dɔʏtn] mean
bedienen (sich) [zɪç bə'diːnən] help oneself
beeilen (sich) [zɪç bə'aɪlən] hurry
Beförderung, -en *f* [bə'fœrdərʊŋ] promotion
befreundet sein mit [bə'frɔʏndət] be friends with
beginnen [bə'gɪnən] start
begrüßen [bə'gryːsən] greet
Begrüßung, -en *f* [bə'gryːsʊŋ] welcome, reception
behandeln [bə'handəln] treat
Behandlung, -en *f* [bə'handlʊŋ] treatment
Behandlungsraum, -räume *m* [bə'handlʊŋsˌraum] surgery
bei [baɪ] at, by, next to
beide ['baɪdə] both, the two
beides ['baɪdəs] both, either
Beilage, -n *f* ['baɪlaːgə] side dish
Bein, -e *n* [baɪn] leg
Beispiel, -e *n* ['baɪʃpiːl] example
bekommen [bə'kɔmən] get
benutzen [bə'nʊtsən] use
Beruf, -e *m* [bə'ruːf] profession
beruflich [bə'ruːflɪç] job-related
besichtigen [bə'zɪçtɪgən] visit
besprechen [bə'ʃprɛçn] talk, discuss
Besprechung, -en *f* [bə'ʃprɛçʊŋ] meeting
Besprechungszimmer, – *n* [bə'ʃprɛçʊŋsˌ-tsɪmɐ] meeting room
besser ['bɛsɐ] better
Bestätigung, -en *f* [bə'ʃtɛːtɪgʊŋ] confirmation
bestellen [bə'ʃtɛlən] order
Besuch, -e *m* [bə'zuːx] visit
besuchen [bə'zuːxn] visit
Betreff, -e *m* [bə'trɛf] subject
Bett, -en *n* [bɛt] bed
bewegen [bə'veːgn] move
bewerben (für) [bə'vɛrbn] apply
Bewerbung, -en *f* [bə'vɛrbʊŋ] job application
Bewerbungsgespräch, -e *n* [bə'vɛrbʊŋs-gəʃprɛːç] job interview
bewölkt [bə'vœlkt] cloudy, overcast
bezahlen [bə'tsaːlən] pay
Bier, -e *n* [biːɐ] beer
Biergarten, -gärten *m* ['biːɐgartn] beer garden
bieten ['biːtn] offer
Bild, -er *n* [bɪlt] picture, image
billig ['bɪlɪç] cheap, inexpensive
Birne, -n *f* ['bɪrnə] pear
bis [bɪs] until, to
Bis bald! [bɪs balt] See you!
Bis später! [bis 'ʃpɛːtɐ] See you (later)!
bitte ['bɪtə] please
Bitte schön! ['bɪtə ʃøːn] Here you are!
bitten (um) ['bɪtn] ask
blau [blau] blue
bleiben ['blaɪbn] stay
Bluse, -n *f* ['bluːzə] blouse
Bodybag, -s *n* ['bɔdiːbɛk] shoulder/cross-body bag
Bonbon, -s *m+n* [bɔŋ'bɔŋ, bõ'bõː] sweet, candy
Bratwurst, -würste *f* ['braːtvʊrst] bratwurst
brauchen ['brauxn] need
braun [braun] brown
brechen ['brɛçn] break
Bretagne *(only Sg)* *f* [bre'tanjə] Brittany
Brezel, -n *f (Brezn, – f)* ['breːtsl ('breːtsn)] pretzel
bringen ['brɪŋən] get, bring
britisch ['brɪtɪʃ, 'briːtɪʃ] British
Brosche, -n *f* ['brɔʃə] brooch

Brot, -e *n* [broːt] bread
Brötchen, – *n* ['brøːtçən] bun
Bruder, Brüder *m* ['bruːdɐ] brother
Buch, Bücher *n* [buːx] book
buchen ['buːxn] book
Buchung, -en *f* ['buːxʊŋ] booking
Buchungsbestätigung, -en *f* ['buːxʊŋs-bɛˌʃtɛːtɪgʊŋ] booking confirmation
bügeln ['byːgəln] iron
Büro, -s *n* [bʏ'roː] office
Bundesland, -länder *n* ['bʊndəsˌlant] German state
bunt [bʊnt] colourful
Burg, -en *f* [bʊrk] castle
Bus, -se *m* [bʊs] bus
Bushaltestelle, -n *f* ['bʊshaltəˌʃtɛlə] bus stop
Business-Netzwerk, -e *n* ['bɪznɛs-nɛtsvɛrk] business network
Butter *(only Sg)* *f* ['bʊtɐ] butter

C

Café, -s *n* [ka'feː] café
Cent, (-s) *m* [(t)sɛnt] cent
Chef, -s *m* [ʃɛf] boss, manager (male)
Chefin, -nen *f* ['ʃɛfɪn] boss, manager (female)
chinesisch [çi'neːsɪʃ] Chinese
Chip, -s *m* [tʃɪp] crisp
Cola, –/-s *n/f* ['koːlaː] coke
Computer, – *m* [kɔm'pjuːtɐ] computer
Consultingfirma, -firmen *f* [kɔn'saltɪŋ-fɪrma] consulting ompany
cool ['kuːl] cool, awesome

D

da [daː] here, there
dabeihaben [da'baɪhaːbn] have
Dame, -n *f* ['daːmə] madam, lady
danach [da'naːx] afterwards
danke ['daŋkə] thanks, thank you
danken (für) ['daŋkn] thank
dann [dan] then
Darf ich ... vorstellen? [darf ɪç 'foːɐʃtɛlən] May I introduce ...?
darauf [da'rauf, 'daːrauf] afterwards; on it
darin [da'rɪn, 'daːrɪn] in that
darum [daː'rʊm] therefore, that's why
dass [das] that
Datei, -en *f* [da'taɪ] file
Daten *(only Pl)* ['daːtn] data
dauern ['dauɐn] take
Daumen drücken ['daumən ˌdrʏkn] keep one's fingers crossed
Daumen, – *m* ['daumən] thumb
davon [da'fɔn, 'daːfɔn] thereof, of it
dazu [da'tsuː] thereto, to it
dazukommen [da'tsuːkɔmən] join
denken (an) ['dɛŋkn] think
denn [dɛn] for, because
der, die, das [deːɐ, diː, das] the
deshalb ['dɛshalp] therefore, thus, hence
Detail, -s *n* [de'taj] detail
deutsch [dɔʏtʃ] German
Deutsche, -n *m* ['dɔʏtʃə] German
Deutschkurs, -e *m* ['dɔʏtʃkʊrs] German class
Deutschland *(only Sg)* *n* [dɔʏtʃlant] Germany
Deutschlehrer, – *m* ['dɔʏtʃleːrɐ] German teacher (male)
Deutschlehrerin, -nen *f* ['dɔʏtʃleːrərɪn] German teacher (female)
Deutschunterricht *(only Sg)* *m* ['dɔʏtʃʊntɐrɪçt] German class/lesson

Dezember *(only Sg) m* [de'tsɛmbɐ] December
Dialog, -e *m* [dia'lo:k] dialogue
Dienstag, -e *m* ['di:nsta:k] Tuesday
dieser, diese, dieses ['di:zɐ, di:zə, di:zəs] this, that
diese *Pl* ['di:zə] these
Ding, -e *n* [diŋ] thing
direkt [di'rɛkt] direct(ly)
Diskussion, -en *f* [dɪskʊ'sjo:n] discussion
doch [dɔx] however, yet
Dokument, -e *n* [dɔkʊ'mɛnt] document
Dom, -e *m* [do:m] cathedral
Donnerstag, -e *m* ['dɔnɐsta:k] Thursday
Doppelbett, -en *n* ['dɔpəlˌbɛt] double bed
Doppelzimmer, – *n* ['dɔpəlˌtsɪmɐ] double room
dort [dɔrt] there
Dose, -n *f* ['do:zə] can
downloaden ['daunlo:dn] download
Drama, Dramen *n* ['dra:ma] drama
draußen ['drausn] out here, outside
dreckig ['drɛkɪç] dirty
dringend ['drɪŋənt] badly
drucken ['drʊkn] print
drücken ['drʏkn] press
du [du:] you
dürfen ['dʏrfn] may
durch [dʊrç] through, by
Durchschnitt, -e *m* ['dʊrçʃnɪt] average
Dusche, -n *f* ['du:ʃə, 'dʊʃə] shower
duschen ['du:ʃn, 'dʊʃn] take a shower
DVD, -s *f* [de:vaʊ'de:] DVD

E

eben ['e:bn] a moment ago
ebenso ['e:bnzo:] the same, likewise
echt [ɛçt] real, really
Ehefrau, -en *f* ['e:əfrau] wife
ehemalig ['e:əma:liç] former
Ehemann, -männer *m* ['e:əman] husband
Ei, -er *n* [aɪ] egg
eigener, eigene, eigenes ['aɪgən] own
eigentlich ['aɪgntlɪç] actually
ein bisschen [ain 'bɪsçən] a bit
ein paar [aɪn 'pa:ɐ] (a) few
ein wenig [aɪn 've:nɪç] a little bit of
ein, eine, ein [aɪn, aɪnə, aɪn] a/an
Einbahnstraße, -n *f* ['aɪnba:nˌʃtra:sə] one-way street
einchecken in ['aɪntʃɛkn ɪn] check in
einfach ['aɪnfax] just, simply
einige [aɪnɪgə] some
Einkauf, -käufe *m* ['aɪnkauf] shopping
einkaufen ['aɪnkaufn] go shopping, shop
Einkaufsliste, -n *f* ['aɪnkaufsˌlɪstə] shopping list
einladen ['aɪnla:dn] invite
Einladung, -en *f* ['aɪnla:dʊŋ] invitation
Einleitung, -en *f* ['aɪnlaɪtʊŋ] introduction
einmal ['aɪnma:l] once
einsammeln ['aɪnsaməln] collect
einscannen ['aɪnskɛnən] scan
einschlafen ['aɪnʃla:fn] fall asleep
einsteigen in ['aɪnʃtaɪgn ɪn] board, get on
einstellen ['aɪnʃtɛlən] hire, employ
eintönig ['aɪntø:nɪç] monotonous
Eintrittskarte, -n *f* ['aɪntrɪtsˌkartə] ticket
einwandfrei ['aɪnvantˌfraɪ] flawless

einzeln ['aɪntsəln] single
Einzelzimmer, – *n* ['aɪntsəlˌtsɪmɐ] single room
Eis *(only Sg) n* [aɪs] ice
eisig ['aɪzɪç] icy
elegant [ele'gant] elegant
Eltern *(only Pl)* ['ɛltɐn] parents
E-Mail, -s *f* ['iːmeːl] e-mail
E-Mail-Adresse, -n *f* ['iːmeːlatrɛsə] e-mail address
empfangen [ɛm'pfaŋən] welcome, receive
Empfänger, – *m* [ɛm'pfɛŋɐ] recipient, receiver
Ende, -n *(mostly Sg) n* ['ɛndə] end
endlich ['ɛndtlɪç] finally
England *(only Sg) n* ['ɛŋlant] England
englisch ['ɛŋlɪʃ] English
Enkel, – *m* ['ɛŋkəl] grandchild (male)
Enkelin, -nen *f* ['ɛŋkəlɪn] grandchild (female)
entscheiden [ɛnt'ʃaɪdn] decide
entschuldigen [ɛnt'ʃʊldigən] excuse
Entschuldigung! [ɛnt'ʃʊldigʊŋ] Sorry!
Entschuldigung, -en *f* [ɛnt'ʃʊldigʊŋ] apology
er [eːɐ] he
erfolgreich [ɛɐ'fɔlkraɪç] successful
ergeben, sich [zɪç ɛɐ'geːbn] come along, arise
Erkältung, -en *f* [ɛɐ'kɛltʊŋ] cold
erklären [ɛɐ'klɛːrən] explain
erleben [ɛɐ'leːbn] experience
erleichtern [ɛɐ'laɪçtərn] make ... easy
Ermäßigung, -en *f* [ɛɐ'mɛːsɪgʊŋ] discount
ermitteln [ɛɐ'mitəln] investigate
erreichen [ɛɐ'raɪçn] reach
erst [eːɐst] first; only
erster, erste, erstes ['ɛɐstɐ, 'ɛɐstə, 'ɛɐstəs] first
Erwachsene, -n *m/f* [ɛɐ'vaksənə] adult, grown-up
erzählen [ɛɐ'tsɛːlən] tell
es [ɛs] it
essen ['ɛsn] eat
Essen, – *n* ['ɛsn] meal
Etage, -n *f* [e'taːʒə] floor, level
etwa ['ɛtva] about
etwas ['ɛtvas] somewhat, a little; something
Euro, (-s) *m* ['ɔʏro] Euro
Europa *(only Sg) n* [ɔʏ'roːpa] Europe

F

fahren ['faːrən] go, ride, drive
Fahrgeschäft, -e *n* ['faːɐgəʃeft] ride
Fahrkarte, -n *f* [CYRCAPfaːɐkartə] ticket
Fahrplan, -pläne *m* ['faːɐplaːn] timetable
Fahrrad, -räder *n* ['faːɐraːt] bicycle, bike
Fahrradverleih, -e *m* ['faːɐraːtfɛɐlaɪ] bike rental
Fahrt, -en *f* [faːrt] journey, trip; drive
Fall, Fälle *m* [fal] case
falsch [falʃ] wrong, false
Familie, -n *f* [fa'miːljə] family
fantastisch [fan'tastɪʃ] great, fantastic
Farbe, -n *f* ['farbə] colour
fast [fast] almost, nearly
faulenzen ['faulɛntsn] do nothing
Februar *(only Sg) m* ['feːbruaːɐ] February
fegen ['feːgn] sweep
fehlen ['feːlən] miss, be missing
Feiertag, -e *m* ['faɪɐtaːk] holiday
Ferien *(only Pl)* ['feːrjən] holiday
fernsehen ['fɛrnzeːən] watch TV

Fernsehen *(only Sg) n* [ˈfɛrnzeːən] television, TV
Fernseher, – *m* [ˈfɛrnzeːɐ] television
Fernsehturm, -türme *m* [ˈfɛrnzeːtʊrm] television tower
Fernsehzeitschrift, -en *f* [ˈfɛrnzeːtsaɪtʃrɪft] TV guide
fertig [ˈfɛrtɪç] ready, done
Festnetzanschluss, -schlüsse *m* [ˈfɛstnɛtsanʃlʊs] landline
Festzelt, -e *f* [ˈfɛsttsɛlt] festival tent
Fieber *(only Sg) n* [ˈfiːbɐ] fever
Film, -e *m* [fɪlm] film, movie
Filmverleih, -e *m* [ˈfɪlmfɛɐlaɪ] film rental
finden [ˈfɪndn] find, think
Firma, Firmen *f* [ˈfɪrma] company
Fisch, -e *m* [fɪʃ] fish
Flasche, -n *f* [ˈflaʃə] bottle
Fleisch *(only Sg) n* [flaɪʃ] meat
fliegen [ˈfliːgən] fly
Flipchart, -s *n* [ˈflɪptʃaːɐt] flip chart
Flug, Flüge *m* [fluːk] flight
Flugzeug, -e *n* [ˈfluːktsɔʏk] plane
Flur, -e *m* [fluːɐ] corridor
folgen [fɔlgn] follow
Formular, -e *n* [fɔrmʊˈlaːr] form
fortfahren [ˈfɔrtfaːrən] continue
Frage, -n *f* [ˈfraːgə] question
Fragebogen, -bögen *m* [ˈfraːgəboːgn] questionnaire
fragen (nach) [ˈfraːgn] ask
Frankreich [ˈfraŋkraɪç] France
französisch [franˈtsøːsɪʃ] French
Frau *(abbr. Fr.)* [frau] woman, wife, Ms
frei [fraɪ] free
Freitag, -e *m* [ˈfraɪtaːk] Friday
Freizeit *(only Sg) f* [ˈfraɪtsaɪt] leisure time
freuen, sich [zɪç ˈfrɔʏən] be pleased/glad/happy
Freund, -e *m* [frɔʏnt] friend (male), boyfriend
Freundin, -nen *f* [ˈfrɔʏndɪn] friend (female), girlfriend
frisch [frɪʃ] fresh
frisch machen (sich) [ˈfrɪʃ maxn] freshen up
froh [froː] glad
früh [fryː] early
früher [fryːɘ] earlier
Frühling, -e *(mostly Sg) m* [ˈfryːlɪŋ] spring
Frühstück, -e *(mostly Sg) n* [ˈfryːʃtʏk] breakfast
frühstücken [ˈfryːʃykn] eat breakfast
fühlen [ˈfyːlən] feel
Führungsposition, -en *f* [ˈfyːrʊŋspozɪtsjoːn] leadership position
für [fyːɐ] for
Fuß, Füße *m* [fuːs] foot
Fußball, -bälle *m* [ˈfuːsbal] football, soccer
Fußballplatz, -plätze *m* [ˈfuːsbalplats] football ground

G

Gabel, -n *f* [ˈgaːbəl] fork
ganz [gants] complete, completely
gar nicht [gaːɐ nɪçt] not at all
Garten, Gärten *m* [ˈgartn] garden
Gast, Gäste *m* [gast] guest
Gästezimmer, – *n* [ˈgɛstətsɪmɐ] guest room
geben [ˈgeːbn] give
Geburtsdatum, -daten *n* [gəˈbuːɐtsdaːtʊm] date of birth

Geburtstag, -e *m* [gə'buːɐtstaːk] birthday
Geburtstagsgeschenk, -e *n* [gə'buːɐtstaːksgəʃɛŋk] birthday present
Gedanke, -n *m* [gə'daŋkə] thought
geeignet [gə'aignət] suitable
gefallen [gə'falən] appeal, please; like
gehen ['geːən] go
gelb [gɛlp] yellow
Geld *(only Sg) n* [gɛlt] money
Gelenk, -e *n* [gə'lɛŋk] joint
gelten (für) ['gɛltn] apply
gelungen [gə'lʊŋən] successful
gemeinsam [gə'maɪnzaːm] common; together
Gemüse *(only Sg) n* [gə'myːzə] vegetable
genau [gə'nau] exactly
genießen [gə'niːsən] enjoy
Genre, -s *n* ['ʒãːrə] genre
genug [gə'nuːk] enough
gepflegt [gə'pfleːkt] neat, groomed
gerade [gə'raːdə] right now
geradeaus [gə'raːdəaus] straight on
Gern geschehen! [gɛrn gə'ʃeːən] You're welcome!
gern, gerne ['gɛrn(ə)] gladly
geschäftlich [gə'ʃɛftlɪç] on business, commercial
Geschäftsfrau, -en *f* [gə'ʃɛftsfrau] businesswoman
Geschäftsmann, -männer *m* [gə'ʃɛftsman] businessman
Geschenk, -e *n* [gə'ʃɛŋk] gift, present
Geschirr *(only Sg) n* [gə'ʃɪr] dishes
Geschirrspüler, – *m* [gə'ʃɪrʃpyːlɐ] dishwasher
geschlossen [gə'ʃlɔsn] closed
Geschwister *(only Pl)* [gə'ʃvistɐ] brothers and sisters
Gesetz, -e *n* [gə'zɛts] law
Gespräch, -e *n* [gə'ʃprɛːç] conversation, talk
gestern ['gɛstɐn] yesterday
gesund [gə'zunt] healthy
Gesundheit *(only Sg) f* [gə'zunthaɪt] health
Getränk, -e *n* [gə'trɛŋk] beverage, drink
Gewitter, – *n* [gə'vɪtɐ] thunderstorm
Gift, -e *n* [gɪft] poison
Glas, Gläser *n* [glaːs] glass
glauben (an) ['glaubn] think, believe
gleich [glaɪç] immediately, soon, same
gleichberechtigt ['glaɪçbəˌrɛçtɪkt] equal
Gleis, -e *n* [glaɪs] rails
Glück *(only Sg) n* [glʏk] luck
Glück haben [glʏk haːbn] be lucky
glücklich ['glʏklɪç] happy
Gott, Götter *m* [gɔt] god
Gramm *(only Sg) n* [gram] gramme, gram
gratulieren zu [gratʊ'liːrən] congratulate
Grippe, -n *f* ['grɪpə] flu
groß [groːs] big
großartig ['groːsartɪç] awesome
Großeltern *(only Pl)* ['groːsɛltɐn] grandparents
Großmutter, -mütter *f* ['groːsˌmʊtɐ] grandmother
Großvater, -väter *m* ['groːsˌfaːtɐ] grandfather
grün [gryːn] green
grüßen ['gryːsən] greet
Gruppe, -n *f* ['grʊpə] group
Gruß, Grüße *m* [gruːs] greeting, salutation
günstig ['gʏnstɪç] low priced
Gurke, -n *f* ['gʊrkə] cucumber

gut [guːt] good
Gute Nacht! [ˌguːtə 'naxt] Goodnight!
Guten Abend! [ˌguːtn 'aːbnt] Good evening!
Guten Morgen! [ˌguːtn 'mɔrgn] Good morning!
Guten Tag! [ˌguːtn 'taːk] Good day/ afternoon!

H

haben ['haːbn] have
Hähnchen, – *n* ['hɛːnçn] chicken
halb [halp] half
Hallo! ['haloː] Hello!
Hals, Hälse *m* [hals] neck, throat
Halsschmerzen *(only Pl)* ['halsʃmɛrtsn] sore throat
Halsweh *(only Sg) n* ['halsveː] sore throat
halten ['haltən] hold
halten von ['haltən fɔn] think
Haltestelle, -n *f* ['haltəˌʃtɛlə] stop
Hand, Hände *f* [hant] hand
Handout, -s *n* ['hɛndaut] handout
Handschuh, -e *m* ['hantʃuː] glove
Handy, -s *n* ['hɛndi] mobile phone
Handzettel, – *m* ['hantˌtsɛtəl] handout
häufig ['hɔʏfɪç] often
Hauptbahnhof, -höfe *m* ['hauptbaːnˌhoːf] main station
Hauptgericht, -e *n* ['hauptgəˌrɪçt] main dish
Hauptteil, -e *m* ['haupttaɪl] main part/section
Haus, Häuser *n* [haus] house
Hausarbeit, -en *f* ['hausarbaɪt] chore
Hausnummer, -n *f* ['hausˌnʊmɐ] house number
heiß [haɪs] hot
heißen ['haɪsn] be called
helfen ['hɛlfən] help
Hemd, -en *n* [hɛmt] shirt
Herbst, -e *(mostly Sg) m* [hɛrpst] autumn
hereinkommen [hɛ'raɪnˌkɔmən] come in
Herr, -en *m (abbr. Hr.)* [hɛr] sir, mister
herrichten ['heːɐrɪçtn] prepare
hervorragend [hɛɐ'foːɐraːgənt] excellent
herzlich ['hɛrtslɪç] dearly
Herzlich willkommen! ['hɛrtslɪç vɪl'kɔmən] Welcome!
Herzlichen Glückwunsch! ['hɛrtslɪçən 'glʏkvʊnʃ] Congratulations!
heute ['hɔʏtə] today
heutig ['hɔʏtɪç] today's
hier [hiːɐ] here
hineingehen [hɪ'naɪngeːən] go inside
hinfahren ['hɪnfaːrən] get/drive there
Hinfahrt, -en *f* ['hɪnfaːrt] journey there
hinfallen ['hɪnfalən] fall over
hinten ['hɪntn] (at the) back
hinter ['hɪntɐ] behind
hinterlassen ['hɪntɐlasn] leave
Hobby, -s *n* ['hɔbiː] hobby
hoch [hoːx] high
Hochhaus, -häuser *n* [hoːxhaus] high-rise building
hoffen ['hɔfn] hope
hoffentlich ['hɔfntlıç] hopefully
holen ['hoːlən] get, fetch
Honig *(only Sg) m* ['hoːnɪç] honey
hören ['hørən] listen; hear
Hose, -n *f* ['hoːzə] trousers
Hosenanzug, -züge *m* ['hoːzənˌantsuːk] pantsuit
Hotel, -s *n* [ho'tɛl] hotel

Hotelangestellte, -n *m* [ho'tɛlˌangəʃtɛltɐ] hotel clerk
Hunger *(only Sg) m* ['hʊŋɐ] hunger
hungrig ['hʊŋriç] hungry
Hurra! [hʊ'ra:] Hooray!
husten ['hu:stn] cough
Hut, Hüte *m* [hu:t] hat

I

ich [ɪç] I
Idee, -n *f* [i'de:] idea
ihr [i:ɐ] you
im Folgenden [ɪm 'fɔlgndən] in the follwing, hereafter
Im Notfall [ɪm 'no:tfal] if need be
immer ['ɪmɐ] always
in [ɪn] in
in der Nähe von [ɪn de:ɐ nɛ:ə] near, not far from
in Ordnung [ɪn 'ɔɐtnʊŋ] all right, be OK/fine
Informatiker, – *m* [ɪnfɔr'ma:tɪkɐ] computer scientist
Information, -en *f* [infɔrma'tsjo:n] information
informativ [ɪnfɔrma'ti:f] informative
informieren [ɪnfɔr'mi:rən] inform
inklusive [ɪnklʊ'zi:və] inclusive
Innenstadt, -städte *f* ['ɪnɛnˌʃtat] city centre
interessant [ɪnt(ə)rɛ'sant] interesting
Interesse, -n *n* [ɪnt(ə)'rɛsə] interest, hobby
international [ɪntɐnatsjo'na:l] international
Internet *(only Sg) n* ['intɐnɛt] internet
irgendwelche [ɪrgnt'vɛlçə] any
Italien [i'ta:ljən] Italy
italienisch [ital'je:nɪʃ] Italian

J

ja [ja:] yes
Jacke, -n *f* ['jakə] jacket
Jackett, -s *n* [ʒa'kɛt] jacket, suit jacket
Jahr, -e *n* [ja:ɐ] year
Jahreszeit, -en *f* [ja:rəstsaɪt] season
Januar *(only Sg) m* ['janua:ɐ] January
Japan ['ja:pan] Japan
japanisch [ja'pa:nɪʃ] Japanese
Jeans, – *f/Jeans (only Pl)* [dʒi:ns] jeans
jedenfalls ['je:dn'fals] anyway
jeder, jede, jedes ['je:dɐ, 'je:də, 'je:dəs] each
jemand ['je:mant] someone, somebody
jetzt [jɛtst] now
Job, -s *m* [dʒɔp] job
joggen ['dʒɔgən] run, jog
Joghurt, -s/– *m* ['jo:gʊrt] yogurt
Judo *(only Sg) n* ['ju:do] judo
Jugendherberge, -n *f* ['ju:gəntˌhɛrbɛrgə] youth hostel
Juli *(only Sg) m* ['ju:li:] July
jung [jʊŋ] young
Juni *(only Sg) m* ['ju:ni] June

K

Kaffee *(only Sg) m* ['kafe:, ka'fe:] coffee
kalt [kalt] cold
Kantine, -n *f* [kan'ti:nə] canteen
kaputt [ka'pʊt] broken, in pieces
kaputtmachen [ka'pʊtmaxn] break
Karate *(only Sg) n* [ka'ra:tə] karate
Karotte, -n *f* [ka'rɔtə] carrot
Karriere *(only Sg) f* [kar'je:rə] career
Karte, -n *f* ['kartə] ticket; map
Kartoffel, -n *f* [kar'tɔfl] potatoe
Karton, -s *m* [kar'tɔŋ] carton
Karussell, -s *n* [karʊ'sɛl] roundabout

Käse *(only Sg) m* ['kɛːzə] cheese
kaufen ['kaufn] buy
Kaufhaus, -häuser *n* ['kaufhaus] department store
kaum [kaum] hardly
kehren ['keːrən] sweep
kein [kaɪn] no
keinmal [kaɪnmaːl] not once, never
Kellner, – *m* ['kɛlnɐ] waiter
Kellnerin, -nen *f* ['kɛlnərɪn] waitress
kennen ['kɛnən] know
kennen (sich) [zɪç 'kɛnən] know each other
kennenlernen ['kɛnənlɛrnən] meet, get to know
Kilo, (-s) *n* ['kiːlo] kilo
Kind, -er *n* [kɪnt] child
Kindergarten, -gärten *m* ['kɪndɐˌgartn] nursery
Kindergärtner, – *m* ['kɪndɐˌgɛrtnɐ] nursery teacher (male)
Kindergärtnerin, -nen *f* ['kɪndɐˌgɛrtnərɪn] nursery teacher (female)
Kinderzimmer, – *n* ['kɪndɐtsɪmɐ] nursery, children's room
Kino, -s *n* ['kiːno] cinema
Kirche, -n *f* ['kɪrçə] church
klappen ['klapn] go off all right
klar [klaːr] clear
Klasse, -n *f* ['klasə] class
Kleid, -er *n* [klaɪt] dress
Kleidung *(only Sg) f* ['klaɪdʊŋ] clothes
Kleidungsstück, -e *n* ['klaɪdʊŋsʃtʏk] piece of clothing
klein [klaɪn] small, little
klettern ['klɛtɐn] climb
Klima *(only Sg) n* ['kliːma] climate
klingeln ['klɪŋəln] ring
Kneipe, -n *f* ['knaɪpə] pub, bar
Knöchel, – *m* ['knœçl] ankle
Knochen, – *m* ['knɔxn] bone
Koch, Köche *m* [kɔx] chef, cook (male)
kochen ['kɔxn] cook
Köchin, -nen *f* ['kœçɪn] chef, cook (female)
Kollege, -n *m* [kɔ'leːgə] colleague (male)
Kollegin, -nen *f* [kɔ'leːgɪn] colleague (female)
komfortabel [kɔmfɔɐ'taːbəl] comfortable
kommen ['kɔmən] come; get to; be on TV
Kommissar, -e *m* [kɔmɪ'saːɐ] detective, commissar
Kommode, -n *f* [kɔ'moːdə] chest of drawers
Komödie, -n *f* [kɔ'møːdiə] comedy
können ['kœnən] can
Könnte ich ...? ['kœntə ɪç] Could I ...?
Kontakt, -e *m* [kɔn'takt] contact
Kontakte knüpfen [kɔn'taktə ˌknʏpfn] make new contacts, socialise, network
Kontinent, -e *m* ['kɔntinɛnt] continent
Kontrolle, -n *f* [kɔn'trɔlə] control
Konzert, -e *n* [kɔn'tsɛrt] concert
Kopf, Köpfe *m* [kɔpf] head
Kopfschmerzen *(only Pl)* ['kɔpfʃmɛrtsn] headache
Kopfweh *(only Sg) n* ['kɔpfveː] headache
kosten ['kɔstn] cost
kostenlos ['kɔstnloːs] (for) free
Kostüm, -e *n* [kɔs'tyːm] female suite
krank [kraŋk] ill
Krankenhaus, -häuser *n* ['kraŋknˌhaus] hospital
Krankenkasse, -n *f* ['kraŋknkasə] health insurance company
Krankenschwester, -n *f* ['kraŋknˌʃvɛstɐ] nurse

Krankheit, -en *f* ['kraŋkhaɪt] illness
Krawatte, -n *f* [kra'vatə] tie
Kreditkarte, -n *f* [kre'diːtˌkartə] credit card
Kreuzung, -en *f* ['krɔʏtsʊŋ] crossroads
Krimi, -s *m* ['krɪmi] crime series, detective story
Kritik, -en *f* [kri'tiːk] criticism
kritisieren [kriti'ziːrən] criticise
Kuchen, – *m* ['kuːxn] cake, pie
Küche, -n *f* ['kʏçə] kitchen
kühl [kyːl] chilly, cool
Kunde, -n *m* ['kʊndə] client
Kurs, -e *m* [kʊrs] class, course
Kurve, -n *f* ['kʊrvə] turn
kurz [kʊrts] short(ly), brief(ly)

L

Laden, Läden *m* ['laːdn] shop
Lampe, -n *f* ['lampə] lamp
Land, Länder *n* [lant] country
lang(e) [laŋ] long
langsam ['laŋzaːm] slow(ly)
langweilig ['laŋvaɪlɪç] boring
Laptop, -s *m/f* ['lɛptɔp] laptop
lassen ['lasn] let
laufen ['laufn] run, jog
Laufstrecke, -n *f* ['laufˌʃtrɛkə] running route
leben ['leːbn] live
Leben, – *(mostly Sg) n* ['leːbn] life
Lebensmittel, – *(mostly Pl) n* ['leːbnsmɪtl] food
lecker ['lɛkɐ] delicious, tasty
legen ['leːgən] lay
Lehrer, – *m* ['leːrɐ] teacher (male)
Lehrerin, -nen *f* ['leːrərɪn] teacher (female)
leicht [laɪçt] easy
leider ['laɪdɐ] unfortunately
leidtun ['laɪdtuːn] be sorry
leihen ['laɪən] borrow, lend
Leistung, -en *f* ['laɪstʊŋ] performance
Lektion, -en *f* [lɛktsi'oːn] lesson
lernen ['lɛrnən] learn
Lerner, – *m* ['lɛrnɐ] student
lesen ['leːzn] read
letzter, letzte, letztes ['lɛtstɐ, 'lɛtstə, lɛtstəs] last
Leute *(only Pl)* ['lɔʏtə] people
lieb [liːp] nice, dear, beloved, good
lieb haben ['liːp ˌhaːbn] like/love you, be fond of
Liebe *(only Sg) f* ['liːbə] love
Liebe/Lieber ... ['liːbə, 'liːbɐ] Dear ...
lieber ['liːbɐ] rather, preferably
liegen ['liːgn] lie
links [lɪŋks] left
Liter, – *m* ['liːtɐ, 'lɪtɐ] litre
Lob *(only Sg) n* [loːp] praise
loben ['loːbn] praise
locker ['lɔkɐ] casual
Löffel, – *m* ['lœfl] spoon
Lust haben auf ['lʊst haːbn auf] be up for sth

M

machen ['maxn] make
Macht nichts! ['maxt nɪçts] Never mind!
Mai *(only Sg) m* [maɪ] May
mal, einmal [maːl] once
man [man] one, you
Manager, – *m* ['mɛnɛdʒɐ] manager
manche ['mançə] some
manchmal ['mançmaːl] sometimes
Mann, Männer *m* [man] man

Mantel, Mäntel *m* ['mantəl] coat
Markt, Märkte *m* [markt] market
Marktplatz, -plätze *m* [marktplats] market place
Marmelade, -n *f* [marmə'la:də] jam
März *(only Sg) m* [mɛrts] March
Maschinenbau *(only Sg) m* [ma'ʃi:nənbau] mechanical engineering
Material, -ien *n* [mater'ja:l] material
Mauer, -n *f* ['mauɐ] wall
Medium, Medien *n* ['me:diʊm] medium
mehr [me:r] more
mehrere ['me:rərə] several
Meine Güte! ['maɪnə 'gy:tə] Blimey!
meinen ['mainən] think, mean
Mensch! [mɛnʃ] Gosh!, Blimey!
Mensch, -en *m* [mɛnʃ] human (being), man
merken ['mɛrkn] notice
Messer, – *n* ['mɛsɐ] knife
Milch *(only Sg) f* [mɪlç] milk
Milchkaffee, -s *m* ['mɪlçkafe:] café au lait
Milchprodukt, -e *n* ['mɪlçpro,dʊkt] dairy product
Minute, -n *f* [mi'nu:tə] minute
mit [mɪt] with
Mitarbeiter, – *m* ['mɪtar,baɪtɐ] personnel
mitbringen ['mɪtbrɪŋən] bring along
Mitglied, -er *n* ['mɪtgli:t] member
mitkommen ['mɪtkɔmən] come along
mitnehmen ['mitne:mən] take along
Mittag, -e *m* ['mɪta:k] noon
Mittagessen, – *n* ['mɪta:k,ɛsn] lunch
mittags ['mɪta:ks] at noon
Mittwoch, -e *m* ['mɪtvɔx] Wednesday
Möbel, – *(mostly Pl) n* ['mø:bl] furniture
Mobiltelefon, -e *n* [mo'bi:ltele,fo:n] mobile phone
möcht- ['mœçt-] would like to
Moderation, -en *f* [modera'tsio:n] moderation
moderieren [mode'ri:rən] moderate
mögen ['mø:gn] like
möglich ['mø:klɪç] possible
Möglichkeit, -en *f* ['mø:klɪçkaɪt] possibility
Möhre, -n *f* ['mø:rə] carrot
Moment! [mɔ'mɛnt] Just a moment!
Moment, -e *m* [mɔ'mɛnt] moment
Monat, -e *m* ['mo:nat] month
Montag, -e *m* ['mo:nta:k] Monday
Mord, -e *m* [mɔrt] murder
Mörder, – *m* ['mœrdɐ] murderer
morgen ['mɔrgn] tomorrow
Morgen, – *m* ['mɔrgn] morning
morgens ['mɔrgns] in the morning
motivieren [mɔti'vi:rən] motivate
Müll *(only Sg) m* [mʏl] rubbish, trash
Müsli, -s *n* ['my:sli] muesli
müssen ['mʏsn] have to, must
Mütze, -n *f* ['mʏtsə] cap
Museum, Museen *n* [mʊ'ze:ʊm] museum
Mutter, Mütter *f* ['mʊtɐ] mother
Muttersprache, -n *f* ['mʊtɐ,ʃpra:xə] native language

N

na (ja) [na] well
Na klar! [na 'kla:r] Of course!
nach [na:x] to, toward, past, after
nach Hause [na:x 'hauzə] home
Nachbar, -n *m* ['naxba:r] neighbour
Nachmittag, -e *m* ['na:xmita:k] afternoon
nachmittags ['na:xmita:ks] in the afternoon

Nachname, -n *m* ['na:xna:mə] last name
Nachricht, -en *f* ['na:xrɪçt] message
Nachrichten *(only Pl)* ['na:xrɪçtn] news
nachschauen, nachschlagen ['na:xʃauən] look up
nächster, nächste, nächstes ['nɛ:kstɐ, 'nɛ:kstə, 'nɛ:kstəs] next
Nacht, Nächte *f* [naxt] night
Nachtisch *(only Sg) m* ['na:xtɪʃ] dessert
nah [na:] close, nearby
Name, -n *m* ['na:mə] name
Nase, -n *f* ['na:zə] nose
natürlich [na'ty:ɐlɪç] naturally, of course, sure, certainly
Nebel *(only Sg) m* ['ne:bl] fog
neben ['ne:bən] at, by, next to
neblig ['ne:blɪç] foggy
nehmen ['ne:mən] take
nein [naɪn] no
nennen ['nɛnən] mention
nervös [nɛr'vø:s] nervous
nett [nɛt] nice
Netzwerk, -e *n* ['nɛtsvɛrk] network
neu [nɔʏ] new
nicht [nɪçt] not
nicht mehr [nɪçt me:ɐ] not anymore, no longer
nichts [nɪçts] nothing
nicken ['nɪkn] nod
nie [ni:] never
niemand ['ni:mant] nobody, no one
niesen ['ni:zən] sneeze
noch [nɔx] still
noch einmal [nɔx 'aɪnma:l] once again
normal [nɔr'ma:l] normal
normalerweise [nɔr'ma:lɐwaɪzə] usually
Notfall, -fälle *m* ['no:tfal] emergency
Notiz, -en *f* [no'ti:ts] note
November *(only Sg) m* [no'vɛmbɐ] November
Nudel, -n *f* ['nu:dəl] noodles
Nummer, -n *f* ['nʊmɐ] number
nun [nu:n] now
nur [nu:ɐ] only, just
Nutzen *(only Sg) m* ['nʊtsən] use

O

ob [ɔp] if, whether
oben ['o:bən] above
Obst *(only Sg) n* [o:pst] fruit
oder ['o:dɐ] or
offen ['ɔfən] open
Öffnungszeit, -en *(mostly Pl) f* ['œfnʊŋstsaɪt] opening hours
oft [ɔft] often, a lot
Ohr, -en [o:ɐ] ear
Ohrenschmerzen *(only Pl)* ['o:rənˌʃmɛrtsn] earache
Oje! [o:'je:] Oh dear!
Oktober *(only Sg) m* [ok'to:bɐ] October
Onkel, – *m* ['ɔŋkl] uncle
online ['ɔnlaɪn] online
Online-Bewerbung, -en *f* ['ɔnlaɪn-bəˌvɛrbʊŋ] online application
Orange, -n *f* [o'rã:ʒə, o'raŋʒə] orange
Ordnung, -en *f* ['ɔrtnʊŋ] order
organisieren [ɔrgani'zi:rən] organise
Overheadprojektor, -en *m* ['o:vɐhɛt-pro:ˌjɛktɔɐ] overhead projector

P

Packung, -en *f* ['pakʊŋ] package, pack
Papier *(only Sg) n* [pa'pi:r] paper
Paprika, -s *m/f* ['paprika] peppers
Park, -s *m* [park] park

Parkplatz, -plätze *m* ['parkplats] parking (space)
Party, -s *f* ['pa:rti] party
Passant, -en *m* [pa'sant] passerby (male)
Passantin, -nen *f* [pa'santɪn] passerby (female)
passen (zu) ['pasn] fit, suit
passend ['pasnt] suitable, appropriate
passieren [pa'si:rən] happen
Pause, -n *f* ['pauzə] break
per [pɛr] by
Person, -en *f* [pɛr'zo:n] person
Personalausweis, -e *m* [pɛrzo'na:lausvaɪs] ID card
Personalchef, -s *m* [pɛrzo'na:lʃɛf] personnel manager
persönlich [pɛr'zø:nlɪç] personally
Pfirsich, -e *m* ['pfɪrzɪç] peach
pflegen ['pfle:gn] maintain; nurse
Pfleger, – *m* ['pfle:gɐ] male nurse
Piepston, -töne *m* ['pi:psto:n] beep, pip
Plan, Pläne *m* [pla:n] plan
planen ['pla:nən] plan, arrange, design
Planung, -en *f* ['pla:nʊŋ] planning
Platz nehmen ['plats ˌne:mən] take/ have a seat
Platz, Plätze *m* [plats] place; seat
plötzlich ['plœtslɪç] suddenly
Polen *(only Sg)* *n* ['po:lən] Poland
polnisch ['pɔlnɪʃ] Polish
Pommes (frites) *(only Pl)* ['pɔməs, pɔmfrɪt] chips, fries
populär [pɔpʊ'lɛ:ɐ] popular
Position, -en *f* [pozi'tsjo:n] position
Post *(only Sg)* *f* [pɔst] mail; post (office)
Posteingang, -gänge *m* ['pɔstaɪngaŋ] in-box
Postleitzahl, -en *f* ['pɔstlaɪttsa:l] postal code
Praktikum, Praktika *n* ['praktikʊm] placement
Präsentation, -en *f* [prɛzɛnta'tsjo:n] presentation
präsentieren [prɛzɛn'ti:rən] present
Preis, -e *m* [praɪs] price
prima ['pri:ma] great
privat [pri'va:t] private
Privatsender, – *m* [pri'va:tˌsɛndɐ] private (TV) station
pro [pro:] per
probieren [pro'bi:rən] taste, try
Problem, -e *n* [pro'ble:m] problem
Professor, -en *m* [pro'fɛso:ɐ] professor
Programm, -e *n* [pro'gram] programme; channel
Projekt, -e *n* [pro'jɛkt] project
prüfen ['pry:fn] check
pünktlich ['pʏnktlɪç] punctual
Pullover, – *m* [pu'lo:vɐ] jumper, sweater
Punkt, -e *m* [pʊŋkt] topic; point
putzen ['putsn] clean

Q

Quartal, -e *n* [kvar'ta:l] quarter
Quizsendung, -en *f* [kvizsɛndʊŋ] quiz show

R

Rad fahren ['ra:t fa:rən] cycle
Rad, Räder *n* [ra:t] bike; wheel
Radio, -s *n* ['ra:djo] radio
Radtour, -en *f* ['ra:ttu:ɐ] bicycle tour
Radverleih, -e *m* ['ra:tfɛɐlaɪ] bike rental
Ratgeber, – *m* ['ra:tge:bɐ] guide
Raum, Räume *m* [raum] room

Rechnung, -en *f* ['reçnʊŋ] bill
recht haben ['rɛçt ha:bn] be right
rechts [rɛçts] right
Rechtsanwalt, -anwälte *m* ['rɛçtsanvalt] lawyer (male)
Rechtsanwältin, -nen *f* ['rɛçtsanvɛltɪn] lawyer (female)
reden ['re:dn] talk
Regal, -e *n* [re'ga:l] shelf
Regen *(only Sg) m* ['re:gn] rain
Regenschirm, -e *m* ['re:gnʃɪrm] umbrella
regnen ['re:gnən] rain
regnerisch ['re:gnərɪʃ] rainy
reichen ['raɪçn] be enough
Reis *(only Sg) m* [raɪz] rice
Reise, -n *f* ['raɪzə] journey, trip, tour
reisen ['raɪzn] travel
Reisepass, -pässe *m* ['raɪzəpɛsə] passport
Reiseziel, -e *n* ['raɪzətsi:l] destination
Rente, -n *f* ['rɛntə] pension
reservieren [rezɛr'vi:rən] book, retain
Restaurant, -s *n* [rɛsto'rã:] restaurant
restlich ['rɛstlɪç] remaining
Rezeption, -en *f* [retsɛp'tsio:n] reception, front desk
richtig ['rɪçtɪç] right, correct; really, quite
Richtung, -en *f* ['rɪçtʊŋ] direction
Riesenrad, räder *n* ['ri:znra:t] big wheel
Rock, Röcke *m* [rɔk] skirt
röntgen ['rœntgn] x-ray
Röntgen *(only Sg) n* ['rœntgn] X-ray
rot [ro:t] red
Rotwein, -e *m* ['ro:twaɪn] red wine
Rücken, – *m* ['rʏkn] back
Rückenschmerzen *(only Pl)* ['rʏknʃmɛrtsn] backache
Rückfahrt, -en *f* ['rʏkfa:rt] return journey
rufen ['ru:fn] call, shout
Rufnummer, -n *f* ['ru:fnumɐ] phone number
Ruhe *(only Sg) f* ['ru:ə] peace, quiet
Ruhestand *(only Sg) m* ['ru:əʃtant] retirement
rund [rʊnt] round
rund um [rʊnt ʊm] about
russisch ['rʊsɪʃ] Russian
Russland *(only Sg) n* ['rʊslant] Russia

S

Sache, -n *f* ['zaxə] thing
Saft, Säfte *m* [zaft] juice
sagen ['za:gn] say
Sahne *(only Sg) f* ['za:nə] cream
Salat, -e *m* [za'la:t] salad
Samstag, -e *m* ['zamsta:k] Saturday
Satz, Sätze *m* [zats] sentence, phrase, clause
sauber ['zaubɐ] clean
Sauerkraut *(only Sg) n* ['zauɐkraut] sauerkraut
Sauna, -s/Saunen *f* ['zauna] sauna
scannen ['skɛnən] scan
Schal, -s *m* [ʃa:l] scarf
Schalter, – *m* ['ʃaltɐ] ticket office
schauen ['ʃauən] look
scheinen ['ʃaɪnən] shine
Scherbe, -n *f* ['ʃɛrbə] shard
schick [ʃik] chic, fashionable
schicken ['ʃɪkn] send
Schinken, – *m* ['ʃɪŋkn] ham
schlafen ['ʃla:fn] sleep
Schlafzimmer, – *n* ['ʃla:ftsɪmɐ] bedroom
Schlagsahne *(only Sg) f* ['ʃla:gza:nə] whipped cream
schlecht [ʃlɛçt] bad

schließlich ['ʃliːslɪç] after all
schlimm [ʃlɪm] bad
Schlüssel, – *m* ['ʃlʏsl] key
Schluss, Schlüsse *(mostly Sg) m* [ʃlʊs] conclusion, end
schmecken ['ʃmɛkn] taste
Schmerz, -en *m* [ʃmɛrts] pain
schmerzen ['ʃmɛrtsn] hurt
Schmuck *(only Sg) m* [ʃmʊk] jewellery
Schnee *(only Sg) m* [ʃneː] snow
schneien ['ʃnaɪən] snow
schnell [ʃnɛl] fast
Schnitzel, – *n* ['ʃnɪtsl] schnitzel
Schokolade, -n *f* [ʃoko'laːdə] chocolate
Schokoladentorte, -n *f* [ʃoko'laːdntɔrtə] chocolate gateau
schon [ʃoːn] already, yet
schön ['ʃøːn] nice, beautiful
Schorle, -n *f* ['ʃɔrlə] juice or wine mixed with sparkling water
Schottland *(only Sg) n* ['ʃɔtlant] Scotland
Schrank, Schränke *m* [ʃraŋk] cupboard
schreiben ['ʃraɪbn] write
Schuh, -e *m* [ʃuː] shoe
Schule, -n *f* ['ʃuːlə] school
Schulung, -en *f* ['ʃuːlʊŋ] training
schwarz [ʃvarts] black
Schwellung, -en *f* ['ʃvɛlʊŋ] swelling
schwer [ʃveːɐ] difficult, hard; heavy
Schwester, -n *f* ['ʃvɛstɐ] sister
Schwimmbad, -bäder *n* ['ʃvimbaːt] swimming pool
schwimmen ['ʃvimən] swim
sehen ['zeːən] see
Sehenswürdigkeit, -en *f* ['zeːənsvʏrdɪçkaɪt] sight
sehr [zeːɐ] very
sein [zain] be
seit [zaɪt] for, since
Seite, -n *f* ['zaɪtə] side; page
selbst [zɛlpst] oneself
selten ['zɛltn] rare(ly)
seltsam ['zɛltzaːm] strange
senden (an) ['zɛndn] send
Sender, – *m* ['zɛndɐ] channel, station; sender
Sendung, -en *f* ['zɛndʊŋ] broadcast, show, programme
September *(only Sg) m* [zɛp'tɛmbɐ] September
Serie, -n *f* ['zeːrjə] serial, series
Service, -s *m* ['zœrvɪs] service
Serviette, -n *f* [zɛrvi'ɛtə] napkin
setzen ['zɛtsn] put, place
setzen, sich [zɪç 'zɛtsn] sit down
shoppen ['ʃɔpn] go shopping, shop
sich [zɪç] oneself
sicher ['ʒɪçɐ] sure(ly), for sure; safe
sicherstellen ['ʒɪçɐʃtɛlən] ensure
sie [ziː] she, they
Sie [ziː] you (formal)
simsen ['zɪmzn] text
singen ['zɪŋən] sing
Single, -s ['sɪŋl] single
Situation, -en *f* [zitua'tsjoːn] situation
sitzen ['zitsn] sit
Sitzplatz, -plätze *m* ['zitsplats] seat
Small Talk *(only Sg) m* ['smɔːltɔːk] small talk
SMS, – *f* [ɛsɛm'ɛs] SMS, text (message)
so [zoː] so, as, such
Socke, -n *f* ['zɔkə] sock
Sofa, -s *n* ['zoːfa] couch
Software *(only Sg) f* ['sɔftvɛːr] software
sogar [zo'gaːɐ] even
Sohn, Söhne *m* [zoːn] son
sollen ['zɔlən] shall, are to
sollt- ['zɔlt-] should
Sommer, – *(mostly Sg) m* ['zɔmɐ] summer

Sonderangebot, -e *n* ['zɔndɐangəbo:t] special offer
Sonne, -n *f* ['zɔnə] sun
sonnig ['zɔniç] sunny
Sonntag, -e *m* ['zɔnta:k] Sunday
sonst [zɔnst] else
Spanien *(only Sg) n* ['ʃpa:niən] Spain
spanisch ['ʃpa:nɪʃ] Spanish
spannend ['ʃpanənt] fascinating
Spaß, Späße *m* [ʃpa:s] fun
spät [ʃpɛ:t] late
später [ʃpɛ:tɐ] later
spazieren [ʃpa'tsi:rən] stroll, walk
Spaziergang, -gänge *m* [ʃpa'tsi:rgaŋ] walk
Speisekarte, -n *f* ['ʃpaɪzekartə] menu
Speiseraum, -räume *m* ['ʃpaɪzeraum dining room
Spezialität, -en *f* [ʃpetsiali'tɛ:t] specialty
spielen ['ʃpi:lən] play
Sport *(only Sg) m* [ʃpɔrt] sport
Sportart, -en *f* ['ʃpɔrtart] sport
sportlich ['ʃpɔrtlɪç] casual; athletic
Sportplatz, -plätze *m* ['ʃpɔrtplats] sports ground
Sportverein, -e *m* ['ʃpɔrtfɛɐ'aɪn] sports club
Sprachkurs, -e *m* ['ʃpra:xkurs] language course/class
sprachlich ['ʃpra:xlɪç] linguistic
Sprachschule, -n *f* ['ʃpra:xʃu:lə] language school
sprechen ['ʃpreçn] speak, talk
Sprudel, – *m* ['ʃpru:dl] sparkling water
Staatsangehörigkeit, -en *f* ['ʃta:tsangə hø:rɪçkaɪt] nationality
Stadt, Städte *f* [ʃtat] town, city
Stadtrundfahrt, -en *f* ['ʃtatrʊntfa:rt] sightseeing tour
Stadtzentrum, -zentren *(mostly Sg) n* ['ʃtattsɛntrʊm] city center
Stand, Stände *m* [ʃtant] (market) stand
ständig [ʃtɛndɪç] all the time, constantly
stark [ʃtark] heavy; strong
starten [ʃtartn] start, set off
Statistik, -en *f* [ʃta'tɪstɪk] statistics
stattfinden ['ʃtatfɪndn] take place
Stau, -s *m* [ʃtau] traffic jam
staubsaugen ['ʃtaupzaugn] hoover
stehen ['ʃte:ən] stand, be
Stelle, -n *f* ['ʃtɛlə] job; position; place
stellen ['ʃtɛlən] put, place
Stellenanzeige, -n *f* ['ʃtɛlən'antsaɪgə] job advertisement
stimmen ['ʃtɪmən] be right
Stimmt! ['ʃtɪmt] True!, Right!
Stock, – *m* [ʃtɔk] floor, level
Stockwerk, -e *n* ['ʃtɔkvɛrk] floor, level
Straße, -n *f* ['ʃtra:sə] street, road
Straßenbahn, -en *f* ['ʃtra:sənba:n] tram(way)
Straßenbahnhaltestelle, -n *f* ['ʃtra:sənba:nhaltəʃtɛlə] tram stop
Strategie, -n *f* [ʃtrate'gi:] strategy
Student, -en *m* [ʃtʊ'dɛnt] student
Studentenausweis, -e *m* [ʃtʊ'dɛntn-ausvaɪs] student ID
studieren [ʃtu'di:rən] study
Studium, Studien *(mostly Sg) n* ['ʃtu:diʊm] studies
Stück, -e *n* [ʃtʏk] piece
stürmen ['ʃtʏrmən] storm
stürmisch ['ʃtʏrmɪʃ] stormy
Stufe, -n *f* ['ʃtu:fə] stair
Stuhl, Stühle *m* [ʃtu:l] chair
Stunde, -n *f* ['ʃtʊndə] hour; lesson
Sturm, Stürme *m* [ʃtʊrm] storm
suchen [zu:xn] search, look for
süß [zy:s] sweet, cute

super ['zu:pɐ] great
Supermarkt, -märkte *m* ['zu:pɐmarkt] supermarket
Suppe, -n *f* ['zupə] soup

T

Tag, -e *m* [ta:k] day
Tageslichtprojektor, -en *m* ['ta:gəs lɪçtpro:jɛkto:ɐ] overhead projector
Tagesordnungspunkt, -e *m* ['ta:gə sortnʊŋspʊnkt] topic
Tante, -n *f* ['tantə] aunt
Tasse, -n *f* ['tasə] cup
Tatort, -e *m* ['ta:tɔrt] crime scene
Team, -s *n* [ti:m] team
Tee, -s *m* [te:] tea
Teilnehmer, – *m* ['taɪlne:mɐ] member, participant
Telefon, -e *n (abbr. Tel.)* [tele'fo:n] (tele) phone
telefonieren [telefo'ni:rən] call, phone, talk over the phone
Telefonnummer, -n *f* [tele'fo:nnʊmɐ] phone number
Teller, – *m* ['tɛlɐ] plate, dish
Tennis *(only Sg) n* ['tɛnis] tennis
Termin, -e *m* [tɛr'mi:n] appointment
Terminkalender, – *m* [tɛr'mi:nkalɛndɐ] diary
Test, -s *m* [tɛst] test
teuer ['tɔʏɐ] expensive
Theater, – *n* [te'a:tɐ] theatre
Thema, Themen *n* ['te:ma] topic
Thriller, – *m* ['θrɪlɐ] thriller
Tipp, -s *m* [tɪp] tip
Tisch, -e *m* [tɪʃ] table
Tischtennisplatte, -n *f* ['tɪʃtɛnɪsplatə] table tennis table
Titel, – *m* ['ti:tl, tɪtl] (academic) title
Tochter, Töchter *f* ['tɔxtɐ] daughter
Toilette, -n *f* [toa'lɛtə] bathroom, lavatory
toll [tɔl] cool, awesome, great
Tomate, -n *f* [to'ma:tə] tomato
Torte, -n *f* ['tɔrtə] gateau
total [to'ta:l] totally
tragen ['tra:gn] carry; wear
Transport, -e *(mostly Sg) m* [trans'pɔrt] transport
treffen (sich) ['trɛfn] meet
Treppe, -n *f* ['trɛpə] stairs
trinken ['trɪŋkn] drink
Trinkgeld *(only Sg) n* ['trɪŋkgɛlt] tip
trotzdem ['trɔtsde:m] anyway
Tschüs! [tʃy:s] Bye!
T-Shirt, -s *n* ['ti:ʃœrt, 'ti:ʃø:ɐt] T-shirt
Tür, -en *f* [ty:ɐ] door
Tüte, -n *f* ['ty:tə] bag
tun [tu:n] do
TV, -s *n* [te:'fau] TV

U

über ['y:bɐ] over
überhaupt [y:bɐ'haupt] at all
übermorgen ['y:bɐmɔrgn] day after tomorrow
übernachten [y:bɐ'naxtn] stay/spend the night
Übernachtung, -en *f* [y:bɐ'naxtʊŋ] overnight stay
übernehmen [y:bɐ'ne:mən] take over
übersehen [y:bɐ'ze:ən] overlook
übersetzen [y:bɐ'zɛtsn] translate
üblich ['y:blɪç] common, normal
übrig ['y:brɪç] left (over)
übrigens ['y:brɪgns] by the way
Uhr, -en *f* [u:r] clock, watch

Uhrzeit, -en *f* ['u:rtsaɪt] time (of day)
um [ʊm] at; about
umdrehen ['ʊmdre:ən] turn around
umknicken ['ʊmknɪkn] twist
umsteigen ['ʊmʃtaɪgn] change
und [ʊnt] and
und so weiter (usw.) [ʊnt zo: waɪtɐ] and so on
Unfall, -fälle ['ʊnfal] accident
ungefähr [ʊngəfɛ:ɐ] about, around
Universität, -en *f (abbr. Uni, -s f)* [univɛrzi'tɛ:t ('ʊni)] university
unnötig ['ʊnnø:tɪç] unnecessary
unten ['ʊntn] below
unter ['ʊntɐ] beneath
Unterlagen *(only Pl)* ['ʊntɐla:gn] documents
unternehmen [ʊntɐ'ne:mən] do, undertake
Unterricht *(only Sg) m* ['ʊntɐrɪçt] class
Unterrichtsstunde, -n *f* ['ʊntɐrɪçtsʃtʊndə] lesson
Unterwäsche *(only Sg) f* ['ʊntɐvɛʃə] underwear
unüblich ['ʊny:blɪç] uncommon
Urlaub, -e *m* ['u:ɐlaup] holiday
USA *(only Pl)* [u: ɛs 'a:] USA
US-amerikanisch [u: 'ɛs amerika:nɪʃ] American

V

Vater, Väter ['fa:tɐ] father
Verabredung, -en *f* [fɛɐ'apre:dʊŋ] appointment, date, rendezvous
verabschieden [fɛɐ'apʃi:dn] say good-bye
Veranstaltung, -en *f* [fɛɐ'anʃtaltʊŋ] event
verbinden [fɛɐ'bɪndn] put through; connect
Verbindung, -en *f* [fɛɐ'bɪndʊŋ] connection
verbringen [fɛɐ'braxt] spend
verdienen [fɛɐ'di:nən] earn
vereinbaren [fɛɐ'aɪnba:rən] agree, arrange
Verhalten *(only Sg) n* [fɛɐ'haltn] behaviour
verheiratet [fɛɐ'haɪra:tət] married
Verkäufer, – *m* [fɛɐ'kɔʏfɐ] salesman
Verkäuferin, -nen *f* [fɛɐ'kɔʏfərɪn] saleslady
Verkehrsmittel, – *n* [fɛɐ'ke:ɐsmɪtl] means of transport
verlassen [fɛɐ'lasn] leave
verleihen [fɛɐ'laɪən] lend
verletzen (sich) [zɪç fɛɐ'lɛtsn] hurt (oneself), injure
Verletzung, -en *f* [fɛɐ'lɛtsʊŋ] injury
vermeiden [fɛɐ'maɪdn] avoid
Verpackung, -en *f* [fɛɐ'pakʊŋ] packaging
verschicken an [fɛɐ'ʃɪkn] send
verschieden [fɛɐ'ʃi:dn] different
verschneit [fɛɐ'ʃnait] snowy
Verspätung, -en *f* [fɛɐ'ʃpɛ:tʊŋ] delay
verstehen [fɛɐ'ʃte:ən] understand
verteilen [fɛɐ'taɪlən] distribute, hand out
verwählen [fɛɐ'vɛ:lən] dial the wrong number
Verwandte, -n *m+f* [fɛɐ'vantə] relative (male and female)
viel [fi:l] much
Viel Spaß! [fi:l 'ʃpa:s] Have fun!
Viele Grüße [ˌfi:lə 'gry:sə] (kind/best) regards
Vielen Dank! [ˌfi:lən 'daŋk] Thank you very much!

vielleicht [fi'laɪçt] maybe
Viertel, – *n* ['fɪrtl] quarter
Visitenkarte, -n *f* [vi'si:tnkartə] business card
Volksfest, -e *n* ['fɔlksfɛst] fair
voll [fɔl] crowded, full
Volleyball, -bälle *m* ['vɔlibal] volleyball
von [fɔn] from, of
vor [fo:ɐ] before, to, in front of
Voraussetzung, -en *f* [for'auszɛtsʊŋ] requirement
vorbei [foɐ'baɪ] over; past
vorbeigehen [fo:ɐ'baɪge:ən] pass
vorbereiten ['fo:ɐbəraɪtn] prepare
Vorbereitung, -en *f* ['fo:ɐbəraɪtʊŋ] preparation
Vorgehen, – *n* ['fo:ɐge:ən] actions
vorgestern ['fo:ɐgɛstɐn] day before yesterday
vorkommen ['fo:ɐkɔmən] occur, happen
Vormittag, -e *m* ['fo:ɐmɪta:k] morning
Vorname, -n *m* ['fo:ɐna:mə] first name
vorn(e) ['fɔrn(ə)] in front
Vorschlag, -schläge *m* ['fo:ɐʃla:k] proposition, suggestion
vorschlagen ['fo:ɐʃla:gn] suggest
vorstellen (sich) ['fo:ɐʃtɛlən] introduce, present
Vortrag, -träge *m* ['fo:ɐtra:k] speech

W

wählen ['vɛ:lən] dial
während ['vɛ:rənt] during; while
Wand, Wände *f* [vant] wall
wann [van] when
warm [varm] warm
Wartebereich, -e *m* ['vartəbəraɪç] waiting area
warten ['vartn] wait
Wartezimmer, – *n* ['vartətsɪmɐ] waiting room
warum [va'rʊm] why
was [vas] what
was für ein [vas fy:r aɪn] what (kind of)
Wäsche *(only Sg) f* [vɛʃə] laundry
waschen (sich) ['vaʃn] wash
Wasser *(only Sg) n* ['vasɐ] water
WC, -s *n* [ve:'tse:] toilet
Webseite, -n *f* ['vɛpzaɪtə] web page, website
Wechselgeld *(only Sg) n* ['vɛksəlgəlt] change
weg [vɛk] away
Weg, -e *m* [ve:k] way
wegen ['ve:gn] because of
wegfahren ['vɛkfa:rən] go away (on a trip)
wehtun ['ve:tu:n] hurt
weil [vaɪl] because
Weile *(only Sg) f* ['vaɪlə] while
Wein, -e *m* [vaɪn] wine
Weinglas, -gläser *n* ['vaɪngla:s] wine glass
Weintraube, -n *f* ['vaɪntraubə] grape
weiß [vaɪs] white
weit [vaɪt] far, long
weit weg [vaɪt 'vɛk] far away
weiter ['vaɪtɐ] continuing, further, next
weiterarbeiten ['vaɪtɐarbaɪtn] continue working
Weiterbildung, -en *f* ['vaɪtɐbɪldʊŋ] further education
weiterhelfen ['vaɪtɐhɛlfn] help
weiterhin ['vaɪtɐhɪn] furthermore
weiterleiten ['vaɪtɐlaɪtn] forward
weitermachen ['vaɪtɐmaxn] continue
welcher, welche, welches ['vɛlçɐ, 'vɛlçə, 'vɛlçəs] which, what

Welt, -en *f* [vɛlt] world
weltweit ['vɛltvaɪt] worldwide
wenig ['veːnɪç] little
wenn [vɛn] when; if
wer [veːɐ] who
werden ['veːɐdən] become
Westen *(only Sg) m* ['vɛstn] west
Wetter *(only Sg) n* ['vɛtɐ] weather
Whiteboard, -s *n* ['vaɪtbɔːɐt] whiteboard
wichtig ['vɪçtɪç] important
wie [viː] how
Wie geht's? [viː 'geːts] How are you?, What's up?
wie lange [viː 'laŋə] how long
wie oft [viː 'ɔft] how often
wie viel [viː 'fiːl] how much
wie viele [viː 'fiːlə] how many
wieder ['viːdɐ] again
wiederholen [viːdɐ'hoːlən] repeat
wieso [vi'zoː] why
willkommen [vɪlkɔmən] welcome
Wind, -e *m* [vɪnt] wind
winden ['vɪndn] blow
windig ['vɪndɪç] windy
Winter, – *(mostly Sg) m* ['vɪntɐ] winter
wir [viːɐ] we
wirklich ['vɪrklɪç] really
Wirklichkeit *(only Sg) f* ['vɪrklɪçkaɪt] reality
wissen ['vɪsn] know
wo [voː] where
Woche, -n *f* ['vɔxə] week
Wochenende, -n *n* ['vɔxnɛndə] weekend
Wochenmarkt, -märkte *m* ['vɔxnmarkt weekly farmer's market
woher [voː'heːr] where from
wohin [voː'hɪn] where to
wohl [voːl] probably
wohlfühlen ['voːlfyːlən] be comfortable, feel good
wohnen ['voːnən] live
Wohngemeinschaft, -en *f (abbr. WG, -s f)* ['voːngəmaɪnʃaft (veː'geː)] flat share
Wohnort, -e *m* ['voːnɔrt] residence
Wohnung, -en *f* ['voːnʊŋ] flat
Wohnungsanzeige, -n *f* ['voːnʊŋs-antsaɪgə] flat advertisement
Wohnzimmer, – *n* ['voːntsɪmɐ] living room
Wolke, -n *f* ['vɔlkə] cloud
wollen ['vɔlən] want
worauf [voː'rauf] what
Wort, Wörter *n* [vɔrt] word
worüber [voː'ryːbɐ] what about
wünschen ['vʏnʃən] wish
würd- [vʏrd-] would
wunderbar ['vʊndɐbaɐ] marvelous
Wunsch, Wünsche *m* [vʊnʃ] wish
Wurst, Würste *f* [vʊrst] sausage
Wurzel, -n *f* ['vʊrtsəl] root

Z

zahlen ['tsaːlən] pay
Zahn, Zähne *m* [tsaːn] tooth
Zahnarzt, -ärzte *m* ['tsaːnartst] dentist
Zähne putzen ['tsɛːnə ˚pʊtsn] brush one's teeth
Zahnschmerzen *(only Pl)* ['tsaːnʃmɛrtsn] toothache
Zebrastreifen, – *m* ['tseːbraʃtraɪfn] zebra crossing
Zeit, -en *(mostly Sg) f* [tsaɪt] time
Zeitschrift, -en *f* ['tsaɪtʃrɪft] magazine, journal
Zeitung, -en *f* ['tsaɪtʊŋ] newspaper
Zelt, -e *n* [tsɛlt] tent
Zeugnis, -se *n* ['tsɔʏknɪs] certificate

ziemlich ['tsi:mlɪç] pretty, quite
Zimmer, – *n* ['tsɪmɐ] room
Zimmerservice *(only Sg) m* ['tsɪmɐzœrvɪs] room service
zu [tsu:] to, toward
Zucchini, -s *f* [tsʊ'ki:ni] courgette
zuerst [tsu'e:ɐst] (at) first
Zufall, -fälle *m* ['tsu:fal] coincidence, chance
zufrieden [tsu'fri:dən] satisfied
Zug, Züge *m* [tsu:k] train
Zugfahrt, -en *f* ['tsu:kfa:rt] train ride
zuhören ['tsuhørən] listen
zukünftig ['tsukʏnftɪç] future
Zukunft *(only Sg) f* ['tsukʊnft] future
zuletzt [tsu'lɛtst] lastly
zum Beispiel *(abbr. z. B.)* [tsʊm 'baɪʃpi:l] for example, for instance
zum einen [tsʊm 'aɪnən] on the one hand
zumachen ['tsu:maxn] close
zurück [tsu'rʏk] back
zurückhaltend [tsu'rʏkhaltnt] conservative, modest
zurückrufen [tsu'rʏkru:fn] call back
zusammen [tsu'zamən] together
Zusammenarbeit *(only Sg) f* [tsu'zamənarbaɪt] cooperation
zusammenarbeiten [tsu'zamənarbaɪtn] cooperate
Zusammenfassung, -en *f* [tsu'zamənfasʊŋ] summary
zusammensitzen [tsu'zamənzɪtsn] sit together
zusätzlich ['tsuzɛtslɪç] additionally
zustimmen ['tsuʃtɪmən] agree
Zutat, -en *f* ['tsuta:t] ingredient
Zwiebel, -n *f* ['tsvi:bl] onion
zwischen ['tsvɪʃn] between

Trackangaben

CD 1

Track no.	Day (Lesson)
1	Introduction
2	L 2/dialogue
3	L 2/d. slow
4	L 2/2
5	L 2/4
6	L 3/dialogue
7	L 3/d. slow
8	L 3/3
9	L 4/dialogue
10	L 4/d. slow
11	L 4/2
12	L 5/dialogue
13	L 5/d. slow
14	L 5/2
15	L 6/5
16	L 6/17
17	L 6/19
18	IT 1/3
19	IT 1/8
20	L 7/dialogue
21	L 7/d. slow
22	L 7/3
23	L 8/dialogue
24	L 8/d. slow
25	L 8/2
26	L 9/dialogue
27	L 9/d. slow
28	L 9/3
29	L 10/dialogue
30	L 10/d. slow
31	L 10/2
32	L 11/dialogue
33	L 11/d. slow
34	L 11/1
35	L 12/dialogue
36	L 12/d. slow
37	L 12/1
38	L 13/dialogue
39	L 13/d. slow
40	L 13/1
41	L 13/3

CD 2

Track no.	Day (Lesson)
1	L 14/3
2	L 14/9
3	L 14/15
4	L 14/18
5	IT 2/3
6	L 15/dialogue
7	L 15/1
8	L 15/4
9	L 16/dialogue
10	L 17/dialogue
11	L 18/dialogue
12	L 18/3
13	L 19/dialogue
14	L 19/1
15	L 20/dialogue
16	L 20/2
17	L 21/dialogue
18	L 21/2
19	L 22/4
20	L 22/7
21	L 22/9
22	L 22/11
23	IT 3/3
24	IT 3/5
25	L 23/dialogue
26	L 23/1
27	L 24/dialogue
28	L 25/dialogue
29	L 25/1
30	L 26/dialogue
31	L 26/2
32	L 27/dialogue
33	L 27/1
34	L 28/dialogue
35	L 28/3
36	L 29/dialogue
37	L 29/3
38	L 30/2
39	L 30/7
40	L 30/13
41	FT 5
42	FT 8
43	FT 13
44	FT 15
45	FT 21

CD 3

Track no.	Day (Lesson)
1	Introduction
2	Vocabulary L2
3	Vocabulary L3
4	Vocabulary L4
5	Vocabulary L5
6	Vocabulary L7
7	Vocabulary L8
8	Vocabulary L9
9	Vocabulary L10
10	Vocabulary L11
11	Vocabulary L12
12	Vocabulary L13
13	Vocabulary L15
14	Vocabulary L16
15	Vocabulary L17
16	Vocabulary L18
17	Vocabulary L19
18	Vocabulary L20
19	Vocabulary L21
20	Vocabulary L23
21	Vocabulary L24
22	Vocabulary L25
23	Vocabulary L26
24	Vocabulary L27
25	Vocabulary L28
26	Vocabulary L29

Picture credits

Getty Images: George Doyle – 159; Niko Guido – 19 (unten); Jasmina007 – 17; Martin Leigh – 143; Photo Alto/Odilon Dimier – 183; Stockbyte – 201; Stephan Zabel – 45

iStock: no_limit_pictures – 144; Sean Warren – 34

Thinkstock: SeanPavonePhoto - U1; akarelias – 19 (oben); Helder Almeida – 166; Eileen Bach – 189; Marcin Balcerzak – 184; Robert Brown – 138; cmfotoworks – 120; Steve Cole – 61; Comstock – 119; dekadi – 149; Digital Vision – 97; Barbara Dudzinska – 137; elxeneize – 68; Petro Feketa – 172; fotobauer – 6; Fuse – 85; gielmichal – 92; Good Mood Photo – 86; Peter Gudella – 114; Ingram Publishing – 165, 171; insagostudio – 178; Brian Jackson – 18, 39, 40; Jupiterimages – 33, 108, 196; Maksym Khytra – 67; Levent Konuk – 126; kosmos111 – 91; lentolo – 22; LuminaStock – 28; Robyn Mackenzie – 62; Maridav – 80; matthewennisphotography – 56; Ryan McVay – 21; mila1974 – 177; Dean Mitchel – 195; moodboard – 74; ronaldino3001 – 132; shironosov – 160; Alison Stieglitz – 131; Maria Teijeiro – 55; wavebreakmedia – 190; Mikkel William Nielsen – 79; xyno – 113; xyno6 – 125: Catherine Yeulet – 27; Hongqi Zhang – 107; Zheka-Boss – 73; Katarzyna Zwolska – 20

Einfach besser nachschlagen!

- Enthält rund 80.000 Stichwörter und Wendungen.
- Das perfekte Wörterbuch zum Lernen, Verstehen, Schreiben und Sprechen.
- Mit zahlreichen Infofenstern zu Grammatik, Wortschatz und Landeskunde.
- 22 Farbzeichnungen zu wichtigen Wortfeldern und Alltagsthemen.
- Die Wörterbuch-Rallye befähigt zum schnellen und effizienten Nachschlagen.

ISBN 978-3-12-514467-5